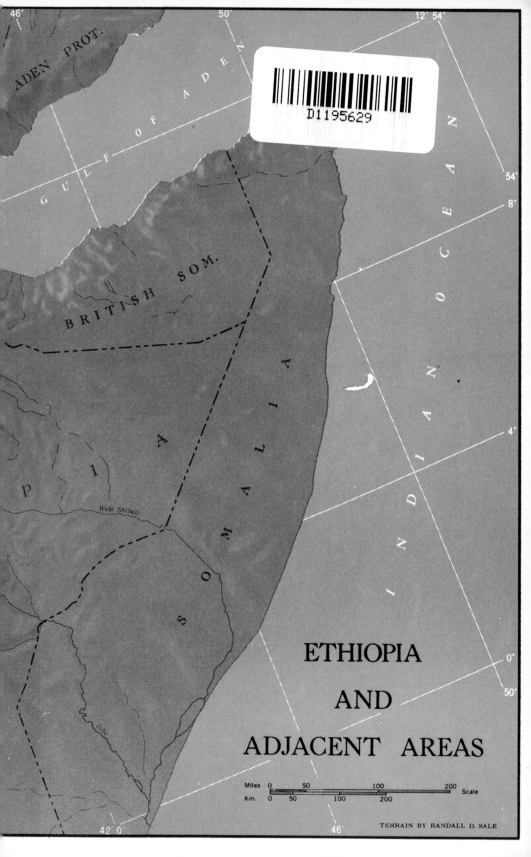

ADEN PROT.

GULF OF ADEN

BRITISH SOM.

INDIAN OCEAN

ETHIOPIA

PIA

SOMALIA

Webi Shibeli

ETHIOPIA

AND

ADJACENT AREAS

Miles 0   50   100   200   Scale
Km.   0   50   100   200

TERRAIN BY RANDALL D. SALE

NORTHWEST ETHIOPIA

NORTHWEST
ETHIOPIA

**PEOPLES
AND
ECONOMY**

Frederick J. Simoons

Madison · 1960
THE UNIVERSITY OF WISCONSIN PRESS

PUBLISHED BY THE UNIVERSITY OF WISCONSIN PRESS,
430 STERLING COURT, MADISON 6, WISCONSIN

COPYRIGHT © 1960 BY THE REGENTS OF
THE UNIVERSITY OF WISCONSIN

PRINTED IN THE UNITED STATES OF AMERICA
BY VAIL-BALLOU PRESS, INC., BINGHAMTON, NEW YORK

PHOTOGRAPHS PRINTED BY CUSHING-MALLOY, INC.,
ANN ARBOR, MICHIGAN

LIBRARY OF CONGRESS CATALOG CARD NUMBER 60-5660

To Stephanie

PREFACE

Ethiopia through most of history has remained a land seldom visited and little known by Western scholars. The meagerness of our rather recently acquired knowledge of Ethiopia is not surprising when we consider the difficulties that visitors in the past underwent to gain access to the mountain heart of the country. European travellers, after a long sea journey, had to pass through coastal lowland areas controlled by Islamized tribesmen who regarded Christians with distrust, contempt, and often hostility. Once in the cool highland, travellers were often troubled and hindered in their work by illnesses in the new environment. In addition, they were hampered by the reserve and suspicion of the conservative mountain people, especially during the times of anarchy which were so common in Ethiopia's turbulent past. The best early European accounts of Ethiopia were written by a handful of sturdy, intrepid, and highly motivated men, usually priests, representatives of European governments, or adventurers of one sort or another. Among these men was Francisco Alvarez, chaplain of a Portuguese mission to the King of Abyssinia in 1520–27, Charles Jacques Poncet, a French doctor who was the first European to visit and write of Gondar in 1669–70, and the Scottish adventurer James Bruce, who was in Ethiopia from 1769 to 1772.

The situation described above has been greatly altered in recent generations, particularly since the accession to the crown of His Majesty, Haile Selassie. Today, the yearning for progress and thirst for knowledge that have seized many Ethiopians smooth the way for field research into the economic and cultural life of the country, and there is a growing literature in French, German, Italian, and English dealing with Ethiopian life. I have taken advantage of the new opportunities to make a study of the peoples and economy of Ethiopia's Northwest, the homeland of the Amhara people and the center of medieval Abyssinia.[1] In the Northwest, which coincides with the Province of Begemder and Semyen,[2] there are, unlike parts of East

[1] "Abyssinia" is a word derived from the tribal name Habashat. Arabs today call the Ethiopians *habash*, which in Arabic means "mixture." Though this is not the actual derivation of "Abyssinia" (Trimingham, 1952: 5), it does show that the Arabs look on the Ethiopians as a mongrel people, an implication the latter dislike. "Abyssinia" in a strict sense has been used either to apply to "an ethnic

Africa, no European farmers, no Indian settlers, no plantations, no railroads, and few motor roads; and there are no reliable statistical data for the area. In studying the Northwest, then, I dealt with local people and relied heavily on firsthand observations made during the eight months that I spent there in 1953–54, supplemented and put into cultural and historical perspective by material gathered during four months travelling elsewhere in Ethiopia, by additional months of travel in the Sudan, Uganda, the Belgian Congo, and Nigeria, and by data gathered from published works. The latter contributed the bulk of the material for the chapter on historical background, but field research contributed substantially to each of the other sections of the book, especially to the chapters on economic life. This material has been organized in an encyclopedic fashion in order to make it available in the most convenient form to those who are interested only in particular aspects of the life of Northwest Ethiopia. The emphasis throughout is on the use the Ethiopians make of their environment, on their plants and animals, their food, their artifacts and technology, their trade, and their attitudes as they have contributed to the development

---

unit roughly identical with the old Aksumite [Axumite] Empire" (Ullendorff, 1955: 4) which was the goal of South Arabian migration, or to "the historic kingdom of the highlands which was influenced by the Semitic civilization of South Arabia and afterwards adopted Christianity, and whose peoples expressed themselves through the Semitic languages, Ge'ez, Tigriña, and Amharic" (Trimingham, 1952: v). In this book, I use the word in the latter sense, of the historic Christian kingdom, because under such a definition the Amhara, who are among the most vigorous propagators of Semitic language and ways, were Abyssinians. "Ethiopia" is derived from a word used by the ancient Greeks meaning people with "burnt faces." It has been used to refer to so many different areas since ancient times that it has created considerable confusion. One Axumite king used the term "Ethiopian" to refer to the kingdoms of the Nile, so it was not appropriated by the Abyssinians until after that time (Trimingham, 1952: 38). "Ethiopia" will be used here to refer both to the present-day Empire of Ethiopia and to the geographic region of that name, which includes both members of the Federation of Ethiopia and Eritrea. "Ethiopians" refers herein to all of the natives of the region, excluding the Arabs, Greeks, and other foreign minorities, but including all other groups of whatever ethnic, religious, or racial type.

  [2] The province, which is shaded on Map 10 and indicated simply as Begemder on Map 2, is legally known by the double name, Begemder and Semyen. Semyen, in addition to being part of the name of the province, is the name of one of the six provincial districts (awradjas) which includes the high mountain section to the north known traditionally as Semyen. Begemder is the traditional name for the area centered on the town of Gondar, which at present is divided among various awradjas, each having its own name. The name "Begemder," according to Hermann Steudner (1863: 121), is derived from the words bög, sheep, and meder, land; thus, Begemder, if Steudner's explanation is accepted, means "land of sheep." The name "Semyen" is said to have originally meant "south," but with the shift in the center of the Ethiopian state, it has come to mean "north" in Amharic (Beckingham and Huntingford, 1954: 16; based on statements by Ludolf, Dillmann, and Basset).

of the cultural landscape. This emphasis is that of the historically oriented cultural geographer who, like the Scandinavian ethnologist, tends to be concrete and earthbound,[3] and who is concerned less with acculturation, comparative sociology, ethos, and problems of personality and culture than with culture as an intermediary between man and the earth.

The procedures followed in field research in Northwest Ethiopia involved first setting up a central base in the small hotel in the provincial capital of Gondar, hiring a full-time interpreter (an Amhara boy of seventeen), and obtaining introductions from local officials to headmen of two villages in which we wished to work. Then, driving from Gondar each morning, we studied first an Amhara hamlet in the village of Mariam Deber, ten miles south of Gondar, and then a Falasha (Jewish) hamlet in the village of Weuleka, three miles north of Gondar. In the hamlets I talked with the men, asking them about their work, and my wife sketched artifacts and talked to the women about their work. Finally, the rains having ceased and the streams becoming fordable, we drove in our Land Rover one hundred miles southeast to Debre Tabor where we camped for three weeks in the compound of the Seventh Day Adventist Mission, studied the market and the regional economy, and also worked with a Christian priest of the village of Wogeda Iyesus in order to better understand the church and its part in economic life. Then, returning to Gondar, we gathered equipment and supplies, drove sixty miles north to Debark, hired mules, and left for a month-long mule trip across Semyen, visiting the Sahalla Agow and the Tekezzay River and then climbing Mt. Ras Dedjen, camping along the way in villages to talk to farmers and others long enough to get a picture of the agriculture and economic life of the region. Returning to Gondar, we were unable to rent mules for a trip to the Sudan border country, so we purchased three mules for riding and seven donkeys for packing, gathered supplies, hired muleteers, and left on a five-week trip to Ch'ilga, Metemma, the Dinder, and the country of the Kumfel, returning by way of Lake T'ana and Gorgora. Everywhere in the field we were accompanied by guides and guards supplied by the government, the number of guards being determined by the safety of the country through which we passed, for there were bandits about. At its largest, our party consisted of forty people including interpreter, guards, guides, and travellers who attached themselves to our group for company and for safety. When we camped

[3] See Sol Tax, Loren C. Eiseley, Irving Rouse, and Carl F. Voegelin, *An Appraisal of Anthropology Today* (Chicago: The University of Chicago Press, 1953), pp. 218–23.

we pitched our pup tent and cooked our own meals over small kerosene stoves we had purchased. After returning from the Metemma
trip, rather than chance a planned trip northwest through Wolk'aīt
to Om Ager before the rains began, I worked around Gondar on my
notes, on gathering information about places not visited, on matters
I had not myself observed, and on the life of the Moslems and other
peoples of Gondar. Thus we spent our eight months in Begemder
and Semyen.

The reader will recognize the deficiencies that may arise from field
work as we did it. Perhaps most serious was the need to rely on English-
speaking interpreters who were usually members of the dominant
ethnic group, the Amhara; this gave an Amharic bias to the material
that was sometimes hard to eliminate and that made some informants
hesitate being frank. The constant presence on mule trips of a police-
man whose duty it was to report to the government on my activities did
not add to the freeness of informants or interpreters. Moreover, there
must have been errors in translation, for among groups whose language
is not Amharic it is common for only a few people in a village to speak
Amharic, and even they may not understand it perfectly. To counter-
act the dangers of this system, whenever possible I questioned more
than one informant on the same question, and checked the information by using other interpreters or by careful cross-checking with the
same interpreter and, where possible, with the literature.

I have followed C. H. Walker (1928) and Alone and Stokes (1946) in
attempting to write Amharic words, as well as the words of other
Ethiopian languages, in Latin characters so that the English reader will
be able to approximate their actual pronunciation. Place names in
common English use such as Addis Ababa and Gondar and names of
well-known people such as Menelik are usually spelled according to
common English usage, though the first time such words are used I
have indicated in parentheses the way they would be spelled in my
system. I have been forced to take many words from the literature
directly because I could not determine how they are pronounced. I
need only caution the reader that there will be inconsistencies and
mistakes even within the simple system used here, for the problems of
phonetics can be solved only by a linguist familiar with all of the
languages involved.

Consonants are generally pronounced as in English. The *g* is hard
as in *go; gn* is like the Spanish *ñ* or the French *gn;* the consonants *ch,*
k, p, and *t* are pronounced as in English, but they also have explosive
forms which are indicated by an apostrophe following the consonant,
as in T'ana and Ch'ilga. Vowels are pronounced as follows: *a* usually

as in *father; e* as in *let; i* as in *kill; ī* (overlined) as in *machine; o* as in *soft; u* as in *lunar.*

To minimize the possibility of confusion, a number of terms which may have cultural, religious, and ethnic connotations will be defined briefly here. "Ethiopia" refers to the modern empire of that name and to the region encompassed by the Federation of Ethiopia and Eritrea. "Ethiopian" in a general sense applies to things past and present found within the region; when applied to people it refers to all natives of the land, excluding the Arabs, Greeks, and other foreign minorities, but including all other groups of whatever ethnic, religious, or racial type. "Ethiopian Plateau," however, refers only to the larger, northwestern plateau of Ethiopia, and "Ethiopian physical type" refers to a particular physical type common in Ethiopia and different from that of the Negro peoples of Ethiopia. "Abyssinia" pertains to the historic Christian kingdom widely known by that name that existed in northern Ethiopia from medieval times to the middle of the nineteenth century, when modern Ethiopia was formed; "Abyssinians" refers to all peoples who were included in the kingdom of Abyssinia, including the Amhara, Tigrinya-speakers, and others. "Semite" is synonymous with "Semitic-speakers" and in Ethiopia includes those who speak Amharic, Tigrinya, Tigre, and one or two lesser languages. "Amharic-speakers" applies to all groups who speak the Amharic language, which in Northwest Ethiopia includes the Amhara, Falasha, Jabartis, and Wayt'o. "Amhara" pertains only to the ethnic group, which comprises only part of the Amharic-speakers. "Cushite" or "Cushitic-speakers" refers to peoples speaking Cushitic languages, such as Agow, Somali, and Galla; in Begemder and Semyen these include the Agow of Sahalla, the K'amant, and the Kumfel. "Negro," when applied to groups, indicates that they are of Negro physical type and not of Ethiopian type and that they do not speak Semitic or Cushitic languages. "Negro" when used to refer to groups within Northwest Ethiopia refers specifically to the Gumis and Hametsh.

Acknowledgment is due to the Board of Overseas Training and Research of the Ford Foundation which financed my field work, the Wenner-Gren Foundation for Anthropological Research and the Emmanuel S. Heller Scholarship at the University of California which supported further library research for the Ph.D. dissertation completed at the University of California (Berkeley), and the University of Wisconsin which provided summer salary support for rewriting the dissertation for publication. I am indebted, too, to Mr. G. Edward Nicholson and to Professors Carl O. Sauer, James J. Parsons, Wolfram Eberhard, Fritz Kramer, and David Ames for suggestions, to Mary Jane

Johnson and her staff for typing, to Paul English for research assistance and help with the index, and to Fritz Kramer, Juan Farfán, and the cartographic staff of the Department of Geography, University of Wisconsin, for map work. Randall Sale designed and drew the shaded-relief map, "Ethiopia and Adjacent Areas." My wife, Elizabeth, assisted in all stages of the research and writing, and drew the sketches appearing in the text. In Ethiopia, Dr. and Mrs. Gordon B. Schilz, Mr. and Mrs. Erling Bjaanes, Mrs. Doris Durell, and others helped in many ways. And Dejasmatch Assrate Kassa, Governor-General of the Province of Begemder and Semyen, gave the warm encouragement and support without which this study would not have been possible. Wondim-Ageghne Kassa, my interpreter, introduced me with pride to his world and helped me to understand. To the many Ethiopian officials and farmers and merchants and police and passers-by who gave me the information I sought and in return asked of my land, I humbly acknowledge indebtedness.

                                                                          F.J.S.

Madison, Wisconsin
January, 1960

CONTENTS

LIST OF ILLUSTRATIONS AND TABLES

XV

NORTHWEST ETHIOPIA

Chapter I

THE NATURAL SETTING

The cool, well-watered plateaus of Ethiopia dominate the dry lowlands of the horn of Northeast Africa, dividing the region into two sharply contrasting landscapes: highland and lowland. The desirable high country, though difficult of access because of its inhospitable borders and rough approaches, has long attracted outsiders, some of whom came to raid and pillage, and others to conquer and settle. This has encouraged extensive and long-continued culture contact in Ethiopia, and has led to large-scale interaction and borrowing among the cultures involved, a situation which is particularly interesting because Ethiopia lies near the border of the Middle East and Negro Africa. The main purposes of this book are 1) to describe the economic life of the peoples of the northwestern part of the main Ethiopian Plateau, the heartland of medieval Abyssinia and a region of great religious and ethnic differences, as well as of striking environmental contrasts, and 2) to assess the role that cultural attitudes have played in the development of the economy and of the present-day cultural landscape. Before considering the activities of man in Ethiopia, however, it is necessary to provide a sketch of the natural setting.

Topography.—Ethiopia extends across a zone of instability in the earth's crust which has been characterized by extensive faulting and the repeated issuing forth of lavas onto the surface from both fissures and volcanoes. In time, the lava deposits were built up into beds thousands of feet thick, to form the Ethiopian highlands and to cover much of the adjacent area. Although few active volcanoes remain today, extinct volcanoes are found in both highland and lowland, and other volcanic phenomena, such as hot springs, are widespread. The faulting that accompanied the outpouring of lava formed a great rift valley which cuts the highland into two parts, the Ethiopian Plateau to the northwest and the Somali Plateau to the southeast [1] (see Map 1).

[1] Some writers have called the upland to the southeast of the Rift Valley the Central Plateau or Massif Central and the slope to the Indian Ocean the Somali Plateau or the Galla-Somali Plateau. I prefer to follow G. Dainelli (1943), who

The Ethiopian Plateau, with which this book is concerned, is not a uniform, level surface, but a rolling upland with an average elevation of about 7,000 feet, and with extreme heights of 15,000 feet. On its eastern margins, the plateau drops by a series of spectacular, north-south tending escarpments into the Danakil Depression, a northward extension of the Rift Valley which is below sea level in a few places and contains some of the lowest spots on the continent of Africa. Except for the Awash River, only short streams drain eastward into the Danakil Depression, to lose themselves in the parched sands or to empty into marshes or dry lakes which have supplied salt to Northeast Africa since prehistoric times. From the eastern escarpments, the highland surface slopes gently to the west, draining largely in that direction by way of streams which eventually reach the Nile. In the southern part of the Ethiopian Plateau, the Omo River drains southward into Lake Rudolf, and smaller streams feed the string of lakes in the Rift Valley.

While the Ethiopian Plateau was being built up by vulcanism and perhaps by faulting, the powerful gradational agents ice and water were acting to wear it down. Gradation by ice was important in the Pleistocene period, when mountain glaciers covered the higher regions; today, though their scars and deposits can still be found in the higher parts of the plateau,[2] the glaciers themselves have disappeared. Gradation by water, on the other hand, continues to be important, for Ethiopia has considerable rain and steep slopes. This has encouraged erosion and led to the development of powerful rivers, the largest of which have cut deep gorges into the plateau to divide it into several semi-isolated segments. In terms of downcutting, one of the most effective of these rivers has been the Blue Nile (Abbai), which rushes through a deep, winding canyon, passing over rapids and falls before it emerges onto the plains of the Sudan. Each section of the Ethiopian Plateau is further fragmented by lesser stream valleys which in many places make travel so difficult during the rainy season that there is little or no contact among neighboring districts at that time. Even during the dry season, travel frequently is a wearisome matter of climbing up and down trails that cling to the sides of stream valleys. A

distinguishes three principal regions: the Ethiopian Plateau, the Somali Plateau, and the sunken zones between them. The term Massif Central or Central Plateau, referring to the highland southeast of the Rift Valley, can easily confuse the reader for he may think of "central" as "main" or "principal," or as that occupying the heart of the country, a designation which applies best to the Ethiopian Plateau proper.

[2] For an account of the deposits left by Pleistocene mountain glaciers in Ethiopia, see Hövermann, 1954.

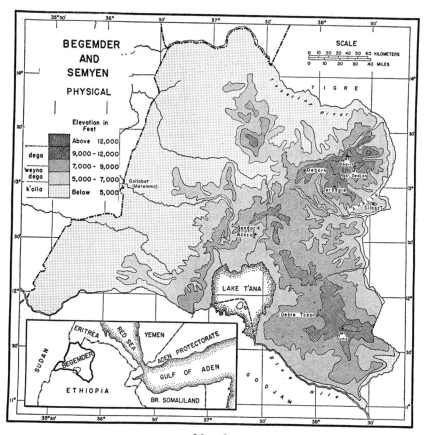

BEGEMDER AND SEMYEN
PHYSICAL

SCALE

0 10 20 30 40 50 60 KILOMETERS
0 10 20 30 40 MILES

Elevation in Feet

dega — Above 12,000
— 9,000 - 12,000
weyna dega — 7,000 - 9,000
k'olla — 5,000 - 7,000
— Below 5,000

TIGRE

Debark Mt. Ras Dedien

Janamora

Silasz?

Gallabat (Metemma)

Gondar
Azezo

LAKE T'ANA

Debre Tabor

Mt. Guna

GODJAM

Blue Nile

SUDAN ERITREA RED SEA YEMEN

BEGEMDER ADEN PROTECTORATE

GULF OF ADEN

ETHIOPIA BR. SOMALILAND

Map 2

5

common product of fragmentation by stream erosion is the *amba,* a
flat-topped mountain which may be protected by resistant rock strata
and which rises high above the surrounding country. *Ambas* are excellent natural forts, difficult of approach and with sufficient water,
grass, and arable land to enable the inhabitants to withstand long
sieges. Ethiopians have long recognized the defensive qualities of the
ambas and they figure prominently in Ethiopian history.

It is not surprising that in such a dissected land the mountain people
should develop strong regional loyalties. Such loyalties are marked in
the Northwest (Map 2), which is almost completely severed from
the rest of the plateau by the deep gorge of the Tekezzay River to
the north and east and by that of the Blue Nile to the southeast,
forming a unit the size of Ceylon that is so distinctive that the Ethiopian government made of it a province, Begemder and Semyen,
which hereafter will be considered synonymous with "the Northwest."
Begemder and Semyen is the homeland of the Amhara, the ruling
group in Ethiopia today and historically a powerful force in shaping
the national character. In topography, Begemder and Semyen is similar
to the rest of the Ethiopian Plateau. In the northeastern part of the
province, the plateau surface is surmounted by lofty mountain peaks
(Fig. 1) which comprise the highest part of Ethiopia. Mt. Ras Dedjen
(Ras Dashan), the highest point, towers 15,158 feet.[3] Nearby, Bwa-ît
(Buahit) rises to 14,797 feet, and Mt. Guna, to the east of Lake T'ana,
reaches 13,881 feet. These peaks, like most of the Ethiopian Plateau,
are comprised largely of extrusive igneous rocks such as basalt.

Along its southern border, Begemder and Semyen encompasses the
major part of Lake T'ana, a large, shallow lake which is the source of
the Blue Nile. To the west, the plateau drops off gradually in a series
of hills, each lower than the last, until at the Sudan border, which is
also the provincial boundary, the elevations average 2,000 to 3,000 feet.
Since volcanic rocks cover the plateau surface to considerable depths,
as much as 9,000 feet in some places, the older Mesozoic sedimentaries,
particularly sandstones and limestones, and Pre-Cambrian crystalline
rocks are exposed only along the Sudan border and in the deepest
stream valleys.

CLIMATE.—The most conspicuous climatic features of Northwest
Ethiopia, a tropical mountain land, are an alternation of a long dry
season with a season of storms, a decrease of temperature and increase
of precipitation with altitude, and a small annual range of temperature.

[3] The reader's attention is called to Maps 9 and 10 on which place names mentioned in the text have been located.

Most precipitation falls in the form of rain during the period of high sun. At Gondar, for example, about 94 per cent of the average annual precipitation of 50 inches falls during the period from April through September, the peak months of July and August alone accounting for almost 60 per cent of the year's precipitation. At the height of the rainy season, some precipitation falls almost every day, with clouds commonly forming in late morning or early afternoon and rain or, rarely, hail, sometimes accompanied by lightning and thunder, falling during the afternoon or evening. The Ethiopians consider the rainy season (Amharic: *keremt*) to be their winter, for it is a period of decreased mobility and, for many places, the time when the lowest daytime maximum temperatures occur. At the height of the rainy season in the Northwest, all of the motor roads except for the main north-south road are made impassable by mud and water. At that time, even cross-country travel by foot and mule is difficult. Indeed, many streams which in the dry season are placid, ponded, or dry become in the rainy season rushing torrents which can be crossed only with considerable difficulty by strong swimmers. Traditionally, all contact between Semyen and Tigre Province across the swollen, swirling Tekezzay River ceased during the period of heavy rains, and caravans headed north for Tigre had to turn back to winter in Semyen. Even today, many administrative centers back from the motor road, such as Derasgie, are cut off at the time of heavy rains from contact with the center of government at Gondar.

During the rainy season, the fields of the Northwest are green with growing plants, the countryside is filled with tender grass, and the cattle are sleek, fat, and contented. In September, at the end of the rainy season, comes the Ethiopian New Year, a time of great joy and festivities. Then, with the end of the rains, the fields slowly, almost imperceptibly, change from green to brown and yellow, the crops are harvested, and the farmers' storage bins are filled with grain. As the dry season progresses, the water level gradually drops, and streams can be forded once again. Flies, which are least troublesome in the rainy season, seem to increase enormously in numbers until, by the middle of the dry season, they are a source of considerable annoyance to foreigners, though Ethiopians, at most, leisurely drive them off with horsehair flicks (Amh.: *ch'ira*). As the field grasses become parched and impalatable, the cattle become thinner and thinner until finally their ribs protrude and they seem like mere bags of bones.

The second climatic contrast in Northwest Ethiopia is that between the hot, oppressive lowlands and the cool, pleasant plateau, a contrast that has been felt and vividly described by many foreign travellers.

Ethiopians themselves are even more sensitive to temperature changes
with altitude, and, as in other tropical highland regions, climatic zones
are given distinct names according to their altitude: the hot lowland
below 5,500 feet (Amh.: *k'olla*), the middle highland between 5,500 and
8,000 feet (Amh.: *weyna dega*), and the cold highland above 8,000 feet
(Amh.: *dega*). A fourth zone, above the limit of farming, is also distinguished (Amh.: *urec*), but this is found only in the highest mountain
areas.

In the cold highland, the temperature is moderately high in the
middle of the day, but drops rapidly once the sun goes down, and it is
low enough at night so that warm sleeping bags are necessary for
foreigners. The Ethiopians from lower elevations, when camping in
the *dega,* are also troubled by the cold, for they are scantily clad in
cotton and are unaccustomed to low temperatures. At night they often
form a shivering, vociferous cluster around a campfire, wrapped in
their blankets and huddled together to keep warm. It is worth noting
that in the Northwest wool is woven in the highest sections of the cold
highland, though not commonly elsewhere. The middle highland, by
contrast, is the temperate section, the preferred country of most Ethiopians, and the region of greatest population densities and most advanced culture. Its daytime temperatures are not excessively high, nor
are its nights too cold; in Gondar (6,900 feet elevation), for example,
maximum temperatures in daytime range from about 75° to 90° F.,
and minimum temperatures at night from 45° to 60° F. Just as the
highland Ethiopians like the temperate middle highland, so they dislike and fear the hot lowland, with its high, oppressive temperatures,
and its virulent malaria and other diseases. When making a mule trip
into the lowland along the Sudan border, for example, we could not
get muleteers to take their animals into that country, and finally were
forced to buy our own animals and pay high wages by local standards
to get men to care for them. In Metemma (Gallabat), in the hot lowland at 2,500 feet elevation, the average monthly temperature of the
warmest month is 87° F., 18 degrees higher than at Gondar. During
the heat of the day in the hot lowland of the Northwest, as in the
northern Sudan, conditions are so uncomfortable that almost all
human activity ceases, and people find some shady spot and rest.

Differences in elevation result in differences of precipitation as well
as of temperature. Thus, at Metemma, at 2,500 feet, the average annual
rainfall is 35 inches, at Gondar, 6,900 feet, it is 50 inches, and at Debre
Tabor, 8,500 feet, perhaps 55 inches. It is possible that places in the
high mountains of Begemder and Semyen have even higher precipita-

tion, but unfortunately there are no meteorological stations in such places.

In Northwest Ethiopia, the lowest average monthly temperatures occur at the height of the rainy season (July-August) and the highest during the late dry season (March-April). Like other tropical highland regions, Northwest Ethiopia has a small annual range of temperature. At Metemma, the difference in average monthly temperatures from the warmest to the coldest month is 13° F., and at Gondar it is only 10° F.

VEGETATION.—In Northwest Ethiopia, there are striking changes with altitude in vegetation type as well as in temperature and precipitation.

When the traveller leaves the plateau on the trail to the Sudan border in the dry season, he passes through rough, brush-covered hills and into woods of leafless trees. Here and there are thickets of a sere, yellow bamboo (*Oxytenanthera abyssinica*) [4] (Fig. 2), and stands of dry brown grasses (Fig. 3) which often reach heights of seven feet or more. The grass is so thick in some sections along the trail that travelling merchants commonly set fire to it to clear the way. From the heat of these fires and the hot sun, long, twisting, deep cracks develop in the dried-out soil in many places, and mules and donkeys have considerable difficulty picking their way across such areas without stumbling.

Farther into the lowland (Amh.: *k'olla*), near Metemma, the woods assume a more open, parklike aspect, with short grass growing beneath the trees (Fig. 4). In this dry forest there are few shrubs or young trees, and full-grown trees usually are only a foot or so in diameter. Here and there among the trees are termite mounds which at their maximum seldom rise higher than a man's head. Along streams in the lowland there is a denser growth of shrubs and trees, some of which reach large size and retain their leaves through the dry season, providing welcome shade for the traveller at the time of noonday heat.

Perhaps the most common lowland trees are leguminous species, such as acacias whose thorny branches hang low over the trails, seeming to clutch at the passer-by, tearing his clothes, and scratching his skin. Other trees in the lowland are the *Dalbergia melanoxylon*, the dom palm (*Hyphaene* sp.) whose nuts provide a vegetable ivory, the sausage tree (*Kigelia aethiopica*) with its long, sausagelike fruits, as well as several large trees which usually occur singly: the baobab (*Adansonia*

---

[4] The botanical classification of plants will be indicated only the first time the English or Amharic word is mentioned in the text. When it is not indicated in the text, the botanical classification can be found in the glossary.

digitata), the tamarind (*Tamarindus indica*), and the sycamore fig tree (*Ficus sycomorus*). Lofty, candelabra-shaped euphorbias, some of which are twenty or more feet tall, grow on shady, steep sides of stream valleys.

The cool middle highland (Amh.: *weyna dega*) is a grassland with scattered thorny brush and small trees found especially on uncultivated hill slopes, near streams, and on the edges of cultivated fields. The absence of extensive woods or forests in the highland regions in central and northern Ethiopia is often surprising to European travellers. Indeed, from a vantage point the viewer sees great distances across the countryside and has a feeling of unlimited space, an experience quite different from that in the confining dry forests and high grass of the lowland. Both the middle highland and the cold highland are reminiscent of some of the Coast Range country of central California in their predominantly grassy cover and their change in aspect from green to brown and yellow with the seasons.

Among the grasses of the middle highland those of the following genera predominate: *Andropogon, Panicum, Pennisetum, Sporobolus,* and *Eragrostis.* The common trees include acacias, the oleaster (*Olea chrysophylla*), several species of fig (*Ficus*), the native juniper (*Juniperus* sp.), *Carissa edulis, Cordia abyssinica,* and *Croton macrostachys.* Candelabra euphorbia is found sometimes on steep, shady slopes and in some places grows in hedgerows. Bamboo (*Arundo donax*) is grown on the edges of some gardens, but I have not seen it growing in natural thickets in the middle highland of the Northwest, although it has been reported by travellers as occurring naturally at similar elevations elsewhere in Ethiopia.

Recently introduced species include the eucalyptus (*Eucalyptus globulus*) and the prickly-pear cactus. The latter plant is widespread in Eritrea where it seems to have been introduced in 1865.[5] Because it is found in Begemder and Semyen largely along the motor road and as a hedge plant in only a few gardens around Gondar, I suspect that it was carried south by the Italians.

The cold highland (Amh.: *dega*) contains more grass and fewer trees and shrubs than the middle highland (Fig. 5). Among the trees of the cold highland are juniper, which is the most common, and species of *Olea,* as well as *Hagenia abyssinica.* From the latter, a purgative, *kosso,* is made. Conspicuous among the cold highland plants are the giant thistle *Echinops giganteus,* giant lobelias, some of which reach heights of twenty feet, and *Protea abyssinica.* Near the summit of Ras Dedjen

[5] Piccoli, 1943: 275.

in the alpine zone beyond the limits of agriculture, giant lobelias are the only conspicuous species, standing like sentinels on the spongy meadows (Fig. 6). At the highest elevations mountain grasses displace all other forms of vegetation.

Chapter II

Historical Background

History of Northern Ethiopia.—Little is known of the prehistory of highland Ethiopia, but it is said that in paleolithic times the Ethiopian Plateau was occupied by hunting and gathering people of two races. In the southwest were Bushmanoid people, and in the northeast were Caucasoids. In time, the Caucasoids, who were of Hamitic stock and spoke Cushitic languages, dominated the entire area. At some unknown date prior to 3000 B.C., Negroid peoples pushed into the plateau from the west, introducing agriculture to the Cushites, and also interbreeding with them. The agricultural Cushites, who by this time were quite mixed racially, gradually evolved into separate groups, including the Agow-speaking peoples who occupied much of the northern and central sections of the plateau. Though the role of the Agow people in the culture history of the region is shrouded in mystery, it has been claimed that they were culturally one of the most creative peoples in all of Africa, that they established Ethiopia as an important center of plant domestication, and that they maintained intermittent contacts with ancient Egypt and exchanged certain domestic plants and animals with them.[1]

From about 1000 B.C. to 400 B.C. the northern plateau was settled by new immigrants, this time Semitic-speaking peoples from South Arabia (see Map 3). The Semitic migrations apparently involved the movement of large groups of farmers who came to Ethiopia with their families as settlers and colonizers.[2] These farmers settled among the Cushitic-speaking peoples of the plateau in regions similar in climate and vegetation to their mountain homeland of Yemen. They kept their ancient tribal names, one of which, Habashat, developed into

[1] This reconstruction is based on Murdock, 1959: 181–83. It has been assumed by others that the Cushitic-speaking Caucasoid peoples were preceded by Negroids (see, for example, Trimingham, 1952: 5–7), and that the Negroid peoples were either killed, assimilated by the Cushites, or pushed into harsh environments, particularly in the lowland to the west of the plateau.

[2] Trimingham, 1952: 33.

the name of the country, Abyssinia, and another, Ge'ez, came to be used for the language.

Since little archeological work has been done in Ethiopia, we can only surmise what new culture traits the Semitic invaders introduced.

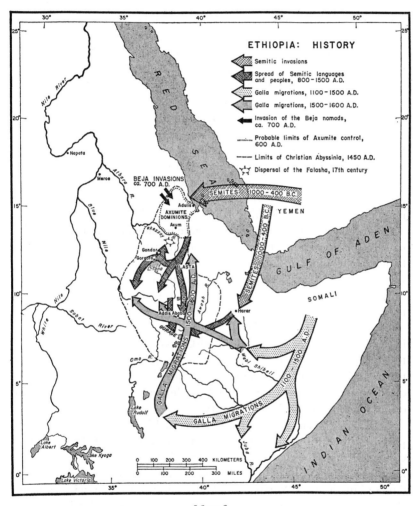

ETHIOPIA: HISTORY

Semitic invasions

Spread of Semitic languages and peoples, 800–1500 A.D.

Galla migrations, 1100–1500 A.D.

Galla migrations, 1500–1600 A.D.

Invasion of the Beja nomads, ca. 700 A.D.

Probable limits of Axumite control, 600 A.D.

Limits of Christian Abyssinia, 1450 A.D.

Dispersal of the Falasha, 17th century

MAP 3

In South Arabia, the Semites knew irrigation, using terraces, canals, and elaborate hydraulic devices.[3] Because of this and because ruins of waterworks are scattered across Tigre and Eritrea, where they settled, it is likely that the Semites introduced advanced systems of irrigation

[3] Trimingham, 1952: 32–33.

agriculture to Ethiopia. Further claims that the Semites introduced the use of metals,[4] the camel and incense,[5] as well as new domestic plants and animals [6] are conjectures without, to my knowledge, specific evidence. Present-day distributions within the country and the available historical evidence suggest that the Semites diffused the plow and various winnowing implements within Ethiopia, as well as the practice of weaving cloth. The latter skill, however, was known in quite early times in the Sudan at Meroe, and both it as well as the plow and the winnowing implements in question may actually have been introduced to Ethiopia in pre-Semitic times.

Perhaps the most striking of the Semitic introductions, however, were the art of writing, superior techniques of building construction, and larger scale political organization. In the centuries after the Semites arrived, they built a number of cities on the Sabaean model of South Arabia. The ruins of one such city have been uncovered at Ava, including monoliths, a temple to the sun god, and Himyaritic inscriptions dating from the seventh to the fifth centuries B.C.[7] The most elaborate of the Semitic ruins are found, however, at Axum in Tigre, which was the center of a city-state founded before the beginning of the Christian era. Though many of the ruins at Axum are buried beneath the modern town, it is clear that the structures there are superior in workmanship to all subsequent Ethiopian construction. Most conspicuous at Axum are the huge, elaborately carved obelisks made of single blocks of granite, all but one of which now lie broken on the ground. The one obelisk remaining standing is seventy feet high. The largest of the fallen obelisks was about 110 feet high. Scattered across the Axumite dominions are the ruins of temples and towns, steles and obelisks, and reservoirs and dams which attest to the cultural attainments of these people [8] who were to leave their imprint on all subsequent Ethiopian history.

Gradually the city-state of Axum extended its rule over the northern part of the Ethiopian Plateau as far south as the Tekezzay River, covering almost exactly the present distribution of the Tigrinya language [9] (see Map 3). The Axumites were in contact with the Sudanese kingdoms of Napata and Meroe along the Nile, with nomadic Beja tribes to the north, as well as with Nilotics, and with the unassimilated Agow-speaking peoples to the south. Such contacts do not, however, seem to have contributed to the flowering of Axumite civilization. Rather, it was contacts with Arabia and the Mediterranean world which affected Axum's cultural growth. The Ptolemies of Egypt

[4] Trimingham, 1952: 33.   [5] Ullendorff, 1955: 5.
[6] Trimingham, 1952: 33.   [7] Trimingham, 1952: 33.
[8] Trimingham, 1952: 34.   [9] Ullendorff, 1955: 14.

ained the literary and ecclesiastical language of the country. In
, there arose a new Christian kingdom, which later was known in
ope as Abyssinia. The Abyssinian kingdom of the ninth and tenth
turies was not restricted to the northern fringe of the highland, as
m had been, but was located in the very heart of the Ethiopian
teau. The Abyssinian kings were at war constantly with the Agow
es whose lands they had entered and who more than once menaced
existence of the kingdom.[13] Indeed, in the twelfth century, an
ow Christian group seized power for a while and moved the capital
th to their homeland of Lasta (Map 3), there to establish a new
nasty known as the Zagwe dynasty. The Zagwes were apparently
ergetic propagators of the faith, both as missionaries and as builders
churches and monasteries. The most remarkable enterprise of the
gwes was the construction at Lalibela of rock-hewn churches which
ll stand today and which are an important pilgrimage center.

While the Zagwes were converting pagan Agow to Christianity in
rthern Ethiopia, Moslems were converting the lowland tribes along
e Red Sea to Islam and moving into central Ethiopia, establishing a
ltanate in Shoa. Prosperous Moslem ports grew along the coast, trad-
g particularly in slaves, and Moslem colonies were established even
the Christian part of the plateau. With the consolidation of the
byssinian Christian state, especially after the accession to power of a
Solomonid" dynasty claiming descent from Solomon and the Queen
f Sheba, it began to expand southward over Moslem regions, and a
ong struggle broke out between Christians and Moslems, apparently
ot so much because of religious zeal as from pressures of territorial
xpansion.[14] The shift of the capital of Abyssinia from Lasta into the
country of the Amhara confirmed the orientation of the emergent state
which, unlike Axum, looked to its southern marches and not to the
Red Sea for military adventures and political expansion.

In the sixteenth century began a series of events which shook the
Abyssinian state to its roots, placed it in brief contact with Europe, and
then returned it to the proud isolation it had so long known. By this
time the Christian Abyssinian state was precariously held together not
by nationalism,[15] but by an adherence to the Ethiopian church and
a vacillating loyalty to the emperor that depended largely on the
effectiveness of his armies. Despite the size (Map 3) and apparent
strength of Abyssinia, powerful regional feelings existed, as well as
strong loyalties to ambitious feudal lords, so that whenever the central
authority weakened there were revolts against the king. Many parts

[13] Trimingham, 1952: 52.   [14] Trimingham, 1952: 65.
[15] Trimingham, 1952: 77.

founded trading posts along the Red Sea whic[h]
lenism; in the first century A.D., Zoscales, K[
quainted with Greek literature, as may have bee[n
In the fourth century, as a result of maritime
with the Byzantine Empire, Monophysite Chris[t
to Axum. At first it was only the court religion
century it had been widely accepted by the Axu[

Their ties with the outside world drew the A[
campaigns abroad, and their armies raided as
Axumite armies invaded the land of their ancest[
the third century, again in the fourth, and aga[i
century. Their period of greatest influence was
fourth century to the seventh century A.D.   At th[e
in the sixth century, Axum held "the richest po[
commercial relations reached as far as Persia, [
and had become a recognized member of the
powers." [11]

Axum's period of power and influence was not
the seventh century the Axumites were driven fro[m
the Persians, who in turn were expelled shortly t[
birth of Islam. From that time on, the Red Sea tra[
safe for Axumite shipping and Axum's ties with the
weakened. Moreover, in the late seventh century,
tribe invaded the Axumite Empire from the nort[h
waste the countryside and overrunning much of Ha[

Isolated from contact with the outside world by Is[l
by hostile nomads, Axum directed its waning stren[
country of the south, a shift in focus perhaps stimu[
placement of large numbers of people by the Beja
tianity, which had assumed an intolerant national [
given powerful impetus to the spread southward of Ax[
Nevertheless, the political unity of Axum had been
Judaism, perhaps spread by Jewish merchants or by
Arabia, had made considerable headway among the
peoples, creating a force which vigorously opposed the [
tianity southward and may have contributed to the
the empire which followed.

The breakdown of Axum's power was followed by se[
about which little is known, but during which the conve[
peoples to Christianity continued and new Semitic langu[
such as Tigrinya and Amharic, though Ge'ez, the langu[

[10] Trimingham, 1952: 40.   [11] Trimingham, 1952: 41.
[12] Trimingham, 1952: 47.

of the country were effectively independent, paying tribute to the king, but having little further obligation to him.

In the late fifteenth century, the Portuguese rounded the Cape of Good Hope, established a sea route to India, and tried to establish a military alliance with Abyssinia against Islam. The Abyssinian kings did not conclude an alliance, but in 1535, after the Moslem warrior Ahmed Gragn, or Ahmed the Left-handed, declared a holy war and led his Moslem army against Christian Abyssinia, the king sent an appeal to the Portuguese for aid. Before the Portuguese force of four hundred men led by Christavão da Gama, son of Vasco da Gama, arrived in 1541, the Moslems had overrun Abyssinia. Most Christians apostatized to Islam and the king became a hunted fugitive who was pursued from place to place. The Christian loyalists, however, eventually joined forces with the Portuguese, defeated their Moslem conquerors, killed Gragn in a battle fought near Lake T'ana, and reestablished Christianity in northern Ethiopia.

The military help given to Abyssinia by the Portuguese led to the settlement of the surviving Portuguese soldiers among the Abyssinians. Moreover, as a result of these contacts, Jesuit priests were sent to Abyssinia to convert the people to Roman Catholicism. At first, the kings were friendly toward the Jesuits who, by 1622, had gained such influence in the court that the king, Susenyos, was converted to Roman Catholicism and tried to make it the state religion. The Jesuits seem, however, to have alienated the Abyssinians by suppressing their ancient religious customs; "they were rebaptized as though they were pagans, their priests were reordained and churches reconsecrated, graven images and the Latin rite and calendar were introduced; whilst deeply rooted customs, like circumcision and the observance of the Sabbath, were prohibited." [16] This led to a reaction against Catholicism, in which the son of Susenyos, Fasiladas, expelled the Jesuits and executed those who refused to leave. He permitted no more Roman Catholic priests to enter the country, and persecuted those of his people who refused to renounce Catholicism. Thus, even the tenuous ties with the Western world established through Catholicism were severed, and Abyssinia remained aloof from Europe until the colonial powers threatened its independence centuries later.

Abyssinian battles with the Moslems left the state in a severely weakened condition in the sixteenth century, at the very moment when a new and even more dangerous threat developed. At about that time, nomadic Galla tribesmen, who were under pressure from the Somali, began to invade the southern part of the Ethiopian Plateau, from

[16] Trimingham, 1952: 99.

what is now Somali country, and to push northward (Map 3). When the Galla acquired horses and became skilled in their use, Galla cavalry pushed into the very heart of the Abyssinian kingdom, even into Begemder and Semyen itself. The Galla came to the highland not as raiders alone, but also as settlers. Wherever they settled, they made travel dangerous and uncertain for the Abyssinians, isolated entire provinces from one another, and broke up the empire.[17] The Abyssinians fought many battles against the Galla, but though individual groups were defeated, the force of the Galla migration could not be stopped. Several large groups of Galla, separated from the main body of their people, settled among the Abyssinians, becoming seminomads or farmers. They remained powerful, however, and were largely independent, though many of them, because of their warlike propensities, were recruited into the armies of the Abyssinian rulers.[18]

The Galla, despite their strength, were themselves too disunited to rule Abyssinia as a people, though groups of them did intimidate and sometimes dominate the kings of Abyssinia. It is said that during this period only the sacred character of the Abyssinian monarchy preserved the dynasty from extinction, so that the Galla, even though they wielded great power, never took over the throne itself.[19] Even so, the power of the Abyssinian king was so nominal and the unity of the country so weakened that the time from 1769 to 1855 is known as the period of regional sovereigns.

Modern Ethiopia dates from the rise of Kassa, who was crowned King Theodore in 1855. From a position as an obscure Amhara bandit chief, Kassa, through his excellent leadership and fighting ability, defeated the regional kings and reunited northern Ethiopia under his rule. His successors, particularly King Menelik, continued the unification of the country, defeating Egyptian and Italian efforts to gain control of it.

From the time of Menelik (1889–1910), Ethiopian leaders have become increasingly aware of the desirability of adopting many of the material elements of Western civilization and there has begun a slow modernization of the country. The Italian occupation of Ethiopia from 1935 to 1941, brief though it was, was the time of most energetic construction, and the motor roads, airports, radio stations, telephone systems, electric plants, hospitals, schools, and public buildings built by the Italians largely for their own ends, proved to be an enormous contribution to the Ethiopian government which succeeded them. Today, this government continues its efforts to develop the country in

[17] Trimingham, 1952: 106.   [18] Trimingham, 1952: 106–7.
[19] Trimingham, 1952: 107.

order to raise living standards and to assure the survival of Ethiopia as an independent land.

THE NORTHWEST IN ETHIOPIAN HISTORY.—During Axumite times, Begemder and Semyen probably were beyond the frontiers of the Semitic state. With the invasion of the Axumite realm by the Beja, Semitic-speaking people are believed to have been displaced, many of them settling south of the Tekezzay River, the southern frontier of Axum. Though these settlers lived among Agow-speaking peoples, their descendants maintained their Semitic language and identity. In time, Begemder in the northwestern plateau became the center of the emergent Abyssinian state. It was, however, an unsettled frontier land quite unlike Axum. The rulers lived in military camps fighting rebellious Amhara lords as well as the Cushites and the fierce Falasha who controlled Semyen, the cold roof of Ethiopia. This was the heyday of the warrior, a period when there was little time for or inclination toward art, literature, or elaborate construction.

After the arrival of the Portuguese, however, castles were built for the Abyssinian kings at the north end of Lake T'ana. First Guzara was built, then Gorgora, and finally, after the expulsion of the Portuguese, Gondar, which remained the capital of Abyssinia for three centuries (Figs. 7 and 8). Arched Portuguese-style bridges spanning the Blue Nile and lesser streams still stand as a tribute to the impetus given to building construction by the Portuguese (Fig. 9). The Abyssinians themselves, despite the establishment of a fixed capital and their Axumite heritage, had little building skill and relied on foreign and half-breed artisans. Therefore, within a few generations after the Portuguese left Ethiopia, their high standards of construction were lost.

The Northwest remained the cultural hearth of Abyssinia until a century ago when King Theodore attempted to reunite the warring segments of the land. To do this, he moved his capital to Magdala on the eastern margin of the Ethiopian Plateau. King Menelik, who completed the unification of the country, moved the capital still farther, to the southern frontier of his day. Now Menelik's capital, Addis Ababa ("New Flower"), is not only the seat of government, but a growing, progressive city, the unquestioned cultural center of the nation, a place of which educated young men speak in enthusiastic terms as the only place in which to live. The Northwest, left behind as the frontier advanced, remains a center of conservatism, a backwash with only its ancient castles to attest to its former greatness.

Chapter III

Peoples, social life,

AND POLITICAL ORGANIZATION

Physical Type and Language

The racial, linguistic, and cultural mélange characteristic of Ethiopia today results not only from its geographic position between the Middle East and Negro Africa, but from the numerous invasions of the region by alien peoples, from large-scale internal migrations, from the diffusion into the area of new culture traits and culture complexes, including Judaism, Christianity, and Islam, and from extensive culture contact, acculturation, and biological intermixing. In ancient times, it is assumed, Ethiopia was occupied by Bushmanoid and Cushitic-speaking Caucasoid peoples, the Cushites gradually gaining ascendancy throughout the area. The subsequent invasions of the region by Negroid peoples led to extensive racial mixing, though the Cushitic languages persisted in most of the area. The invasions of Semitic-speaking peoples from South Arabia later brought new languages and additional Caucasoid people to Ethiopia. Eventually, the Semitic languages largely displaced the Cushitic tongues in the northern parts of the Ethiopian Plateau, though the latter continued to be the principal languages elsewhere in the region. Biologically, however, there was such extensive mixing that today the Semitic-speaking groups are indistinguishable physically from the Cushitic-speaking groups; indeed, it has been estimated that the original Cushitic-speaking groups contributed far more genetically to the present-day Semitic-speaking peoples of Ethiopia than did the Semitic invaders.[1]

Many writers consider both the Cushitic-speaking and Semitic-speaking peoples of Ethiopia to belong to a common "Ethiopian" physical type, which is different from both South Arabian and Negro physical types. The man of Ethiopian physical type (Figs. 11, 12, 13, 14, and 15) is fairly tall,[2] and of slender to moderate body build. His

[1] Trimingham, 1952: 6.

[2] The 248 Amhara men measured by the Missione di Studio al Lago Tana averaged five feet seven inches in height, the tallest being about six feet one inch in

skin color may vary from brown to black. He usually has a long head and a narrow to medium broad nose with a high bridge. His hair is black, and curly or kinky. There is a tremendous variation in appearance among the Semitic and Cushitic peoples of Ethiopia, some individuals having more pronounced Negroid features and others more pronounced Caucasoid features. Regardless of this variation, they can readily be distinguished from the highland Arabs of Yemen, the homeland of the ancient Semitic invaders of Ethiopia, for the Arabs are much lighter in color, their hair is straight or wavy, and they are usually of slighter build. Ethiopians can be distinguished from Negroes in most cases, too, but with greater difficulty.

Within Begemder and Semyen, most people of the several ethnic groups are of the Ethiopian physical type. There are, however, two groups living along the Sudan border (see Map 4), the Gumis and the Hametsh, who are Negroes. These people are, on the average, slightly shorter in stature, somewhat heavier in build, and darker in skin color than the Semitic- and Cushitic-speaking groups (Figs. 22, 23, and 24); they have wide, low-bridged noses, and hair that is kinky or, in a few cases, peppercorn in form. The other peoples of the area recognize the difference in physical type between themselves and the Gumis and Hametsh, for they call the latter two groups *shank'illa* (blacks) or *baria* (slaves), as they do Negro peoples of Africa. Hereafter, when the term "Negro" is used with reference to Northwest Ethiopian groups, it will apply specifically to the Gumis and Hametsh.

Amharic, which is spoken by more of the world's people than any other Semitic language except Arabic, is the most important language of Northwest Ethiopia. It is spoken not only by the Amhara themselves, but by most Ethiopian Moslems (Jabartis) and Jews (Falasha) as well as the Wayt'o of Lake T'ana. Even among groups whose native tongue is not Amharic, there are at least a few men in every village who know it, for government affairs are conducted in Amharic and most merchants are Amharic-speakers. After Amharic, Tigrinya is the most widely spoken Semitic language in Ethiopia; in the Northwest, there is a considerable section bordering Tigre Province which is occupied by people who speak this language (see Map 4). In addition, there are many Tigrinya-speaking people, migrants from northern Begemder and Semyen or from Tigre or Eritrea, who live and work in towns and cities throughout the province.

The Cushitic languages are represented in the Northwest by Agow

---

height (Cipriani, 1940: 443); Amhara women averaged five feet two inches in height (Cipriani, 1940: 432).

(Agau), dialects of which are spoken by three unassimilated groups: the Agow of Sahalla, the K'amant, and the Kumfel. The K'amant, the largest of these groups, are located northwest of Lake T'ana, entirely within Begemder and Semyen, centering on the towns of Ch'ilga and Tikil Dingaī. The Agow of Sahalla are simply an extension into the Northwest of a larger Agow group which is centered in the prov-

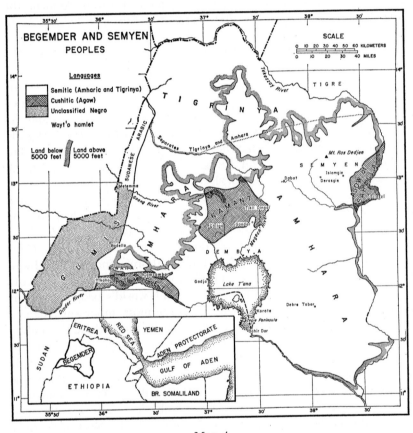

MAP 4

inces to the east, and the Kumfel are one section of a group found also in Godjam Province, where there are also large additional groups of Agow-speaking people.

The Negro Gumis and Hametsh of the western lowlands of Begemder and Semyen are not related in language to the Semitic- and Cushitic-speaking peoples of Ethiopia. Moreover, Joseph Greenberg, in his 1950 classification of African languages, was unable to relate the language of the Gumis to any of the large language families of Africa. Instead, he grouped the Gumis with several other groups from nearby sections of the Sudan into an independent "Koman" language family.

ETHNIC GROUPS

Ethiopians of the Northwest recognize nine principal native ethnic groups, all of which have folk societies whose members strongly identify with the place in which they live. They differ, however, in language, in religion or other aspects of culture, or, to some extent in the case of the Gumis, in race. The persistence of group differences is encouraged by the widespread notion that peoples of other religions, or even, in some cases, people of the same religion but of a different group, are ritually impure, and that one should not eat the flesh of animals slaughtered by them and should avoid contact with them as much as possible. The Amhara, who are Christians and speak a Semitic language, are the most numerous and the most powerful politically. The Tigrinya-speakers, who are also Semites, are probably second in numbers; since they are also Christians and since there seem to be few significant cultural differences between them and the Amhara, I will not describe them further. The Falasha, or "Black Jews of Ethiopia," and the Jabartis, or native Moslems, speak the language of the people among whom they live, and are set apart on the basis of their religions. The Wayt'o are a small group of Moslem fishermen-farmers who live along the shores of Lake T'ana and who, despite the fact that they speak Amharic, are the lowliest group in the Northwest, looked down upon because they eat certain types of flesh which other groups regard as unclean.

Three of the remaining groups are Agow-speaking: the Kumfel of the inhospitable lowlands along the southern borders, the Agow of Sahalla who live in the hot, unpleasant Tekezzay Valley, and the K'amant who live on the western edge of the plateau. These three groups are probably the unassimilated remnants of the Agow farmers who occupied the entire highland of the Northwest before the movement of Semites into the region. Although both the Kumfel and Agow of Sahalla are Christians, the K'amant still adhere to their ancient pagan religion. The Gumis of the Sudan border are the only Negro group of significance, a group distinctive not only because of physical characteristics, but also because of language and culture. There is one village of Negroes of another tribe, the Hametsh, in the Kumfel country, who are important principally because they illustrate one way in which acculturation may have taken place in the Northwest.

All the Semitic- and Cushitic-speaking groups are surprisingly similar, not only in their physical appearance, but also in their material culture, their agricultural methods, and cultivated plants, though some of them differ in religion and social life. Only the Gumis, who live in a harsh environment on the borders of the Ethiopian culture area, stand out as a totally distinct group; not only are they distinguishable in dress and physical appearance from the other peoples of the region, but they lack certain elements of material culture common to the other groups, they possess a smaller variety of domestic plants and animals, they employ different agricultural methods, and they have a less elaborate social and political organization.

Amhara

ORIGIN AND HISTORY.—The origin of the Amhara, like that of the other peoples of Ethiopia, is obscured by traditions interwoven with religious beliefs. Perhaps they had their origin south of the Axumite dominions in a Semitic-speaking Christian tribe which gathered strength and consciousness with the decline of the power of Axum, though this is not certain. It is known, however, that the ancient Amhara pushed southward and eastward conquering and assimilating earlier Agow-speaking Cushitic tribes. Many Amhara today consider their homeland to be Begemder, but, though this has long been their center of power, there is evidence in place names and traditions that Begemder was Agow country not long ago.

An agricultural and herding people with great pride and warlike tendencies, the Amhara, though a minority in numbers in the country as a whole, have been the ruling power in Ethiopia through much of medieval and modern times, and have supplied Ethiopia with its present Emperor, Haile Selassie. Though powerful regional loyalties exist among the Amhara, and have led to the division of the country into warring segments during large parts of its history, the group has had a consistent political consciousness and a belief in its right to unite and rule Ethiopia. These attitudes have been coupled with persistence and a genius for organization unmatched by other Ethiopian peoples. Unification of the country has been accomplished despite fierce opposition by other groups, who often demonstrated great individual bravery and skill in battle, but finally succumbed to the Amhara.

The Amhara have contributed far more to Ethiopia than political unity. They have kept the country in touch with Western civilization through their adherence to Christianity. Their churches and monasteries, moreover, have traditionally been storehouses of religious and historical documents, which are one of the major untouched sources of material on the ancient life and ways of the country. Their priests also have maintained a formal system of education, which recently has been supplemented by a system of state schools. In addition, the fact that Amharic is the only modern language of the country that is written facilitated its use as the language of government and commerce. The Amhara have also had a great effect on the landscape through the diffusion of the plow, which has increased the amount of land under cultivation and has hastened the destruction of woodland on the plateau. Accompanying the plow has been the acceptance of the idea that grains are superior food to green vegetables and root crops. This attitude has led to the expansion of grain cultivation, particularly that of the Amhara's favorite cereal, t'eff (*Eragrostis teff*), and may have led, too, to the abandonment of the cultivation of many root crops and the banana-like ensete (*Ensete edulis*), which are still important in southern highland Ethiopia. Thus, even though the Amhara today seem conservative to Western educators and planners, they are and have been the most important cultural innovators in Ethiopia.

RELIGION AND SOME SOCIAL ATTITUDES.—There are probably more churches in the Amhara country than in any other region of comparable size in the world. Almost every village has its own church (*beita kristyan*), which is usually a circular building with a thatch roof (Fig. 84), conspicuous because it is perched high on a hill, enclosed by a stone wall, and surrounded by a grove of trees, the latter apparently a survival of pagan Agow custom. Larger settlements have more than one church, the number varying according to the size and importance of the place. In the Gondar area, there are, for example, a reputed forty-four churches, a number which testifies to the importance of Gondar, which is the provincial capital and a city of perhaps 22,000 inhabitants. Churches are so numerous in Christian Ethiopia because it has been customary for wealthy lords and kings to build them as acts of piety and as symbols of their greatness. The chronicles of the Gondar kings thus not only relate their triumphs and failures in war, but list the churches constructed by them. Since an important man gains more prestige by building a new church than by renovating an old one, Ethiopian churches, though numerous, are generally in poor condition. Churches commonly bear the name of Jesus, Mary, or one of the saints and sometimes, too, the name of the locality. The Church of Mary in Derasgie, for example, is known as Derasgie Mariam, and the famous churches of Gondar include *Fit Mikael* ("First Michael"), *Gimja Beit Mariam* ("Treasury of Mary"), *Adebabaī Iyesus* ("Court Church of Jesus"), and *Debre Birhan Selassie* ("Trinity of Debre Birhan"). The church is so inextricably a part of

Amhara life that people, when asked the name of their village, often give the name of their church instead. When he arrives at a village, it is considered an act of courtesy for the foreign traveller to visit the local church, which is the most impressive structure of the village and contains the greatest treasures of the neighborhood, including vividly colored paintings of Biblical scenes, the bright vestments and umbrellas of the clergy, and intricately designed crosses, cups, drums, and other gold and silver objects, which are the pride of the local people.

Clergy are so common in the Christian parts of Ethiopia that some European travellers have estimated that one man in every five serves the church in some capacity. Ordinarily, a church is staffed by a large group, including not only priests, but choirmen-scribes (*debtera*) and boy deacons (Fig. 10). Priests and choirmen-scribes can be distinguished by their turbans (Fig. 11), which Christian laymen do not wear, and boy deacons by their skin cloaks and by the wooden staffs they characteristically carry. The priesthood is not hereditary, though priests are chosen from traditional priestly families.[3] This, together with the tendency of priests to marry daughters of other priests, has in fact made the priesthood almost a hereditary caste.[4] Priests are supported by the people's voluntary offerings, by tithes, and by tax-free land provided by the government for their use.[5] Despite this, most of them have about the same standard of living as the general populace. Choirmen-scribes, unlike priests, are not ordained, even though they are the learned men of the church and the choristers who have to learn all the words of the church services. Certain choirmen-scribes receive payment from the church, but most of them support themselves by farming or other activities. Boy deacons are attached to a church in order that they may learn Christian ritual and beliefs. Each boy deacon, during his period of service, subsists in part by begging, and by constructing the fiber parasols (Figs. 75 and 76) that are carried by many Ethiopian women. When boy deacons reach the age of puberty, many of them end their service to the church,[6] though others become priests or choirmen-scribes. In addition to the churches, there is a monastic movement within Ethiopian Christianity, with monks living as celibates in the seclusion of their monasteries, which are usually located far from the corrupting influences of secular life. Sex is so completely eliminated from the life of the monastery that not only are women excluded, but all female animals as well. Monks, because of

[3] Trimingham, 1952: 26.   [4] Perham, 1948: 110.
[5] Trimingham, 1952: 26.   [6] Perham, 1948: 113.

their reputation for great spirituality, are generally held in higher regard than priests, whose failings are known to everyone.

The Ethiopian Church has been affiliated with the Coptic Church of Egypt since ancient times, and the head of the Ethiopian Church, or *Abuna*, has traditionally been an Egyptian Copt appointed by the Patriarch of Alexandria. Through most of history, however, the contacts with the Coptic Church of Egypt were tenuous, for the vast expanses between Egypt and Ethiopia were dangerous to travel, and the Moslem rulers of Egypt did not always facilitate such contacts. It often happened that when an *Abuna* died, the Ethiopian Church was without a replacement for many years. Moreover, there were frequent conflicts of personality and culture between the Egyptian *Abuna* and his Ethiopian associates. Usually the *Abuna*, though revered as the highest figure in the church, had little power, and in some cases was little more than the tool of the reigning king. Today, as the result of an agreement signed between the Ethiopian Church and the Coptic Church in 1948, there is an Ethiopian-born *Abuna*, and the only formal tie remaining with the Coptic Church is in the appointment of the Ethiopian *Abuna*. The Ethiopian church thus has gained open recognition of the near independence it has so long enjoyed.

In beliefs, Ethiopian Christians, like Egyptian Copts, recognize the Monophysite belief as to the nature of Christ, a doctrine which separates them from Western trinitarian Christians. Despite their adherence to the Monophysite doctrine, the Ethiopian Christians have incorporated or tolerate so many pagan and Jewish elements as to warrant their church being considered a separate entity rather than as one with the Coptic Church. Thus, pagan gods continue to exist as good or evil spirits. The extraordinary role of the Virgin Mary, who haunts high mountains, springs, and trees, suggests, moreover, that she has taken the traditional part of pre-Christian spirits.[7] The wearing of amulets, the practice of exorcism, the slaughtering of animals at the dedication of a church, and the observing of the Sabbath as well as Sunday seem equally incongruous practices.

The position of the Ethiopian Church in Amhara life is reminiscent of that of the medieval church in Europe. It plays a conspicuous role throughout a man's life, but particularly at birth, marriage, and death. In times of serious or incurable illness, people sometimes go to the church for alms and spiritual comfort. Once, for example, at a church compound in Gondar I saw a group of these people, including some afflicted with such diseases as elephantiasis and leprosy, waiting for

[7] Trimingham, 1952: 27–28.

food to be provided to them. In a tent set up within the compound, a priest was reading the Bible in Ge'ez to a young woman, apparently to instill faith in her. Traditionally, the church has been a money-lender, too, providing funds to merchants and others at interest rates that are high by Western standards. Such activities are still carried on, though it is not known how widespread they are, or how important a factor they are in the Ethiopian economy today. Churches own land, but they do not seem to be great landowners, though many of them have surplus land which they rent.

Ethiopian Christians may be married sacramentally within the church, or outside the church by a civil ceremony or by agreement. People who have not been married sacramentally may not enter the church while services are being conducted, but must stand outside. Since most people are so married, only a small share of the people see much of church ceremony, except on special occasions when parts of the ceremony are carried on outside.

Ethiopian Christianity is thus a religion with carefully limited participation. It is, moreover, a religion of fast and celebration. There are, for example, no less than two hundred fast days in a year, including each Wednesday and Friday, as well as Lent.[8] Though only the clergy and devout Christians observe all these fasts, everyone is careful to observe the church food taboos, especially the distinction between the flesh of clean and unclean animals, the latter including the pig, camel, horse, mule, donkey, dog, cat, and locust, among others. Christian festivals are greeted with great enthusiasm in Ethiopia, especially *mesk'el,* the celebration of the finding of the true Cross by St. Helena,[9] and the Epiphany (*t'imk'et*). For the festival, the treasures of the church are brought forth, including the *tabot* or ark, a "consecrated slab of stone or wood which symbolizes at once the Ark of the Covenant and the Tables of the Law"[10] and which gives sanctity to a church.

It should be borne in mind that converts to the faiths of foreign missionaries, whether Protestant or Catholic, are not considered true Christians and are generally regarded with suspicion as representatives of alien creeds. In Begemder and Semyen there are two foreign missions: that of the Seventh-Day Adventists at Debre Tabor, a considerable establishment with a well-run school and hospital, which in 1953 was staffed by Norwegians, and the London Mission to the Jews at Dabat, founded by Europeans to convert Falasha to Ethiopian Christianity. The Ethiopian government does not permit foreign

[8] Perham, 1948: 117.   [9] D. Buxton, 1950: 81.   [10] D. Buxton, 1950: 63.

missionaries to proselytize Ethiopian Christians, but even among non-Christian groups they are making few genuine conversions.

Traditional Amhara social attitudes apart from religious ones include respect for the landowning farmer, priest, scribe, and warrior [11] (Fig. 12), and disrespect for most kinds of craftsmen. The ordinary man defers to his feudal lords. The lord, in turn, usually has a haughty bearing before his subordinates, but a humble one before his superiors. Thus, perhaps because most men have ample experience both as superiors and subordinates, two Amhara of different rank, it has been claimed, could change positions and each be perfectly at home in his new role. Moreover, it has always been possible for a man to raise himself in rank and prestige. Perhaps the most notable example of such upward mobility has been Kassa, a bandit, who, through his fighting and leadership ability rose a century ago to the position of Emperor of Ethiopia. Today, the possibility of social advancement through banditry and war has largely been lost, though a clever boy can reach a position of influence by success in the new educational system of the country.

ECONOMIC LIFE.—The bases of Amhara economic life are agriculture and animal husbandry, for the Amhara disdain trade as well as some types of craft work such as smithing and pottery making. Amhara agriculture is based on the use of the ox-drawn plow in the field and the cultivation of cereals, pulses, and oilseeds. Though they have small gardens for spices, medicinals, and other plants which need special care or are cultivated in small quantities, the Amhara direct their main efforts to their field crops. Among the common domestic animals of the Amhara are cattle, horses, donkeys, mules, sheep, goats, chickens, and dogs. The Amhara value their cattle highly not only for the usefulness of oxen for draft purposes and of cows for milk, but for the prestige that possession of cattle gives to the owner. Though the Amhara are largely subsistence farmers and herdsmen, they exchange whatever small surplus they have in the marketplace for the few foods and manufactured products they need.

ROLE IN CULTURE CHANGE IN THE NORTHWEST.—The transformation of the Amhara from what may have been a single tribe into a formidable ethnic group numbering perhaps two million people, has been accomplished largely through the assimilation of other ethnic groups, most of whom were Agow-speaking. This assimilative process, which is here called "Amharization," is a form of acculturation similar to the widespread "Arabization" of native groups in Moslem Africa,

[11] Messing, 1955: 431.

under which the members of the group being assimilated adopt a new
genealogy and a new language, and modify certain aspects of their old
way of life, including some religious and magical beliefs, modes of
dress, and food habits, while retaining certain former traits and attitudes even though they may prevent the new culture from forming a
harmonious whole.

There is much evidence in Begemder and Semyen that Amharization
is continuing today. In regions that were occupied a few hundred
years ago by Agow-speaking K'amant, people today are indignantly
Amharic. In discussing the distribution of the K'amant people with
an old K'amant man in Gondar, I found that people of villages he
considered as K'amant insisted that they were Amhara, an indication
perhaps that within the old man's lifetime these groups have changed
their ethnic affiliations. Such people often have succeeded in elimi-
nating those aspects of their ancient life which distinguish them from
the Amhara. The first changes made are the formal acceptance of
Christianity and the food and ceremonial observances which are
associated with it. Then, if the process continues, certain additional
traits, such as language and dress, are modified to conform with
Amhara ways, though others may persist and eventually become part
of the broader Amhara culture.

It frequently happens that people of one village or of one region
consider themselves to be Amhara, or at least present themselves as
such to strangers, whereas their neighbors, who are unquestionably
Amhara, regard them as impostors. Thus, in any linguistic map of
areas in which people at various stages of assimilation are found, it is
important to consider not only the language the people speak and the
ethnic group they consider themselves to belong to, but the ethnic
group that their neighbors consider them to belong to.

It has been observed that "Amhara" is often used in Ethiopia as
synonymous with "Christian." It is true that should an Amhara for-
sake Christianity, he would no longer be considered an Amhara. On
the other hand, all Christians are not considered to be Amhara, but
only those whose language and ways are Amharic. Thus, in Semyen,
Agow Christians are still considered Agow; the Kumfel, another Agow-
speaking Christian group living along the Dinder River, are considered Kumfel; and those members of the Negro Gumis tribe of the
Sudan border country who have accepted Christianity are still regarded as Gumis. In view of this, the term "Amhara" is used herein
to refer only to the ethnic group, "Amharic" to the language, and
"Amharic-speakers" to all peoples whose first language is Amharic,
even though they may belong to ethnic groups other than the Amhara.

The prestige and advantages of being a Christian and an Amhara exert a powerful attraction on members of other groups. A recent Gumis convert to Ethiopian Christianity, who seemed to know little about Christian teachings and practices, told me in a pathetic manner that now that he and his people were Christians, Amhara merchants would no longer consider them dirty and refuse to eat their food, and they could be friends.

Accompanying the assimilation of other ethnic groups with the Amhara, there has often been strong resistance on the part of the Amhara to the acceptance of foreign ways, which was often accompanied by narrow xenophobic behavior. There has, however, been a significant recent shift in the attitude of the Amhara-dominated national government toward Western ways, motivated by a desire to strengthen and maintain the independence of Ethiopia, and having considerable effect on the nature and means of culture change. This shift, which became more pronounced when Haile Selassie was crowned Emperor in 1930, has led to increased centralization of authority in Addis Ababa and to an emphasis on modernization and national unity. As a result of the shift, and in considerable part because of the Emperor's role in what Simon Messing has called "directed change," [12] new forces of culture change have been unleashed, among the most powerful being an educated elite. The new policy is drawing Ethiopia's various ethnic groups more fully into the national life through greater tolerance of Islam and Judaism, through the greater opportunity granted them in the educational system, and through the increased possibility of advancement to important government positions. Moreover, the Ethiopian Church has been encouraged to convert the pagans to Christianity, which, in the past, they have not always been eager to do. So far, the culture change that has resulted from the policy has been greatest in Addis Ababa, where the agents of change, including a considerable foreign population, have been concentrated; new ways and attitudes have, however, also been introduced in the Northwest, especially in Gondar, the provincial capital. In most sections of the Northwest, which are far removed from the modern currents of life, the forces of inertia and passive resistance inherent in the family organization, the class stratification, and the Christian church are dominant, and the life of the people continues in large part as it always has. It may be, on the other hand, that the new ways may prove more effective in assimilating other groups to the Amhara culture than any that have been followed in the past.

[12] Messing (1955) has given the best account of the mechanisms of culture change in modern Ethiopia and in this paragraph I rely on him to a considerable extent.

Jabartis

ORIGIN AND SOCIAL POSITION.—Following J. Spencer Trimingham, I
have used the term Jabartis to refer to native Moslems living in
Christian areas of Ethiopia,[13] where they constitute perhaps one-tenth
of the population. The Jabartis are similar in race to the Cushitic and
Semitic peoples among whom they live, for many are the direct descendants of local people who were converted to Islam by other Ethiopian Moslems, especially at the time when the Sultanate of Shoa
was flourishing,[14] and when the Moslem armies of Ahmed Gragn
conquered Christian Abyssinia in the sixteenth century.[15] Other
Jabartis are descended from Arabs and other foreign Moslems who
have become assimilated in language and in some customs, though
not in religion.[16]

The Jabartis are scattered across Northwest Ethiopia as individual or
small groups of families among the Christians, or in villages of their
own. Generally they are on good terms with their Amhara Christian
neighbors, and there has even been some intermarriage between leading
Moslem and Christian families in Ethiopia.[17] On the other hand, at
many times in the past there has been considerable anti-Moslem feeling, stemming partially from the fear that the Jabartis would side
with the foreign Moslem enemies of Ethiopia in times of danger. Such
feeling has led to the levying of special imposts on the Jabartis, to
their persecution, and even to their forced conversion. King Theodore,
for example, dealt with the Jabarti problem in 1864 by simply issuing
a decree forbidding Islam and declaring that those Moslems who refused to become Christians would be regarded as rebels. Most Moslems
submitted to Theodore's will and became Christians, but others left
their homes and possessions and took refuge in the woods.[18] Several
times in the past, moreover, Imperial decrees have deprived Jabartis
of land held by hereditary right, which has led many rural Moslems
to turn to weaving and trade to supplement their agricultural income.
Others left the land altogether, settling in towns and cities and earning
their livelihood entirely as merchants. Largely because of this, the

---

[13] Trimingham, 1952: 150–51. As Trimingham points out, Ethiopians themselves
commonly use the term Jabartis to refer to Ethiopian Moslems in general, though
sometimes they use it in the narrow sense of native Moslems living in Christian
parts of the country. Trimingham, however, uses the term Jabartis in a somewhat
different sense than that used in this book, for he does not consider the Jabartis to
comprise an ethnic unit, which is implied here despite the fact that some of them
speak Amharic, and others Tigrinya, or Agow.

[14] Trimingham, 1952: 152.   [15] Grottanelli, 1939: 152.
[16] Trimingham, 1952: 152.   [17] Trimingham, 1952: 152.
[18] Trimingham, 1952: 118.

Jabartis today are on the average more prosperous than their Christian neighbors. Nevertheless, they are looked down upon because of their alien creed and because they work at merchandising and weaving, which are inferior occupations in the eyes of most Christian Ethiopians.

ECONOMIC LIFE.—Jabarti farmers do not differ in their agricultural techniques from their neighbors, and they raise the same crops, with a few additions such as tobacco and *ch'at*. Some rural Jabartis, however, supplement their agricultural earnings or replace them entirely by income gained from trading or from weaving cloth.

Jabarti homes are similar in form to those of other Ethiopians, though they tend to be larger and many have two entrances instead of one,[19] the latter a characteristic that may have developed because of the need for a means of escape. Jabarti villages in Northwest Ethiopia, too, give one the feeling that the inhabitants do not consider themselves secure, for commonly the houses are clustered together in sites away from the main trails that cross the country, and in spots that can readily be defended. In the Jabarti village of Islamgie in Semyen, house compounds are even walled with stone, because the settlement is occasionally raided by bandits, who may be encouraged to do this because of the alien status of its inhabitants. In larger towns, Moslems have traditionally occupied separate quarters. In Gondar even today the Moslems still live in their ancient quarter, Addīs Alem ("New World"), which is located on a hill slope to the south of the city proper. Addīs Alem is a settlement difficult of access, with crooked, narrow paths and a stone wall surrounding each house and mosque compound.

Their ties with the Islamic world which almost surrounds Ethiopia have given the Jabartis an advantage over other Ethiopians in trade, for they have had a greater awareness of the nature of commerce and the variety of goods available in the outside world. Still, the Ethiopian Moslems have not been as successful as the many Yemen Arab merchants who have established shops in the larger towns, for success in shop trade involves stocking a variety of goods and planning future needs carefully, abilities which seem to come much more readily to Yemen Arabs than to Ethiopian Moslems.

RELIGIOUS AND SOCIAL LIFE.—Jabarti villages usually have a mosque (*mesgīd*) which looks much like the other houses and is far less elaborate than the Christian churches. In Gondar, however, there is an impressive white minaret and mosque of Italian construction, a structure reminiscent of the outside Islamic world, but not typical of Moslem places of worship in the province. Jabartis have *sheikhs* who perform much the same functions that priests do in Christian society.

[19] Grottanelli, 1939: 155–56.

Many villages also have *kadis* who usually serve both as Koranic teachers and priests.[20] The Jabartis are not rigid in prayers or fasting, and few go on pilgrimage to Mecca or other holy places. Moreover, few Jabartis except clerics and religious people know in detail the Moslem proscriptions or the Koran,[21] for they speak Amharic and most of them know little, if any, Arabic.

In their social life the Jabartis are like the Christians, except that they acknowledge polygamy, though few men in fact have more than one wife. If a man has two wives, he maintains two residences, one wife living in each. Neither wife is above the other in status and the husband spends half of the month with each.[22] Jabartis claim that there is greater marital fidelity and less divorce among them than among the Christians. Jabarti wives are usually unveiled and, like Ethiopian women in general, they have considerable liberty and are honored.

Jabartis, like all other religious groups of Northwest Ethiopia, refuse to eat pork or the flesh of animals killed by someone of another religion. They have food taboos generally similar to those of the Amhara. Unlike the Amhara, however, they acknowledge the camel as a clean animal, and have taken up smoking tobacco and, to some extent, chewing the stimulant *ch'at*. They drink liquor even in public bars, though Yemen Arabs generally avoid such places. Unlike Christian laymen, many Moslems wear the turban, though otherwise their dress is indistinguishable.

Falasha

ORIGIN AND HISTORY.—The Falasha, or "Black Jews of Ethiopia," have attracted considerable attention abroad because of their dark color and uncertain origins. Calling themselves *"Isra'el"* or *"beita Isra'el"* ("the House of Israel"), many Falasha trace their origin to the Jews who accompanied Menelik, son of King Solomon and the Queen of Sheba, to Ethiopia. Other Falasha claim that when the Hebrews left Egypt in Moses' time, some of them migrated south to Ethiopia; still others assert that they have descended from Jews who came later.[23] The Amhara call them "Falasha," a name which is explained as coming from the Ethiopic word *fälläsä*, "to emigrate." [24] It has been suggested that the term may have been used first by the older native population to designate Jewish immigrants from abroad.[25]

In the absence of reliable historical evidence, the origin and early

---

[20] Trimingham, 1952: 153.
[22] Grottanelli, 1939: 158.
[24] Leslau, 1951: ix.

[21] Grottanelli, 1939: 158.
[23] Leslau, 1951: xliii.
[25] Leslau, 1951: ix.

history of the Falasha remain a matter of speculation to Western scholars. "Whether they are ethnically Jews; whence and when they migrated to Ethiopia, or, on the other hand, whether they represent a part of the native Ethiopian population which was converted at some remote time to Judaism, and if so, by whom—all of these problems still go unsolved." [26] Most Western scholars believe today that the Falasha are a part of the pagan Agow population which was converted to Judaism.[27] Wolf Leslau, an authority on the subject, is inclined to think, in view of the fact that there is more evidence of contact between Yemen and Ethiopia than between Egypt and Ethiopia, that the conversion was accomplished by Jews from Yemen.[28] J. Spencer Trimingham,[29] on the other hand, seems to think that evidence is better for conversion by Jews who reached Ethiopia from Egypt by way of Nubia.

The belief that the Falasha are the descendants of an indigenous people converted to Jewry stems largely from the facts 1) that most of them are indistinguishable in physical appearance from their fellow Ethiopians (Fig. 13), 2) that they do not know Hebrew, but speak the language of the people among whom they live, 3) that Falasha culture, other than religion, is substantially the same as that of other Ethiopians, and 4) that even their religion shows a mixture of pagan, Christian, and Jewish elements.[30] Wolf Leslau has shown that even today the way remains open for the conversion of non-Falasha to Judaism,[31] another indication of the possibility that the Falasha are Jews by conversion. Leslau has also noted that the Bogos, a native Agow tribe of Eritrea, are quite similar in physical appearance to many Falasha,[32] suggesting still further a racial tie with the Agow. Further, a few Falasha in Semyen speak Agow dialects such as K'warenya (Quarenya) and Khamir.[33] Moreover, some old Falasha of K'wara, a district west of Lake T'ana whence K'warenya presumably was derived, still know an Agow dialect they call Dembinya which presumably was derived from the Dembya district just north of Lake T'ana. Moreover, some of the Falasha festivals and fasts bear Agow names and Agow is still used in many prayers and benedictions.[34]

Though their origins and early history remain obscure, we know that the Falasha developed a strong sense of ethnic unity and that the mountains of Semyen became their stronghold, zealously defended by them for many generations. Abyssinian chroniclers record a long series

[26] Leslau, 1949: 216.   [27] Leslau, 1951: xliii; Trimingham, 1952: 20.
[28] Leslau, 1951: xliii.   [29] Trimingham, 1952: 19–20.
[30] Trimingham, 1952: 20–21.   [31] Leslau, 1949: 221.
[32] Leslau, 1949: 217.   [33] Leslau, 1951: xx–xxi.
[34] Leslau, 1951: xxi.

of wars between Christians and Falasha. There is a tradition that in
the tenth century a Falasha princess, Judith, led a revolt which over-
threw the Christian government, laid waste the churches and monasteries, and reigned as Queen for forty years.[35] This tradition, whether
true or not, seems to confirm the position of the Falasha as one of the
important politically coherent groups in medieval Abyssinia. It was
not until the sixteenth century that the Falasha apparently were completely subjected by the Abyssinian kings [36] after hard fighting. In de-
scribing this fighting one Abyssinian writer admires "the courage of
some Falasha women who hurled themselves into an abyss with the
cry 'Adonai, help me,' rather than be captured by the victors." [37] In
the seventeenth century, after further revolts, the Falasha were again
defeated and then expelled from Semyen and scattered over Northwestern Ethiopia (Map 3).[38]

Today, the Falasha live scattered among the general Ethiopian population mostly in Begemder and Semyen and Tigre provinces. Estimates
of their numbers range from 15,000 or 20,000 [39] to 60,000 or 70,000; [40]
30,000 is probably not far from their actual numbers today. The
Falasha own no land, but rent land from other Ethiopians, farming
it and also working as craftsmen for their Christian and Moslem
neighbors. In some places they live in villages but more usually they
occupy hamlets within the villages of other ethnic groups. Other
Ethiopians look down on them because of their religion and because
they participate in the crafts of ironworking and pottery, which are
considered menial work by both Christians and Moslems.

Their lowly position does not seem to trouble the Falasha, who
in general want to remain apart and to maintain their separate identity
and ritual purity. The Falasha who live in Gondar are considered by
Falasha in the villages to be unclean because they come into contact
with non-Falasha.[41] The Falasha attitude of apartness has led to some
Ethiopians calling them the *attĕnkuñ,* meaning "do not touch me." [42]
This attitude has prevented them, unlike Jews elsewhere, from becoming merchants or traders, for they will not travel on the Sabbath,
nor will they eat food prepared by non-Falasha.[43]

RELIGIOUS AND SOCIAL LIFE.—Though it is the religious life of the
Falasha which distinguishes them from other Ethiopians, their beliefs
and practices are similar in many ways to those of the Christians. Thus,
the synagogue (*mesgĭd*), like the church among Christians, is the center
of religious life and there is one in every large village. The synagogue

[35] Budge, 1928, I: 213.   [36] Leslau, 1951: xxxix.   [37] Leslau, 1951: xxxix.
[38] Trimingham, 1952: 20.   [39] Leslau, 1951: xl.   [40] Trimingham, 1952: 21.
[41] Leslau, 1951: xvi.   [42] Leslau, 1951: xl.   [43] Leslau, 1951: xiv.

is a simple structure either circular or rectangular in shape, and often is indistinguishable in appearance from Falasha dwellings, though traditionally it has a red earthenware pot placed on a pinnacle on its roof. Sometimes the synagogue, like the Christian church, contains a sacred place set apart, known as the Holy of Holies, in which the Torah and religious objects are kept.

Priests, chosen from the general populace, perform the rites of the religion. Falasha priests, like Christian priests, can marry, but cannot be divorced. Again like Christian priests, they wear turbans as a sign of their status. There has been a monastic movement among the Falasha, apparently derived from Christian example, though there are few monks among them today. Like Christian monks, Falasha monks live in seclusion, cannot marry, and seem to be held in higher regard than priests. The scriptures are the basis of Falasha religious life, and like the Christian scriptures, are written in Ge'ez, or ancient Ethiopic. "The Old Testament and especially the apocryphal 'Book of Jubilees' constitute the chief sources of Falasha religious law and precept . . . Falasha Judaism is completely pre-Dispersion and therefore the Talmud or any of the other post-Biblical literary works, with the exception of fragmentary pieces of apocrypha, are unknown." [44]

Wolf Leslau says that though the "Falashas fervently believe in 'the God of Israel, the invisible, the creator of heaven and earth,'" they also believe, "with obvious Christian undertones, in a Paradise and a Hell, in angels, and the Last Judgment." [45] The translations of Falasha prayers included by Leslau in his *Falasha Anthology* reveal an attitude that in its wonder and joy at the majesty of God is reminiscent of the Psalms. Nevertheless, Falasha beliefs are tinged with ideas alien to modern Hebrew belief. They are said to worship *Sanbat*, goddess of the Sabbath, to whom they make offerings of meat, drink, and incense. [46] Moreover, like Ethiopian Christians and Moslems, they believe in the evil eye, and Falasha women wear strings of charms around their necks for protection against it.

Falasha worship is focused on sacrifice on the altar, [47] though animal sacrifice has been seriously curtailed. [48] Like Ethiopian Christianity and Islam, the Falasha religion involves feast and fast. There are weekly, monthly, lunar, and yearly festivals and fasts. [49] The Sabbath is very scrupulously observed. Wolf Leslau observes: "On Friday evening the Falasha women start their elaborate preparations; before cooking the Sabbath food, they must first wash their clothes and bodies in the river. The men also quit work at midday and perform the same ritual

---

[44] Leslau, 1949: 219. [45] Leslau, 1949: 220. [46] Trimingham, 1952: 20.
[47] Trimingham, 1952: 51. [48] Leslau, 1949: 221. [49] Leslau, 1949: 220.

ablutions. As soon as the sun sets, all the fires in the village are extinguished until the Sabbath is over. Throughout the Sabbath no work of any kind is permitted." [50]

Falasha will in no event eat meat of animals killed by non-Falasha. Generally they eat the same foods as other Ethiopians except that they do not eat raw meat. Following Biblical proscription, they eat only those animals that are cloven-hoofed and chew the cud, and they obey the commandments about birds and fish in the Book of Leviticus.[51] They do not eat animals which have died natural deaths or those which have been bitten by a wild animal.[52] If the bitten animal is a cow, neither its milk nor its butter may be used, though it may be sold in the market.[53]

Many observers have noted the relative cleanliness of the Falasha, a condition which results from the ritual ablutions they are required to perform frequently. One Falasha told Wolf Leslau that Ethiopians believe they can recognize a Falasha by his odor which results from his frequent ritual bathing.[54] Indeed, some writers [55] say that Falasha settlements are established near streams because so much washing is required.

Like other religious groups of Begemder and Semyen, the Falasha allow marriage only within their own group. Falasha girls are said to be considered marriageable at nine years of age and boys at seventeen. Divorces are frequent, as among other peoples of Ethiopia. Circumcision of boys and excision of girls is practiced. A child may be given either an Ethiopic name or a Hebrew name from the Bible.

The Falasha of Northwest Ethiopia today are still an isolated group, harassed by Protestant missionaries and weakened somewhat by acceleration of the processes of Amharization accompanying the introduction of Western education and customs. The policy of tolerance of the Imperial Ethiopian Government is drawing more and more Falasha, particularly youth, into greater participation in Ethiopia's political and social life and into its new educational system. Such a situation can only lead to a still further weakening of the traditional life of the small and isolated, but persistent and conservative group.

K'amant

POSITION.—The K'amant, the largest remaining Agow-speaking group in Begemder and Semyen, are looked on by the Amhara with a mixture of curiosity and contempt. There is a tradition that formerly they

[50] Leslau, 1949: 221.   [51] Leslau, 1951: xix.
[52] Leslau, 1949: 223; Leslau, 1951: xx.   [53] Leslau, 1951: xx.
[54] Leslau, 1949: 217.   [55] Leslau, 1949: 218; Trimingham, 1952: 21.

lived in the forests by hunting and eating the fruits of trees. For this reason, many Amhara believe the K'amant originally sprang from wood, and they call them "sons of wood" and "fruit of wood." [56] Such traditions may have developed because the K'amant, desiring to avoid assimilation by the powerful Amhara, tried to remain inconspicuous so that they might not be molested. According to some local traditions, when the Amhara first met the K'amant, they asked them what their religion was, and the K'amant answered *"kama anta"* or *"kama antè,"* that is, "like you," intending to say that they were Christians, too.[57] Such folk explanations may or may not have any basis in fact, but they serve to show that the Amhara regard their weaker neighbors to be compliant rustics.

RELIGION.—The religious life of the K'amant, the last surviving pagan Agow group, is still little understood, for they are secretive about their beliefs and rituals. It is clear, however, that their religion parallels in many respects the tribal religions that were common in ancient times in the Mediterranean region and the Middle East. At the same time, the striking resemblances it bears to Ethiopian Christianity and Judaism attest to extensive borrowing from and contributions to these religions. Like Ethiopian Christians, the K'amant worship a world god, *Īdera,* who is said to have created man in his own image and is believed to have power over all nations. According to the K'amant, *Īdera* smote the Egyptians when they pursued the Hebrews across the Red Sea, an act which firmly establishes him as parallel to or identical with Jehovah. Unlike the Ethiopian Christians, the K'amant also have a tribal god, *Kibirwa,* who seems to be the local representative of the world god, and who has power over the country of the K'amant and everyone in it. Even K'amant who apostatize to Christianity and their descendants are considered subject to the tribal god, a situation which eventually may lead to his taking a place among the spirits and gods who still survive in Christian Ethiopia.

Like the other peoples of Ethiopia, the K'amant have a concept of clean and unclean animals. In the past they are said variously to have eaten only the flesh of animals killed by their own people [58] or that of animals killed by themselves and by Christians.[59] Like some peoples of Ethiopia, though not the Amhara or Falasha, they have detested fish in the past,[60] though I do not know what their attitude is toward fish today. Like Christians of past generations, they avoided coffee,[61] which they regarded as a Moslem beverage, and even today their priests

[56] Wolda Mariam, 1940 (Eth.): 106.
[58] Rassam, 1869, I: 209.
[60] Bruce, 1790, IV: 275; Rassam, 1869, I: 209.

[57] Grottanelli, 1939: 250.
[59] Bruce, 1790, IV: 275.
[61] Rassam, 1869, I: 209.

are not permitted to drink coffee or the distilled liquor *arak'i*. Further, like the Falasha, the K'amant traditionally practiced ritual bathing and avoided letting their eating utensils be handled by people of other groups. James Bruce, the Scottish explorer, noted that the K'amant bathed thoroughly after going to market or any other place where they might have come in contact with non-K'amant, who were considered unclean.[62] When some K'amant heard that Bruce and his travelling companions were not descended "from the prophet Jonah," they hid all their pots and drinking vessels so that they should not become contaminated.[63]

Around their necks the K'amant sometimes wear the black cord (Amh.: *mateb*) which Ethiopians consider to be a sign of Christianity. Often they also wear a small silver cross on the cord, as many Christians do. Though they were forced by King Theodore to wear the black cord,[64] apparently they adopted the cross for decorative purposes.

Since their language is unwritten, the K'amant have no religious documents or books. Instead, they pass on their religious precepts, which seem strangely akin to Judaeo-Christian teaching, by word of mouth. The K'amant are required to be monogamous, to refrain from stealing and killing, and to help others, particularly strangers.

The K'amant sometimes use a grain beer, *miskī,* in their religious services, but unlike Christians they do not use raisin or grape wine as a sacramental drink. Indeed, the K'amant head priest at Ch'ilga did not seem to know what raisins were when I showed some to him. The recipe and the actual ingredients of *miskī* are a secret known only to K'amant priests, as the secret of making sacramental wine is known only to priests among the Amhara.

The affinities of the K'amant religion with Judaism and Christianity are shown again in the K'amant observances of the Sabbath, of holidays, and of festivals. Though in the eighteenth century the K'amant observed only the Sabbath,[65] today, like Ethiopian Christians, they observe both the Sabbath and Sunday, though the Sabbath is still more sacred to them. Moreover, at Ch'ilga, where culture change is especially marked, they observe not only their own holidays and festivals, but those of the Christians as well. K'amant religious services are not held regularly every week; instead, people gather together to worship only on holidays or when someone asks the priests to conduct a service for him.

In the past the K'amant worshipped in groves of trees and did not

[62] Bruce, 1790, IV: 275.   [63] Bruce, 1790, IV: 276.
[64] Rassam, 1869, I: 209.   [65] Bruce, 1790, IV: 275.

have church buildings.[66] At the town of Ch'ilga, one of the centers of the K'amant, the head priest insisted that his people have church buildings today, a situation which, if true, may indicate borrowing from the Falasha or Amhara. The K'amant are said to worship kneeling around their leader who is seated on a stool and who is given the title *womber* or stool,[67] the entire situation being curiously parallel to that which is found in parts of West Africa and is so well developed among the Ashanti, who regard the stool as the symbol of kingly rank.

Like the Christians, the K'amant have a church organization and a clergy who are said to be recruited from all walks of life. Such men are required to serve periods of training as boy deacons, much as do Christian scribe-choristers. There are two head priests, who are likened to the head (*Abuna*) of the Ethiopian Christian church. K'amant head priests are not appointed on the basis of merit, but are selected from certain priestly families. One is in charge of all the K'amant to the northeast of the Goang River (Fig. 14), and the other is over those to the southwest. The former maintains his headquarters at the town of Tikil Dingaī, and the latter near Ch'ilga. Though both are of equal rank, the head priest at Tikil Dingaī has more prestige, for he rules Kerker, the traditional homeland of the K'amant. Thus the head priest of Ch'ilga on occasion travels to Tikil Dingaī to participate in holiday festivities, though the head priest of the latter area does not return the visit. There is no clear separation between civil and religious authority among the K'amant. Their leader has both civil and religious rights and political leaders are sanctified and venerated after death.[68]

ECONOMIC LIFE.—There seem to be no differences in agricultural practice between K'amant and Amhara. Both use the plow and similar agricultural implements. They grow the same types of domestic plants. It has been said that the K'amant live exclusively on agriculture and pastoralism, ignoring the forms of artisanship which are characteristic of Falasha life.[69] My observations confirm the deficiency of the K'amant in craft skills. There are few K'amant potters, ironworkers, or weavers, and no professional minstrels. The K'amant who follow these professions have learned their skills from Falasha craftsmen who do most of the K'amant craft work.

Unlike some other minorities living in the highland, such as the Wayt'o and Falasha, the K'amant are not land poor. Where they are in close contact with Amhara, as around Lake T'ana, it is true, they

[66] Rassam, 1869, I: 208; Grottanelli, 1939: 248.   [67] Trimingham, 1952: 17.
[68] Grottanelli, 1939: 249–50.   [69] Grottanelli, 1939: 247.

may be tenants of Amhara landlords, but elsewhere they own their land.[70]

DECLINE.—Today the K'amant language and religion are in decline. The present-day distribution of the K'amant in Begemder, the surviving place names of Agow origin, and the traditions of the K'amant all suggest that they once occupied a much larger region and that they have been pushed back or assimilated by the Amhara. In the last few centuries, Christianity and Amharization have made notable gains in Dembya. Amharic is now the dominant language almost to the Goang River, not far from the K'amant center of Ch'ilga itself. Even in the Ch'ilga area there are numerous converts to Christianity, though the K'amant, who are hostile to Islam, claim that none of their people have become Moslems. Today, if a Christian girl marries a non-Christian K'amant, she usually requires him to become Christian. The young couple ordinarily live with his parents for a while, but despite their differences in religion parents and children apparently get along amicably. Thus, a hamlet often includes both Christians and K'amant. Conversion is exclusively in one direction, from the K'amant religion to Ethiopian Christianity.

The K'amant are apparently willing to sit back and watch the gradual disappearance of their religion. Even the head priest of the Ch'ilga region said nothing to me to indicate that he wished for or hoped for a revival of the ancient religion of his people. The passivity of the K'amant toward the decline of their religion and language may be due to the fact that their religious beliefs and their culture are very similar to those of the Amhara. Since their language is unwritten and since they have no literature or religious "book," the gradual lapse of the language may not be a shocking experience. Today the K'amant live aside from the main currents of innovation in Ethiopia, but it seems as if they can look forward only to further losses by Amharization until they are completely assimilated into the general Amhara population.

Agow of Sahalla

The Agow of Sahalla (Fig. 15) are the last remaining group of Agow-speaking people in the northern part of Begemder and Semyen. Probably Agow-speaking people related to those of Sahalla occupied much of highland Semyen at an early date, but were either assimilated or pushed into the hot, dry, disease-ridden lowland scrub and thorn country (Fig. 16) the Agow now occupy along the Tekezzay River and its tributaries. The Agow have probably survived as an ethnic group

[70] Grottanelli, 1939: 247.

in Sahalla in large part because the Amhara do not like such country, and have felt no incentive to settle there. It is striking that today the boundary between Amhara and Agow in Semyen in many places follows closely the escarpments, with the Amhara on the plateaus and the Agow in the lowlands and river valleys. In Sahalla, the traveller is aware not only of the inhospitableness of the country, but of the poverty of the people as compared to the people of the highland, a poverty which is aggravated by frequent locust infestations. The meagerness of the environment seems also to be reflected in the size of the people and animals, for not only are the Sahalla Agow smaller and slighter than the Amhara, but their oxen are smaller than those of the Amhara.

The Agow of Sahalla are Christians but their churches are staffed by Amhara priests from the highland, an indication, perhaps, of the recency of the conversion of the Agow. The priests and the Amharic-speaking officials, craftsmen, and merchants they encounter are the principal agents of culture contact, though contact through them appears to be far less effective than the continuous, large-scale contact the K'amant have with the Amhara. As a result, though there are some villages on the borders of Sahalla where there has been considerable biological and cultural mixing, most Agow have probably changed little except in the formal acceptance of Christianity.

Despite the apparently limited effect of contact today, the Agow of Sahalla differ from the Amhara in agriculture and economic life very little, and then principally in ways that can be explained by differences in environment. Thus, they possess few mules and no horses, though they have donkeys as well as herds of cattle, sheep, and goats. Their assemblage of domestic plants is in no way different from that of other lowland regions. Their agricultural implements are similar to those of the highland, though they are commonly smaller and less sturdy.

In economic organization, however, the Agow of Sahalla differ somewhat, for they have no markets of their own and instead travel for days to get to highland markets to exchange goods. Moreover, like the K'amant but unlike their relatives across the Tekezzay River in Lasta, they have no professional craftsmen, and their ironwork, weaving, and pottery are done by craftsmen from other ethnic groups.

Kumfel

The Kumfel, a small Christian Agow-speaking group, occupy a few villages at elevations of from 3,000 to 6,000 feet in the dry forest country along the valley of the Dinder River at the southern edge of

Begemder and Semyen. According to their traditions, the Kumfel came
from the Atchifer and Kumbil (the derivation of the word Kumfel?)
districts of Godjam Province a century ago at the invitation of King
Theodore. Amhara of the highland of K'wara nearby claim, on the
other hand, that the Kumfel are descended from slaves set free by
Theodore and allowed to settle along the Dinder. Because they believe
the Kumfel to have been slaves, the Amhara are very contemptuous
of them and regard them as only a little more acceptable than the
Wayt'o fishermen of Lake T'ana. The physical appearance of the
Kumfel casts little light on the problem of their origin, for some of
them are quite Negroid and others indistinguishable from the peoples
of the highland (Fig. 17).

The Kumfel gain their sustenance largely through shifting cultivation. They grow the same types of domestic plants as their neighbors
to the west, the Gumis, though they also cultivate t'eff and a few other
crops not found among the Gumis but common in the highland. The
Kumfel now use the plow for field cultivation to some extent, but they
say that it is an introduction of the last dozen years, before which they
used only the hoe for turning over the soil of their fields. They keep
only a few cattle, though they have larger numbers of sheep, goats,
and chickens. The shelters in which the latter animals are kept at
night are circular in form, roofed with thatch, and raised above the
ground on stilts (Fig. 18); like the sun shelters also found in Kumfel
villages, the animal shelters are of a type common in the Sudan but
not found in highland Ethiopia. The Kumfel country contains an
abundance of wild and semidomesticated bees, and the traveller knows
when he is approaching a Kumfel village by the presence of cylindrical
beehives tied high in the branches of trees, some as far away as five
or six miles from the village. Honey is an important trade item for
the Kumfel today, and when they first settled in the Dinder Valley
they even paid their taxes in honey.

Since the Kumfel have no markets of their own, they must either
exchange their honey, cotton, and grain with travelling merchants or
journey to a distant market in the highland. Only a few Kumfel are
themselves traders and, as among the K'amant, few are craftsmen.

In the village of Camcamba, in the heart of the Kumfel country, I
found several families of Hametsh, Negroes who had migrated from
their home country in the Sudan forty or fifty years before to settle
among the Kumfel. The Hametsh appear to have agricultural implements and practices similar to those of the Kumfel. Moreover, they
have become Christians, and, though they remain a separate group
maintaining their own language at home, they speak Agow with the

Kumfel. Though the Kumfel and Hametsh together number only a few hundred and comprise an insignificant fragment of the population of the Northwest, they are nevertheless interesting because they illustrate one way in which Ethiopic and Negro groups have come into contact and adjusted to each other.

Wayt'o

The Wayt'o are a small Moslem group who traditionally have been hippopotamus hunters and fishermen and who live in hamlets scattered along the shores of Lake T'ana and sections of the Blue Nile nearby.[71] Estimates of the numbers of the Wayt'o have ranged from 200 or 300 [72] to 1,500.[73] The most carefully considered estimate, made after a complete census of seven Wayt'o hamlets in the 1930's, is that of Vinigi Grottanelli, who believed the total number to be about 750.

ATTITUDES TOWARD HUNTING GROUPS IN NORTHEAST AFRICA.—In Northeast Africa, as in other parts of East Africa, there are separate groups of hunters who commonly comprise submerged endogamous classes and in some places also include certain other craftsmen. Everywhere these hunters are despised because, it is said, they eat types of flesh prohibited by local food taboos. Among the Somali, for example, members of the hunting group, the Mijan, even though they are Moslems, eat unclean meat such as head, tripe, and claws, a practice which keeps them in a state of ritual impurity.[74] Among the Gurage, the hunters, there known as Fuga, who eat domestic animals that have died, are often despised by the "noble" Gurage and do not mix with them.[75] Some groups carry their avoidances of hunting groups still further; the Galla, for instance, will not even eat plants cultivated by the hunters, whom they call Watta.[76]

So far as I can determine, the Wayt'o of Lake T'ana, despite their reputation for eating anything, transgress the food taboos of other peoples of the region only by eating the flesh of hippopotami and that of certain forbidden wild fowl. They deny eating other animals, such as turtles, frogs, snakes, bush pigs, and wart hogs, which fall under the food taboos of their neighbors. Nevertheless, their violations of the food taboos are severe enough so that they are the most despised people of Northwest Ethiopia, far lower in status than any other group. James

[71] E. Cerulli heard from an Amhara informant that hunters living along the Tekezzay River are the northernmost group of the Wayt'o. To my knowledge, however, no other writer mentions Wayt'o along the Tekezzay, though Pearce (1831, II: 33) speaks of hippopotamus hunting there.
[72] R. E. Cheesman, 1936: 93.
[73] Rava, 1913: 157.
[74] Trimingham, 1952: 224; I. M. Lewis, 1955: 53.
[75] Leslau, 1950: 62.
[76] Cerulli, 1922: 179.

Bruce writes that in his day the Abyssinians held the Wayt'o "in utter abhorrence, so that to touch them, or anything that belongs to them, makes a man unclean all that day till the evening, separates him from his family and friends, and excludes him from the church and all divine service, till he is washed and purified on the following day." [77] It has also been reported that other Moslems despise them [78] and even refuse to consider them Moslems.[79] Despite the persistence of the general pattern of avoidance today, the strength of feeling involved may be weakening, for the Amhara who accompanied me entered a Wayt'o home without objection and freely ate the parched grain offered them by their Wayt'o hostess.

Not only are the Wayt'o considered unclean and avoided, but at least in James Bruce's time, they were feared as sorcerers who could kill people with their charms.[80] Similar beliefs have also been reported held by the Galla about the Watta hunters,[81] by the Somali about the Mijan and Yibir,[82] and by the Amhara about other minorities and craft classes. These beliefs apparently have provided protection for some of the hunting groups. William Harris, for example, said that no Galla would molest the Watta, and that others who received protection from them could travel in perfect safety throughout Galla country.[83] I do not know whether the Lake T'ana Wayt'o enjoyed such safe-conduct, but it is said that they were never involved in the wars which have swept around them, a situation like that of the Manjo in Kaffa, who were exempt from service in wartime.[84]

ORIGIN OF THE HUNTING GROUPS OF NORTHEAST AFRICA.—Various theories have been advanced to account for the origin of the hunting groups of Northeast Africa. Many writers have assumed that such groups are unassimilated remnants of the aboriginal populations.[85] Support for this assumption is claimed in various local traditions [86] that such people were the original natives of the region. If this were true, we might expect members of the hunting groups to have more pronounced Negroid physical features, and, indeed, the descriptions of some of the hunting groups seem to indicate that they are more Negroid than the peoples among whom they live. The Watta of central Ethiopia, for example, are said to be small in stature, but with robust, supple bodies, a darker skin color than that of the Galla, and coarse,

[77] Bruce, 1790, III: 402.   [78] Rassam, 1869, I: 314.
[79] Grottanelli, 1939: 188.   [80] Bruce, 1790, III: 403.
[81] Harris, 1844, III: 50.   [82] I. M. Lewis, 1955: 53.
[83] Harris, 1844, III: 50.   [84] Huntingford, 1955: 126.
[85] Castro, 1915, II: 338; Grottanelli, 1939: 171–72; Trimingham, 1952: 223; I. M. Lewis, 1955: 52.
[86] Huntingford, 1955: 16.

curly hair.[87] Moreover, the Fuga hunters are said to be darker than their Gurage neighbors,[88] and the Watta in Kaffa to have the features of Negroes.[89] Cardinal Massaja speaks of a Watta custom (in Kaffa?) of hanging weights in the ear lobes of their children, a custom common among some Negro groups farther south,[90] which suggests a relationship between the Watta and these groups. This latter is poor evidence, however, for in Bruce's time the K'amant, who are Cushites, used ear weights, too. Casting more doubt on the racial status of the hunting groups are the statements of other writers who say that the hunter castes in Limmu [91] and among the Somali [92] are not Negroid. Moreover, the Lake T'ana Wayt'o are not Negroes (Figs. 19 and 20) nor, indeed, can they be distinguished physically from the other peoples of the highland areas of the Northwest.

The hunting groups of Ethiopia at home usually speak the language of the people among whom they live; the Wayt'o of Lake T'ana, for example, speak Amharic, whereas the Watta living among the Galla speak the Galla language. Some of the hunting groups, such as the Mijan and Yibir among the Somali [93] and the Fugas among the Gurage,[94] do, it is true, have other "secret" languages known only to themselves. An analysis of the dialects of some of the groups living among the Somali, however, shows no relationship with languages other than Somali.[95] It seems probable, then, that such "secret" languages are merely argots related to the local dialects of the country, and not ancient tongues preserved by ethnic minorities, for argots are also used by certain Ethiopian occupational groups, such as minstrels and merchants.

The terms "Wayt'o," Amharic for the northern group of hunters, and "Watta," Galla for the hunters of central Ethiopia, appear to be related etymologically, and add further confusion to the question of the origin of the hunting groups. They may be, it is said, the names the hunters called themselves originally, or they may have been derived from a Cushitic root, from which also came the Amharic word *wāttata*, "to wander without permanent occupation." [96] If the latter is the case, the use of similar names for such submerged groups would indicate, not that the groups had a common origin, but that names derived from similar roots were applied to several groups.[97] That this may have been the case is suggested by the statement a Wayt'o man

[87] Cerulli, 1922: 203.
[88] Huntingford, 1955: 16.
[89] Cerulli, 1922: 203.
[90] Cerulli, 1922: 203–4.
[91] Cerulli, 1922: 203.
[92] I. M. Lewis, 1955: 52.
[93] I. M. Lewis, 1955: 52.
[94] Leslau, 1950: 62.
[95] I. M. Lewis, 1955: 52.
[96] Cerulli, 1922: 202.
[97] Grottanelli, 1939: 172.

once made to me that the name "Wayt'o" was given to his people by the Amhara. Today, however, the term has acquired a different connotation, meaning, as the Amhara will tell you, "people who eat anything," which refers to the unorthodox eating habits of the group. In Kaffa, the term "Manjo" has acquired similar connotations,[98] though it is said to derive from a root meaning "to tan," indicating that the name for the tanners' class has probably simply been extended to include other submerged groups, including hunters.[99]

The fact that the hunting groups of Ethiopia possess neither a common language nor identical physical characteristics suggests that either they did not develop from a common ancestral group or that, if they did, they have become so mixed biologically and culturally with the groups among whom they live that they have lost their original character. I am inclined to the view that the hunting groups of Ethiopia did not have a common origin, but developed, as Enrico Cerulli suggests,[100] by similar historical processes. The origin of the groups may lie within Northeast Africa in pariahs of various groups, or in various unassimilated ethnic groups, Negro or Cushitic, whose numbers were supplemented by pariahs of the peoples among whom they lived. On the other hand, some hunting groups may have originated outside of Northeast Africa, and entered the region with the sufferance of the local people; in time they became mixed biologically and culturally, especially through pariahs who joined the group. If the view is correct that the hunting groups did not have a common origin, we must determine what the origins of each of the large groups of hunters were.

Maurizio Rava [101] has suggested that the Lake T'ana Wayt'o were originally Moslems who came to live along the shores of Lake T'ana, far from Moslem religious centers, and gradually degenerated in their religion and were repudiated by other Moslems. There are two principal objections to this suggestion: 1) the Wayt'o of Lake T'ana are not isolated from other Moslems and, indeed, are quite close to Gondar, which is a minor center of Islamic culture, and 2) James Bruce [102] called the Wayt'o of his day pagans, which suggests that, instead of being degenerate Moslems, the Wayt'o have probably accepted Islam only in fairly recent times. Because of these objections, most observers have rejected Rava's suggestion. An alternate view, that of R. E. Cheesman,[103] is that the Lake T'ana Wayt'o were earlier arrivals on Lake T'ana than the Amhara and were not evicted because they were the

[98] Grottanelli, 1939: 177.
[100] Cerulli, 1922: 212–13.
[102] Bruce, 1790, III: 402.
[99] Cerulli, 1922: 203.
[101] Rava, 1913: 123–24.
[103] R. E. Cheesman, 1936: 92–93.

only people skilled in water transport and, therefore, of value to the Amhara. Vinigi Grottanelli [104] inclines toward the belief that the Wayt'o had a Nilotic origin and at first were quite distinct from both the Cushites and Semites of Ethiopia, a view which fits with Amharic tradition [105] and with James Bruce's observation [106] that the language of the Wayt'o in his time was radically different from all other languages of Ethiopia. Thus, while the general view is that the Wayt'o were originally a distinct group in language and in race, it is not known whether they were natives of Ethiopia or whether they migrated up the Blue Nile to Lake T'ana from the Sudan, perhaps in pursuit of the hippopotamus.

R. E. Cheesman has reported a story that Emperor Menelik moved some Wayt'o from Lake T'ana to Lake Zwai in the Rift Valley to make and use reed balsas there. If this story is true, the T'ana Wayt'o and the hunters of Lake Zwai are related groups, but it is probably not true, for the Wayt'o of Lake T'ana deny that they are related to similar groups on other lakes or in other provinces.[107]

DISTRIBUTION OF WAYT'O HAMLETS.—Wayt'o hamlets around Lake T'ana are not distributed evenly (see Map 4). Perhaps the greatest concentration of Wayt'o is along the southern shore of the lake from Bahir Dar to just north of Zegie Peninsula. Another concentration is found on the northern shore around the Megech' River. Among the factors determining the distribution of Wayt'o hamlets, according to Grottanelli,[108] are 1) the attraction exercised by larger Amhara settlements near the lake, as, for example, proximity to the markets of Zegie and Korata at the south shore and to Gondar and Dembya on the northeast rim, 2) the favorable nature of the shore for landing balsas, 3) the presence of good agricultural land that the Amhara are disposed to allow tenants to cultivate and that is reasonably close to the quarries of scoraceous lava used for the manufacture of grinding stones, one of the typical occupations of the Wayt'o, and 4) the healthiness of the place. Another factor contributing to the location of some villages is proximity to the papyrus (Cyperus sp.) that is needed by the Wayt'o every month or so for the construction of new balsas. There is, in fact, a concentration of Wayt'o hamlets on the southern shores of Lake T'ana, where the principal stands of papyrus are found. On the other hand, some hamlets, such as that of Godja which I visited, are far from the nearest supply of papyrus and the Wayt'o boatmen must make long trips to get it.

[104] Grottanelli, 1939: 177–78.   [105] Wolda Mariam, 1940 (Eth.): 108.
[106] Bruce, 1790, III: 403.   [107] R. E. Cheesman, 1936: 93.
[108] Grottanelli, 1939: 178.

ECONOMIC LIFE.—In the eighteenth century, James Bruce wrote that the only profession of the Lake T'ana Wayt'o was "killing the crocodile and hippopotamus, which they make their daily sustenance." [109] Since that time, however, the hippopotamus herds have gradually been killed, until today there are few, if any, hippopotami in the lake. This has meant that the Wayt'o have increasingly had to turn to farming to satisfy their needs, a development which has presented them with many new problems. Perhaps the greatest of these problems is that of obtaining land to farm, for all of the land along Lake T'ana is owned either by Amhara or by Jabartis. Some Wayt'o have gone to work as laborers for Amhara and Jabarti farmers, and others have rented land from them, but neither arrangement has been very satisfactory for the Wayt'o.

V. Grottanelli [110] provides a good sketch of the problems encountered by Wayt'o farmers in the 1930's. Since they had no land of their own, the Wayt'o cultivated land of others under the *gabbar* system, whereby a tenant had to pay about 10 per cent of his total harvest to the landlord. Moreover, few if any Wayt'o had oxen for plowing, and they had to "borrow" them from their Amhara or Jabarti neighbors. For this service, the Wayt'o farmer repaid in labor at a rate of four to five days work for each day he used a pair of oxen. After paying for land and for the use of oxen, the Wayt'o had to pay imposts to the government, though he paid less than his Jabarti co-religionists, who were far wealthier. Though they labored faithfully, Wayt'o farmers commonly suffered from shortages of grain. In years of good harvest, for example, a Wayt'o family was estimated to have from eighteen to twenty-three *madigas* [111] of grain left after paying tribute, whereas thirty *madigas* are needed to feed an average family of three persons. To make ends meet, the Wayt'o tried many things. In some cases, a Wayt'o hired himself out to other farmers for part of the year, receiving food and clothing for the time of his service and a *madiga* of *t'eff* at the end of his period of work. In addition, the Wayt'o made and sold grinding stones and mullers of scoraceous lava, and they continued their ancient occupation of making reed balsas for merchants and for others who needed them. Often, too, Wayt'o men worked for the Amhara and Jabartis as boatmen, punting reed balsas loaded with merchandise from place to place on the lake shore. A few Wayt'o turned to weaving cloth for home consumption, although previously

[109] Bruce, 1790, III: 402.

[110] This paragraph and the description of Wayt'o economic life in the 1930's is based on Grottanelli, 1939: 197–211.

[111] A *madiga* is an Ethiopian pot used as a measure of volume which is the equivalent of about 27 to 30 liters.

they had purchased all their cloth from Amhara, Jabarti, and Falasha weavers. Moreover, as much as possible, Wayt'o men followed their ancient fishing and hunting activities (Fig. 21), though only along the Blue Nile were hippopotami still found.

The situation of the Wayt'o seems to have improved a little since the 1930's, for some now own cattle, though most of them still have no other domestic animals, and though they still own no land of their own. Nevertheless, Wayt'o hamlets look like temporary settlements, perhaps because their position as tenants gives them little incentive to make improvements. At the Wayt'o hamlet at Godja, for example, a farmer told me that he buys *gesho* (*Rhamnus prinoides*) leaves for flavoring beer from his Amhara neighbors, rather than grow his own, because he does not own his own land and considers his situation too tenuous to warrant the planting of perennials such as *gesho*. The feeling of impermanence the Wayt'o have is undoubtedly stimulated by their relations with their landlords, some of whom threaten to deny them the right to rent land. The Wayt'o nevertheless staunchly refuse to abandon the land, and claim that as long as they pay rent they cannot be dispossessed. If a Wayt'o man dies, they say, his son inherits the right to rent the land his father has used. Thus far, the Wayt'o have been able to survive in this tenuous way.

RELIGIOUS AND SOCIAL LIFE.—Though the Wayt'o are believed to have lost the religious rites and ceremonies they possessed as pagans, they have only a limited understanding of Islam and deviate from accepted Moslem practices to a considerable extent. They neither participate in prayer regularly nor perform ablutions, nor are they devout in their beliefs.[112] Nevertheless, Islam, in however heretical a form, plays an important role in their way of life. They have, for example, arbiters of religious law (*Kadīs*) who handle problems within the group,[113] though they themselves are said to be ignorant of Islamic precepts. Moreover, the Wayt'o have their own *sheikhs*, or priests, who conduct religious services. The *sheikh*, who visits each hamlet only once or twice a month, holds services in an unpretentious place of worship (*mesgīd*). At that time the entire community assembles at the *mesgīd* with flat bread (*injera*), coffee, and mead and sometimes even a chicken, to eat in the company of the *sheikh*. After the meal, the *sheikh* reads the Koran to the assembled group in an Arabic which is neither correct nor understood. While he remains in the hamlet, usually from a few days to a week, prayers are held five times a day, but once he leaves this practice ceases until he arrives again. The *sheikh* is fed

[112] Grottanelli, 1939: 187–88.
[113] The material in this paragraph is based on Grottanelli, 1939: 187–88.

by the people of the hamlet while he stays there, and at night he sleeps in the *mesgīd*.

Not only do the Wayt'o eat the flesh of certain animals that other Ethiopian Moslems refuse, but they differ from them in other habits and customs, generally following Amhara ways instead. They do not, for example, use tobacco, though some of them grow it for sale to other Moslems. Nor do they chew the leaves of the indigenous stimulant *ch'at (Catha edulis)*, though, curiously, holy men use it on holy days and at times of prayer, apparently for inspiration. Like other Ethiopian Moslems, on the other hand, but contrary to the strict practices of many Yemen Arabs, the Wayt'o drink alcoholic beverages, though they do not permit them in the *mesgīd*. In addition, the Wayt'o are monogamous, though they recognize that Islam permits polygamy; their marriages are readily dissolved, however, for all men except priests.

The unity of the Wayt'o is maintained through their religious ties and through the practice of marrying only within the group. On the other hand, they do not comprise a political unit, each group instead recognizing the Amhara chief of the region in which they live.

FUTURE OF THE WAYT'O.—With the destruction of the T'ana hippopotamus herds, the Wayt'o no longer eat hippopotamus flesh. This, and the fact that their holy men, through studies in Eritrea, the Sudan, and even Mecca, are learning accepted Islamic ways, may cause Wayt'o beliefs and practices to conform in the future more closely with those of other Moslems. Moreover, the expanded culture contact between the Wayt'o and other Ethiopians through the increased importance of farming for the Wayt'o may also lead to the gradual breaking down of the barriers against them and eventually to their assimilation into the general Jabarti population. Other despised Ethiopian groups have sometimes followed craft activities which are considered beneath the dignity of the Amhara, and which usually serve to reinforce their lowly position. It is interesting to note, however, that the Wayt'o are not going in that direction. They now make no pottery, iron products, or leather goods, but buy these products from members of the established craft classes. There are, it is true, some Wayt'o weavers, but there are also Amhara, Jabarti, and Falasha weavers and the practice of this craft should not place an additional stigma on the Wayt'o to hinder their eventual assimilation.

Gumis

The Gumis are a subject Negro tribe who live in the hot, dry, thinly settled Sudan border country of Northwest Ethiopia from

Metemma (Gallabat) southward. The Gumis not only differ from the highlanders in material culture, but they have no written language, no such glorious historical tradition as the Amhara, and no organized church or elaborate political organization to bind the tribe together.

Everywhere the Gumis cluster together in agricultural villages, a practice that in the days of slave-raiding of past centuries provided them a greater measure of security than dispersed homesteads would have. Gumis houses are circular, with wattle walls and thatch roofs, like those of the highland but less substantial. Despite the similarity of Gumis and highland house types, Gumis villages have a few structures, usually raised or stilted, which are unknown in the highland and which give the villages a quite distinctive appearance. One of these is the flat-topped sun shelter (Fig. 25) under which the men gather for refreshment and conversation during the heat of midday. Another distinctive structure is the small bamboo hut, raised on stilts, where goats and sheep are kept at night (Fig. 26). In some places quaint, circular chicken coops (Fig. 18) are also set up on high stilts. In addition, scattered about each Gumis village are storage bins, used for grain and cotton, and made of woven bamboo strips or of sorghum stalks set upright and tied together, and plastered over with a mixture of mud and straw (Fig. 49). Each storage bin is raised slightly off the ground on a bamboo platform supported by rocks and when in use is covered with a conical thatch roof.

Perhaps more interesting to the cultural geographer than the distinctive structures of the Gumis, are their domestic plants and animals, and their agricultural practices and implements. As in other lowland areas of Ethiopia, the most important food crop in the Gumis country is sorghum and the most important cash crop is cotton, which is usually interplanted with sorghum. Other food crops besides sorghum are maize, finger millet, sesame, peanuts, and squash. Many plants that are common in the highland, such as garlic, shallots, safflower, chick peas, green peas, *t'eff*, barley, wheat, rye, and flax, are not grown at all by the Gumis, for their country is hot and arid and unsuited to most of these. Curiously, the Gumis have neither root crops nor fruit trees, and they seem to know nothing of the techniques of vegetative reproduction. Whereas the highlanders generally practice sedentary farming, the Gumis practice shifting cultivation, the cultivator abandoning a field when, after several years of cultivation, its soil is too exhausted to provide good yields. Like most shifting cultivators, the Gumis farmer does not cultivate with the plow; instead, he simply makes a small hole in the soil, which is usually sandy and friable, with a bamboo planting stick (Gumis: *siluka*), and then drops a few seeds of sorghum or cotton into the hole, and covers them with a swipe of his foot. The Gumis also have a unique, graceful hoe (Gumis: *t'eba*) which is used for covering the seeds of the few cultivated plants which are sown broadcast, such as *nug*, sesame, and finger millet, as well as for weeding. Since the country of the Gumis is hot, dry, and disease-ridden, most of them keep only a few goats and sheep, for neither camels, cattle, horses, nor even mules and donkeys do well there.

The Gumis of Begemder and Semyen hold no markets but either exchange goods with travelling merchants or visit markets in the highland or in the Sudan. Unlike the highlanders, they do not look down on craft work, or discriminate against craftsmen or place them in separate classes. Nevertheless there are few craftsmen among them; I saw, for example, only one Gumis weaver and was told that there were no tanners at all. Moreover, though the Gumis hold dances and like music, they have no professional musicians such as are found in the highland.

The styles of clothing worn by men among the Gumis are quite varied and include combinations of native and European dress borrowed from the Sudan as well as from highland Ethiopia. Perhaps most common are short cotton pants, gathered around the waist with a string, and sleeved or sleeveless shirts of varied lengths. Gumis women wear a cotton skirt wrapped around the waist and reaching a few inches below the knee. They sometimes tie another cloth under their armpits, covering their breasts. Most Gumis women wear strings tied tightly around their arms, one group of strings just above the elbow and another just below the shoulder (Fig. 28). Around their necks they wear strings of colored beads, and both men and women wear ear rings. Women usually have decorative scars on the back, stomach, upper arm, and cheeks, whereas men have scars on their faces and sometimes on their arms and necks. Boys receive their facial scars, which seem to be tribal marks, at puberty, a practice which is also followed by the Nilotic tribes of the Sudan, but not by the peoples of highland Ethiopia.

The Gumis woman carries heavy loads such as water and grain by means of a carrying stick, unlike the highland woman who carries her goods either on her back or balanced on her head. The woman balances the carrying stick over her shoulder (Fig. 27). From each end of the stick hang long net bags into which fit large gourds or baskets which contain the load. Carrying sticks were also found among the ancient Egyptians and today are used in East Africa among a few tribes such as the Cunama,[114] Barīa, and Hametsh.[115] Gumis women, when they go walking, often carry a short stick (Gumis: *gumba*), usually forked at one end and with an iron point at the other; this stick (Fig. 27) is used only for digging wild roots and for killing snakes.

Unlike the Nilotic tribes and the early Galla, the Gumis have no age classes. The Gumis practice polygyny; the husband maintains a separate household for each wife in the same village, and each works in his fields. Like most Ethiopians, the Gumis fear evil spirits and use charms to protect themselves and their crops from them. Moreover, they venerate certain trees and fear the anger of the elements to such an extent that they sometimes avoid work in order to placate them.[116] Though some Gumis acknowledge Islam and others have been converted to Ethiopian Christianity, most Gumis still worship a tribal God named *Musa* (Moses?), who is said to have no power over peoples other than the Gumis, the Hametsh, and the Datch, the latter being a subject people living in Gumis villages. The Gumis have no organized clergy and no regular ceremonies or holidays except at the time of plant germination and at harvest time. Usually men appeal to *Musa* only in times of sickness or trouble. Those Gumis who have been converted to Christianity call God *Musa,* an interesting example of syncretism. The Gumis converts to Christianity, many of whom were encouraged to become Christians by promised reductions in taxation, say that they became Christians partly because the Amhara who visited them would not eat the flesh of animals they slaughtered, making it necessary for them to provide additional animals for the visitors. More than this, the Gumis say they wish to be considered equals by the Amhara, and accepting Christianity, they feel, is one step toward achieving equality.

The survival of Gumis culture against the pressures of Islam from the Sudan and against Amharization from Ethiopia seems remarkable at first glance. On the other hand, similar small unassimilated tribes of Negroes are found all along the border between Ethiopia and the Sudan, aided in their resistance to acculturation by the unattractiveness of their country for man and most domestic animals. For these reasons there are few people living in the country of the Gumis, and both villages and people give an impression of poverty greater than that found in the highland. Nevertheless, it does seem that the Gumis are in a far better position to resist Amharization than any other minority group of Northwest Ethiopia, and they will probably con-

[114] Grottanelli and Massari, 1943: 57.   [115] Grottanelli and Massari, 1943: 59.
[116] Cerulli, 1956: 32.

tinue their ancient way of life unmolested except, perhaps, for a nominal acknowledgment of Christianity or Islam.

POLITICAL ORGANIZATION

The Province of Begemder and Semyen is one of the twelve provinces of Ethiopia proper. The provincial government in Gondar is headed by a Governor-General assisted by a Director, a Secretary, and local representatives of various departments of the central government, such as the Ministry of Education and the Ministry of the Interior. The province is divided into six districts (*awradja*), each with its own governor and staff. The six districts of Begemder and Semyen and their capitals are Gondar (Gondar), Ch'ilga (Ch'ilga), Debre Tabor (Debre Tabor), Gaīnt (Nifas Moch'a), Semyen (Debark), and Woggera (Dabat). Each district is further divided into smaller units (*wereda*), of which there are twenty-four in Begemder and Semyen, and further into *mikitil-wereda,* which number two hundred fifty-five. The smallest unit of administration is the village with its headman (*ch'ik'a-shum,* literally "mud chief"). The Governor-General is responsible directly to the central government in Addis Ababa and as much, or more, of his time is spent there as in his province. Today the Governor-General appoints only the chiefs of the *mikitil-wereda* and higher chiefs are appointed or confirmed from Addis Ababa.

The present system of government retains some aspects of the hierarchical structure of the political system of ancient Ethiopia, under which every official owed his loyalty to the lord above him. The major change has been to make the Governor-General of a province a political appointee who derives his authority directly from His Majesty and can be transferred or removed by him.

Many changes in social and economic life come through the government and the influences filter down to the people from the higher authorities. Because of the organization of the government, these changes are concentrated in Addis Ababa and in the provincial capitals, and modernization touches the people in isolated villages hardly at all.

Chapter IV

Settlement and House Types

Settlement Pattern and Location.—In the plateau areas of the Northwest, the common settlement pattern is one of agricultural hamlets of perhaps ten to twenty houses located near the fields. An agricultural hamlet is usually occupied by people of a single ethnic group, all of whom may be related to one another. Here and there are larger settlements, either villages or towns, where there are traders, government officials, police, and schools. Isolated farmsteads of only a few buildings are not the rule in the highland, though in some places, such as the area south of Gondar and on the Lake T'ana plain, they occur scattered among the agricultural hamlets. In the lowland regions occupied by the Agow, Kumfel, and Gumis peoples, on the contrary, there are no isolated farmsteads and few hamlets. Instead, most people live in relatively few, widely separated villages, perhaps because these groups need protection from the bandits and slave raiders who have preyed on them since ancient times.

Settlements in the highland regions of Northwest Ethiopia are usually located on hilltops or on well-drained slopes, as elsewhere in highland Ethiopia,[1] and rarely along streams or in other low-lying areas. Because of this, housewives commonly haul water for household use considerable distances, and it is a characteristic sight to see women struggling homeward laden with large earthen water jugs on their backs (Fig. 29). Even in the arid lowland regions of the Northwest, where sources of water are few, riverine sites are avoided in locating villages. Instead, lowlanders either obtain their water from shallow pits and mud puddles or carry water from streams that are considerable distances away. In Sahalla, for example, Agow villages are usually perched in the hills far above the Tekezzay and its tributaries (Fig. 30). In the village of Silaszī in Sahalla, housewives travel for an hour each way at the height of the dry season to fill their water jugs; similarly, David Buxton observed that in the Wollamo country north of Lake Abaya people carry water 2,000 feet upslope to their villages.[2] In the

[1] Plowden, 1868: 135. [2] D. Buxton, 1950: 108.

Sudan border country of the Gumis, villages are usually found not along the large rivers, but near small streams that in the dry season either shrink into stagnant pools or dry up completely. People there obtain water by digging shallow pits in moist sections of the stream bed or near the stagnant pools (Fig. 31).

Probably the most important factor leading people to settle away from low-lying areas is the prevalence of malaria in such places. Lowlanders are fearful enough of malaria, but to highlanders it is a terrifying disease, from which they suffer a frightful mortality. This has not only been a deterrent in keeping highlanders from settling in low-lying sections of the plateau and in the lowland, but has made them reluctant even to travel through the lowland, their fear of malaria being supplemented by a traditional dislike of the high temperatures that prevail there.[3] Many Amhara of highland Begemder and Semyen flatly refuse to go into the lowland along the Sudan border, which is particularly dangerous during and immediately after the rainy season when the risk of contracting malaria is greatest; even at the height of the dry season when the danger is at its minimum, highlanders need strong inducement to venture into the Sudan border country. We found it necessary, for example, to pay much more than the prevailing wages to the highlanders who accompanied us on our trip to the lowland village of Metemma, and even then their friends tried to dissuade them from going. Metemma is considered a punishment post for the police, civil officials, and schoolteachers who are assigned there by the government. Many of the Amhara sent to Metemma leave their families safely behind in the highland and besiege their superiors with petitions requesting permission to return to the cool, pleasant, relatively healthy plateau. To the present-day European traveller equipped with liberal supplies of antimalarial drugs, the highlanders' fear of the low country may seem exaggerated, but he has only to read some of the earlier accounts of travellers to realize that there is a solid basis for the fear. When, for example, R. E. Cheesman took a group of highlanders with him into the lowland in 1927 to explore the valley of the Blue Nile, two strong young men of his group died in a short time. The rest of Cheesman's highlanders understandably refused to remain in the low country, and he found it necessary to make a series of excursions into the valley, accompanied only by his Sudanese guards, and to leave his main party on the plateau.[4]

One effect of the fear and dislike the Amhara and other highland peoples have of the hot, malarial lowland is that it has enabled weaker

[3] Salt, 1814: 212–13; Harris, 1844, III: 225; Rey, 1935: 172.
[4] R. E. Cheesman, 1936: 262–63.

groups, such as the Agow of Sahalla, the Kŭmfel, and the Gumis, who live in such country, to avoid assimilation. Moreover, it has led in many places to the development of a pronounced ethnic boundary at the edge of the plateau, separating the Amhara from these groups. This situation is found not only in Ethiopia, but in certain other parts of the tropics, such as south Yunnan,[5] where politically unified groups with higher cultures have settled in the highland and shunned the hot, malarial lowlands bordering it.

The middle highland itself is not free of malaria, and some places, such as the Lake T'ana area,[6] are known for the prevalence of fever. Indeed, there are few permanent villages along the low-lying east and north shores of the lake because of the unhealthiness of the country during the rainy season. Apparently, this situation has prevailed for a long time, for James Bruce [7] mentions that a mortal fever raged in Dembya, at the north end of Lake T'ana, from March to November. In the year 1953/54 there was a similar scourge during which 5,000 people died in Dembya of malaria and other diseases. Entire settlements were abandoned during the recent scourge, and the government gave orders to move two settlements to higher locations, including the market town of K'olediba. The Ethiopian army post at Gorgora, at the northern tip of Lake T'ana, moreover, has suffered such a high disability rate that army officials there have repeatedly petitioned their headquarters in Addis Ababa to move the post back to a healthier site. The shift of the capital of Abyssinia from Gorgora to higher land at Gondar in the seventeenth century probably was also motivated by a desire to escape the ravages of malaria along the lake.

House Types and Other Structures.—The nomadic peoples of the semidesert to the east and southeast of the highland areas of Ethiopia live in temporary oval-shaped huts made of a framework of curved sticks covered with camels' hair cloth, dum palm fiber, or plaited fiber mats.[8] Such huts serve the nomads well, for they can be dismantled readily and carried about on the backs of camels or other pack animals. Among settled peoples, on the other hand, though herdsmen and crop guards commonly build temporary shelters and grass huts in the field that are no more substantial than the nomads' huts, dwellings are of more permanent construction. Perhaps the most common house

[5] Rock, 1947, I: 3.

[6] Grabham and Black, 1925: 103–4; R. E. Cheesman, 1936: 124–25; Grottanelli, 1939: 11.

[7] Bruce, 1790, II: 265.

[8] For a detailed consideration of the house types of Ethiopia and Eritrea see Pavari, 1936; Dainelli, 1936; Grottanelli, 1939. Pavari includes maps of the distribution of house types.

type in Ethiopia is circular and wattle-walled, and has a conical thatch roof and a dirt floor (Sketch 3). This type, which is characteristic of most of the central and southern parts of the country, is strikingly similar to the houses found in neighboring parts of Negro Africa. The circular Ethiopian house is built by first arranging upright poles in a circle (Fig. 32), then forming a wall by fastening small branches, brush, or large grass stalks in an upright position between the poles (Fig. 33), and then, in some cases, plastering the walls or sections of them with mud. The conical roof is made of a framework of branches which are then covered with thatch; in small houses, the roof is supported by a center pole and by the walls, whereas in larger houses it may be supported without a center pole by four or five forked poles set up at intervals of six to ten feet in a circle concentric with the house walls.

Rectangular houses are also found in Ethiopia, and are characteristic of the city of Harar, parts of Tigre Province, and Eritrea,[9] a distribution which reflects strong South Arabian influences in these places; rectangular structures are common also in towns and cities elsewhere in Ethiopia, where they serve either as houses or as shops. In Tigre, Eritrea, and Harar, the walls of the rectangular houses are made of stone and are usually plastered with mud; their roofs are flat and made of wooden beams laid side by side and covered with twigs, straw, and mud. Some of the rectangular structures found in towns and cities elsewhere (Fig. 82) have walls of stone, and others have walls of wattle and daub; their roofs are most commonly ridged and made either of thatch or of corrugated iron, which is preferred and has prestige value.

The typical house of Begemder and Semyen is circular and wattle-walled and has a dirt floor, a conical thatch-roof, and one entrance. Though there are considerable variations, especially in the size and quality of construction, the basic form is the same everywhere among the peoples of the highland, the Agow of Sahalla (Fig. 30), the Kumfel (Fig. 18), and the Gumis (Fig. 25). As a rule, one part of the house is set aside as a storage area, and the rest serves as living quarters (Sketch 1). In the storage area are the cooking utensils and various basketry and pottery containers of grain and other foodstuffs, and nearby are grindstones and mortars for crushing them. In the living section on the ground and against the walls are beds, some fixed and others movable, which serve as benches in the daytime.[10] In the mid-

---

[9] Pavari, 1936: 340.

[10] There are two types of fixed beds. One type is a clay bench 18 to 25 inches high which is built out from the house wall for four or five feet in a roughly rectangular shape and covered with sheepskins to make it comfortable. The other kind is a rectangular wooden frame made of poles which are fastened into the house wall at

dle of the living section is an open fire to provide warmth and a place to cook. In some houses, there is a second fire in the storage area where most of the cooking is done, in which case the fire in the living section

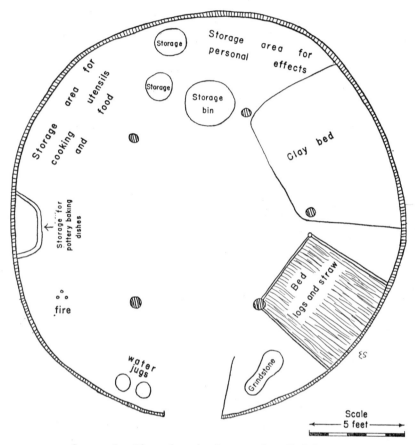

SKETCH 1.—Plan of a circular, wattle-walled house.

serves as a center around which the family and friends gather for talking and gossiping. Smoke from the fires escapes through the thatch roof, the walls, and the doorway, since there are no chimneys and, ordinarily, no windows. During the daytime enough light enters

one end and supported at the other on thick forked sticks, laid across with shorter poles and covered with straw. The movable beds are made of a rectangular wooden frame over which strips of leather are interlaced. In the western lowland where this type of bed is common, they are freely moved in and out of the house as the need for a place to sleep or sit occurs.

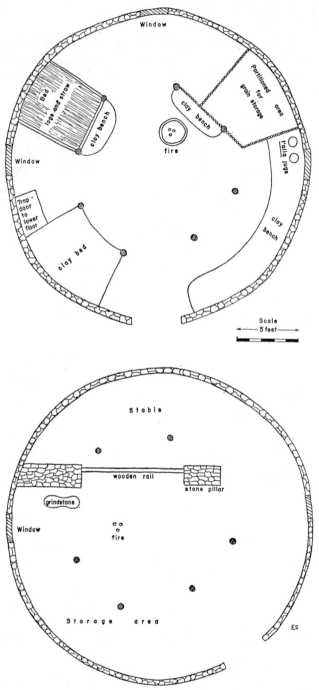

SKETCH 2.—Plan of a two-story, stone-walled house. *Above*, upper floor; *below*, lower floor.

through the roof, walls, and door to see by, and at night the house is lighted by the fire, by oil lamps, or by lanterns. Besides storage and living space, some houses also have a stall inside for a favorite mule or, in large houses, the space between the inner ring of poles and the wall may be used for housing several mules. An agricultural compound in the highland, which is usually occupied by a great family, characteristically includes three or four living houses such as the one just described, as well as a storehouse, a goat house, and a few outdoor grain storage bins with thatch roofs, the whole often ringed by a brush fence.

In addition to the circular houses described above, which are typical of Begemder and Semyen, there are some rectangular houses and shops, most of which are found in the towns and cities. There are also some circular or oval-shaped stone houses, either one or two stories high (Sketch 2; Fig. 34), with thatch roofs and, quite commonly, with windows. Besides houses and shops, there are some more elaborate structures, including churches (Figs. 10 and 84), the stone castles of Gondar (Figs. 7 and 8), a few largely unused arched bridges inspired by the Portuguese (Fig. 9), and many buildings and ruins left from the time of the Italian occupation. Perhaps the strangest of the Italian ruins are the stone-walled forts, found on commanding hills near road camps or large towns, which were built for repelling the raids of the patriot forces.

Though the old Moslem city of Harar in southern Ethiopia is surrounded by a high stone wall with elaborate gates, walled settlements are not typical of Christian Ethiopia. In Begemder and Semyen, for example, only churches, homes of nobles and kings, and occasional house compounds are surrounded by stone walls. The closest approach to the walled settlements so common in parts of the Near East is the palace compound of Gondar, where many buildings have been enclosed as a unit by a high stone wall. This compound was built, however, as a result of Portuguese stimulus and is exceptional.

Chapter V

Agriculture

CHARACTERISTICS AND METHODS

The Soils of Ethiopia

HIGHLAND SOILS.—Though no soil survey of Ethiopia has yet been published, it is known that most Ethiopian soils are derived from fairly recent and fine-textured volcanic parent materials,[1] and that many of the plateau soils provide such good yields as to suggest a high level of fertility. Indeed, some writers have been so impressed with the inferred fertility of Ethiopian soils that they have compared them to the regur soils of India,[2] the terra rossa soils of the Mediterranean countries, and the chernozen soils.[3] The principal work on the soils of the Northwest has been done by Professor H. F. Murphy, who took forty-eight soil samples, mostly in an eighty-five-mile stretch along the motor road from Gorgora northward. He found that the samples were mainly fine textured, many of them stony, and that they ranged in color from light brown through the shades of brown, and from gray to very dark gray. Analysis revealed that 71 per cent of the samples were medium to strongly acid (below pH 6.0), 27 per cent were slightly acid to very mildly alkaline (from pH 6.1 to 7.3), which includes most of the range that is considered most favorable for the common agricultural plants, and 2 per cent were mildly alkaline or above (above pH 7.3). Though acidity is often connected with chemical poverty, all or almost all of the samples were medium or high in available magnesium and potassium, and 58 per cent were medium to high in available phosphorus.[4]

Ethiopians of the highland recognize various differences among their soils, but they commonly distinguish between two principal

[1] Holm, 1956: 7.   [2] Blanford, 1870: 176; Prassolov, 1933: 373.
[3] Prassolov, 1933: 371, 373.
[4] The data above were provided by Professor H. F. Murphy of Oklahoma State University, whose report on the soils of Ethiopia is in press at the time of this writing.

types: black and red. Black soils of the highland commonly occur in areas liable to waterlogging in the wet season, such as shallow valleys and enclosed plains. Red soils tend to be found on hillsides and in better drained sites. Though the black soils tend to be heavy and sticky, they hold moisture well and are commonly planted to late-maturing crops; moreover, they are more fertile than the red soils, and can be cultivated without fallowing for a longer period of time. In one village, for example, black soil could be cultivated up to twelve years without fallowing, whereas red soils had to be fallowed after only four or five years of cropping. In another village, black soils were said to be so fertile that they could be cropped indefinitely if the farmer was careful to include in his rotation scheme such crops as chick peas and the yellow-flowered oil plant *nug* (*Guizotia abyssinica*), which renew the fertility of the soil.

LOWLAND SOILS.—Less is known about the lowland soils of Ethiopia than about those of the highland. In most of the arid section of Ethiopia along the Red Sea and the Indian Ocean, sandy and gravelly desert soils are typical. The soils along the Sudan borders of Northwest Ethiopia, on the other hand, are dark and seemingly fertile, and thus are believed by some to be similar to the soils of the cotton-producing sections of central Sudan. Because of the assumed similarity of these soils, some Ethiopian officials regard the Sudan borders of their country as a region of great potentiality for producing cotton, which is in short supply in the country.

CHARACTERISTICS OF AGRICULTURE IN THE NORTHWEST

The most important food crops in Northwest Ethiopia are cereals and pulses, including wheat, barley, rye, sorghum, the tiny-seeded grass *t'eff*, finger millet, maize, green peas, chick peas, haricot beans, broad beans (horse beans), and lentils (see Map 5). Oilseeds are also important in the Northwest and include *nug*, sesame, castor bean, flax, and the seeds of Amharic cabbage. Spices, of which cayenne pepper is the most important, are also cultivated everywhere in small quantities.

There seem to be no ethnic barriers to the use of any of the cereal grains in Begemder and Semyen, though there are differences in their suitability for particular soils, as well as climatic limits to their cultivation based on altitudinal differences. In the hot lowland below 5,500 feet, sorghum and maize are the most important cereals, though finger millet and sesame are common, too. In the middle highland between 5,500 and 8,000 feet, *t'eff*, wheat, and barley are the important cereals, but maize, sorghum, and finger millet are also significant. Above 8,000 feet, barley and wheat are the most important cereals, and rye is of minor importance. On Mt. Ras Dedjen, highest mountain in Ethiopia, at 11,000 feet I found wheat, barley, rye, and flaxseed to be the only cultivated plants. At Shumlala village (*ca.* 12,000 feet), at the upper limit of agriculture, only barley and rye are cultivated; of the two, barley does better at such altitudes.

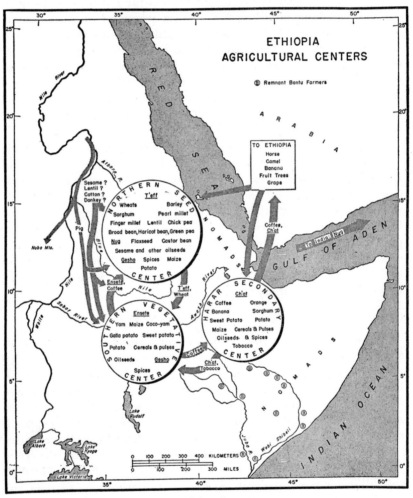

MAP 5

In Northwest Ethiopia, farmers devote considerable effort to cultivating their fields of cereals, pulses, and oilseeds. Nevertheless, they also maintain, near their houses, gardens which provide supplementary food and spices. On the other hand, they largely ignore the possibilities of cultivating fruit trees and root crops, a situation which is surprising in view of the fact that Ethiopia is not far from both the Persian and Mediterranean centers of stone fruit domestication, nor very distant from tropical Africa, where root crops are very important. The neglect of root crops in Northwest Ethiopia is even more conspicuous because in much of the southern plateau areas of Ethiopia root crops, such as the sweet potato (*Ipomoea batatas*), yam (*Dioscorea*), coco-yam or taro (*Colocasia antiquorum*), and the Galla potato (*Coleus edulis*), are important food plants, and the remarkable, banana-like ensete (*Ensete edulis*) in some places is the base of subsistence. It has been suggested that the ensete was formerly cultivated more widely in northern Ethiopia and that with the spread of Amhara influence its cultivation was abandoned in favor of grains because ensete, like root crops and green vegetables, is considered to be inferior food by the Amhara.

The emphasis on seed reproduction and broadcast sowing is as strong in the Northwest as the preference for grains and pulses. It is so overwhelming, in fact, that many farmers there seem to have no understanding of vegetative techniques of reproduction, and so much prefer broadcast sowing that this method is used almost exclusively, even when the seed does not lend itself to broadcasting. I was told, for example, that some farmers will even sow potatoes broadcast rather than plant them. Though some planting of seeds in holes is done, it is generally limited to certain of the garden plants. This insistence on broadcast sowing of seed, as well as the almost exclusive concern with seed reproduction, suggests that cultural attitudes may be more important than environmental opportunities in determining the limits of the areas of vegetative reproduction and seed reproduction, as defined by Carl O. Sauer.

There are similarities between the agriculture of highland Northwest Ethiopia and that of Europe, such as the use of the plow and the combination of agriculture with animal husbandry. On the other hand, there are differences between the two areas. Perhaps the most noticeable difference is the neglect, in Northwest Ethiopia, of manuring,[5] for manure is not collected in piles and only seldom is it applied to fields, though it is sometimes used in gardens. Further, Northwest Ethiopian farmers do not plant fodder crops for their domestic animals, though the animals are permitted to feed on the grain chaff left after threshing is finished, and on the stubble left in the grain fields. Like the farmers of Europe, they rotate their field crops and fallow their fields when the soil is exhausted, practices which contrast

[5] See, for example, Pearce, 1831, I: 343; and Dove, 1890: 23.

with the practice common in rainforest Africa of abandoning a field when it no longer yields well.

Terracing is not common in Northwest Ethiopia, though stone-walled or earth-walled terraces are found occasionally on steep slopes. More usually in rough country, fields, even on slopes as steep as forty-five degrees, are not terraced. Along the gorge of the Shikina River near the village of Bīlaza in Semyen, for example, cultivated fields are on slopes so steep that stacks of grain awaiting threshing in the field are supported on the downhill side by rocks to prevent their slipping. There are no extensive irrigation systems in Begemder and Semyen; at best, irrigation is used only for special crops, and most crops are wholly dependent on rain.

Agricultural Implements

The agricultural implements of Northwest Ethiopia include the plow, the hoe, the digging stick, the planting stick, the sickle, and a variety of threshing and winnowing tools. The plow (Figs. 35 and 36) is the most important implement of field cultivation in the highland areas and in much of the lowland, though it is not used by the Gumis and appears to be only a recent introduction to the Kumfel. The hoe is also important in the Northwest, serving highlanders both in garden cultivation and in the field for weeding and other tasks for which the plow is not suited; moreover, the hoe and the planting stick are the primary implements of field cultivation among the Gumis and Kumfel. The striking things about the hoes of Begemder and Semyen are their versatility, their diversity in form,[6] and the interchangeability of the blades of some of them with those of axes and digging sticks. The digging stick and the hoe cannot be completely separated in function. Nevertheless, the hoe tends to be a chopping tool used for weeding, cutting brush, turning over soil, and digging shallow holes, and the digging stick an implement for digging the deeper holes needed for construction of buildings, for planting the few seeds that are planted, and for harvesting roots and tubers, and not generally for weeding or turning over the soil.

In harvesting most field crops in the Northwest, the sickle is the implement used. For winnowing the great variety of seed crops, there are several winnowing tools, including a wooden pitchfork (Fig. 38), a wooden winnowing scoop (Fig. 39), a grass or wood brush (Fig. 40),

---

[6] For a general description of Ethiopian agricultural implements, see Vitali and Bartolozzi, 1939, and for detailed information on those of the Northwest, see Simoons, 1958.

a skin fan, and sieves and baskets. Such a diversity of winnowing implements is, to my knowledge, unmatched elsewhere in Africa.

PREPARATION AND PLANTING OF THE FIELDS

CLEARING OF LAND FOR PLANTING.—In Northwest Ethiopia, the clearing of land is a greater problem in the lowland than in the highland, for the lowland is wooded and the characteristic shifting cultivation makes necessary the clearing of new plots every few years for planting. Everywhere in the lowland, farmers clear woodland during the dry season and by similar means: first barking the trees or chopping them down and cutting with sickles whatever brush there is, then permitting the wood to dry in the field (Fig. 41), and finally burning it just before the rains begin in the spring. Among the Kumfel, some farmers simply strip the branches from the larger trees and leave them standing to save the labor of cutting them down. After a few years, branches commonly sprout again on the stripped trees, giving the impression that the trees have been left standing untouched in the field. Since there is little woodland left on the plateau, I observed only one field cleared from woodland there, in Zutarīa village in Semyen; juniper trees had been cut down, and, while some of the branches were burned in the field, others were piled at the edge of the field together with branches of thorn acacia to form a fence for protection against domestic animals. Even though there are few wooded areas in the highland to be cleared for planting, commonly brush grows in fallowed fields and must be cut down when the field is again needed for cultivation. In that event, the brush is cut down and allowed to dry, the larger pieces are carried home for fuel, and the smaller bits are gathered into piles in the field and burned. To control the growth of brush, fields under cultivation in both highland and lowland are burned after the harvest either every year or every few years. When Gumis farmers grow sorghum or other annuals in the same field with cotton, they gather the sorghum stalks into small piles away from cotton plants and burn them.

Nowhere in Begemder and Semyen do farmers grub tree stumps from the ground. Even in highland areas where oxen are available for pulling stumps, they are left intact, and the plowman carefully maneuvers around them when turning over the soil. In the Gumis and Kumfel country where there are few, if any, plows, stumps present no problem, for the farmer simply cultivates around them with hoe and digging stick (Fig. 42).

In some parts of the highland, there are numerous stones and boulders in cultivated fields (Fig. 37). Nevertheless, farmers prefer to plow around them, rather than laboriously remove them from the field. As a matter of fact, the presence of rocks in the field may actually help retard soil erosion and thus contribute to the maintenance of soil fertility. Walter Plowden observed, for example, that the best crops were obtained on the stoniest ground, and that people made a point of not removing the stones.[7] In some cases, however, there are so many rocks in a field that the farmer must remove some of them to enable him to plow at all. In such cases, the rocks are gathered into mounds here and there in the field or they are piled at the edge of the field to form walls or low ridges.

TIMES AND METHODS OF SOWING.—Little irrigation is practiced in Northwest Ethiopia and most field crops depend wholly on rainfall. The sowing of seed begins with the first rains, as early as April if the season is early, but more often in May and June. Farmers often sow another crop in September to take advantage of the late rains.

As previously explained, broadcast sowing is the preferred method of seeding in the highland areas of the Northwest. This work is done by the men. In some cases, after sowing such small-seeded cereals as *t'eff* and finger millet, the highland farmer drives sheep, goats, donkeys, or cattle over the field to cover the seed, or he simply brushes soil over it with the branches of trees. More commonly, however, the plow is used to cover the seed after broadcasting. Planting of individual seeds is normally done in the highland only in the garden, and even there only for the seeds of certain plants, such as gourds and squash. Among the Kumfel, seeds of a few plants such as beans, squash, and gourds are planted in holes dug with the hoe, whereas cereal seeds are broadcast and then covered by hoe. The Gumis plant most of their seeds in individual holes which are made with the digging stick, though they broadcast some crops with small seeds and then scrape soil over them with the hoe.

MIXTURE OF FIELD CROPS.—Usually a farmer sows only one type of seed in a field, but sometimes he mixes two or even three different types in the same field. Sometimes he mixes such seed before sowing, and sometimes he sows first one type of seed and then, often within a few days, a second and, rarely, even a third type.

There are many possible mixtures of field crops. Perhaps the most common mixture is wheat and barley, which around Gondar is called *duranya* and is sold in the market places as such. *Duranya* seed is often sown already mixed, and the grains are harvested, threshed,

[7] Plowden, 1868: 136.

winnowed, and stored together. *Duranya* is used in making beer (Amh.: *t'alla*), and is occasionally parched for use in making flat bread (Amh.: *injera*). Sometimes wheat and barley seed, though grown and harvested separately, are mixed intentionally for particular uses, and the mixture is also called *duranya*. Other common mixtures include the following: 1) green peas and horse beans, 2) *t'eff* and the medicinal plant *feyt'o* (*Lepidium sativum?*), 3) lupine (*Bipinus termis;* Amh.: *gibto*) and *t'eff*, flaxseed, or barley, 4) sorghum and finger millet, 5) sorghum and chick peas, 6) safflower and chick peas, 7) safflower and *t'eff*, 8) sorghum, sesame, and haricot beans, 9) maize and squash or gourds, and 10) maize and Amharic cabbage. Occasionally, too, coriander and basil seeds are sown in plots of cayenne pepper (Amh.: *berberei*).

There are plants other than those listed above which are sown mixed, but it is sufficient here to point out that many plants are included in the practice. Farmers explain their mixing of some field crops, such as lupine, by saying that they enrich the soil, and of others by asserting that where different types of plants grow together in a field, they compete with one another, grow larger, and consequently provide a more abundant harvest. Though the practice of sowing such crops as lupine with others probably did, in fact, result from the farmers' recognition that they enrich the soil, the practice of mixing others, such as wheat and barley, may not have developed for the reason suggested, but as a measure of security against crop failure. It would, in fact, have taken an unobservant farmer not to recognize the value of sowing together plants of different growth habits, different soil and moisture requirements, and different resistance to diseases and pests, as insurance against the failure of an entire crop. Some of the plants involved in the practice, such as *t'eff*, may even have originally been weeds in cultivated fields, and come into cultivation because they survived when the main crops failed.

TWO CROPS A YEAR.—It is a common, but by no means universal, practice to grow two crops in succession in the same field in a year. This practice is most common in the highland areas, where a heavier rainfall makes more certain the maturing of the late field crop. Almost any field plant may be used for the late crop. Near Derasgie in Semyen, emmer wheat is often grown as the second crop, and in December the fields of young, green emmer wheat are conspicuous there among the stubble of the first planting. In the village of Mī Abo in Semyen not only emmer wheat, but barley, other types of wheat, and lentils are commonly sown as second crops.

ROTATION, FALLOWING, AND SHIFTING CULTIVATION.—The term "shifting cultivation" is not used in a consistent way in the literature; [8] here, it is defined simply as "that system of agriculture in which an individual's personal rights to a field lapse when, usually after several years of cultivation, he abandons it because of soil exhaustion and low crop yields." The emphasis in this definition is on the lapsing of individual rights after abandonment, for this, however subtle it may be, is the clearest and most universally applicable factor in distinguishing the agricultural systems of the Gumis and Kumfel, the shifting cultivators, from those of the sedentary farmers of Ethiopia's Northwest. Among the sedentary farmers, the farmer retains ownership of the land even when he does not cultivate it, though the fallow period lasts many years.[9] Because of the concern with the ownership of land and the fact that the land has not been surveyed, litigation over land occupies more court time than any other kind of case in the areas of sedentary farming in the Northwest. By contrast, the Gumis and Kumfel farmer, when he abandons a plot, loses his rights to it, though it is considered proper for the farmer who takes over the plot to confirm the abandonment with the person who last worked it.[10]

In other respects, the differences between sedentary and shifting systems of agriculture are less sharp. It is clear, for example, that there are no significant differences in methods of clearing fields between the shifting cultivators and the sedentary farmers of the Northwest, for both slash and burn the woody vegetation in making ready

[8] Attention is directed here to the discussion of shifting and sedentary cultivation by Karl Pelzer (1945). Even so carefully thought-out a definition of shifting cultivation as Pelzer's, however, cannot be applied in precise detail to the situation in Begemder and Semyen. Pelzer defines shifting cultivation as "an economy of which the main characteristics are rotation of fields rather than crops; clearing by means of fire; absence of draft animals and of manuring; use of human labor only; employment of the dibble stick or hoe; short periods of soil occupancy alternating with long fallow periods" (Pelzer, 1945: 17). As will be shown below, some of the groups here considered as practicing shifting cultivation, rotate crops as well as fields and sometimes use draft animals and the plow. Moreover, the sedentary farmers as well as those shifting fields clear by means of fire.

[9] Plowden (1868: 138) makes this observation: "In forest or plain, covered only with grass and jungle, and here and there a heap of ruins, should a village be rebuilt and cultivation resumed, some such ancient peasant is soon found, who demands his post, and points out from memory the boundaries; the descendants of the former inhabitants are sought out under his directions, and under a lenient governor all is restored to its former condition." Thus, one should be very hesitant to conclude that in Ethiopia unused land is in fact abandoned.

[10] Elsewhere in the world where shifting agriculture is practiced, the individual, though seemingly abandoning his field, may retain rights to cultivate it again or, at least, his family or clan may retain these rights. The distinction made here between shifting and sedentary systems in terms of giving up or maintaining rights in the uncultivated field is probably of no general applicability.

their fields. Moreover, there is no complete distinction in agricultural implements, though the planting stick and hoe are the characteristic tools of field cultivation among the shifting cultivators, and the plow among the sedentary farmers. Even in rotation of crops, the differences between shifting and sedentary systems of cultivation are not everywhere sharp, though it is true that the farmers using sedentary methods have a complicated system of crop rotation, whereas the rotation of crops is at best of less concern and less elaborate among the shifting cultivators. The Gumis, for example, have no clear-cut, thought-out rotation, though they do practice an inadvertent rotation, since the same crops are probably not grown in a field year after year. Moreover, as Harold Conklin has suggested for shifting cultivators elsewhere,[11] interplanting does provide a sort of limited crop rotation. The Gumis do practice such interplanting, but it is, we must hasten to add, something qualitatively different from the carefully planned annual rotation of the sedentary farmer, who also practices intercropping in his mixture of seeds. The shifting agriculture of the Kumfel, unlike that of the Gumis, involves a conscious rotation of crops, like that of the sedentary folk of the region. Thus, at Yīkaho village, a farmer might cultivate sorghum the first year after clearing, and the second year do no sowing and instead simply harvest a volunteer crop of sorghum. In successive years, he might sow finger millet and *t'eff* mixed, then sorghum, and so forth, until the field is exhausted about eight years after the first clearing. The practice of allowing a field to remain unplanted for the second year and simply harvesting the volunteer crop of sorghum is common, too, among sedentary farmers in the highland area of K'wara not far from Yīkaho. The Kumfel are, however, not alone among the shifting cultivators in Africa who rotate their crops; the practice is also followed by shifting cultivators in Uganda,[12] and similar systems may be widespread among shifting cultivators elsewhere in Africa.

In the highland, sedentary farmers follow far more complicated systems of rotation, which vary from place to place as well as according to recognized differences in soil. At Weuleka village near Gondar, for example, farmers distinguish between red and black soil. Black soil is so fertile that farmers seldom fallow it, though they rotate crops on it carefully. A typical rotation on the black soil that was suggested to me is as follows: the first and second years a crop of *t'eff* might be grown, the third year *nug,* and then the fourth year *t'eff* again; the fifth year chick peas might be planted, and the sixth year *t'eff* again. The people of Weuleka say that only if a man has many fields

[11] Conklin, 1954: 138. [12] Tothill, 1940: 42.

does he give a field a complete rest, though he is careful to include in his rotation such plants as *nug*, chick peas, and green peas, which renew soil fertility. On red soil people ideally fallow a field every few years (a third year's rest is called *dibila*, which means "starting a new field"). Thus, they might plant *t'eff* the first year, finger millet the second, and then fallow the field for a year or, if the soil is still productive, barley might be sown for a year, then green peas for a year, then barley again, then green peas, then the field is given a complete rest. This fallowing comes no sooner than necessary, and though farmers recognize the value of a fallow third year, actually they often cultivate a field every year until it is exhausted.

When fields are fallowed, domestic animals graze in them and their droppings accumulate. Such droppings and the volunteer plants that fall to the earth and decay are probably the principal means of restoring the fertility of the soil, for only rarely are fertilizers added to fields, and then principally to those that are near home. Moreover, farmers never sow seed in fallow fields for turning under as green manure.

CARE AND PROTECTION OF CROPS

IRRIGATION AND DRAINAGE.—The farmers of the Northwest are faced with problems both of water surplus and water deficiency. Water surplus is common during the rainy season in poorly drained fields, where, in some cases, farmers plow shallow ditches to provide outlets for excess water. Water deficiency occurs when the rains are not sufficient to enable the maturing of plants, or when the cultivator attempts to grow crops during the dry season. Although most farmers rely principally on rainfall to water their fields, and accept an occasional failure of the rains rather than develop elaborate irrigation works, many of them have established small irrigated plots to make cultivation possible during the dry season.

In the highland, irrigated plots are small and inconspicuous and everywhere it is the naturally watered fields that dominate the landscape. Irrigated plots are commonly found only along streams where water can readily be channeled onto nearby land by means of shallow ditches. Wells are not common and even where they exist water is not taken from them for irrigating fields.

In the lowland regions of Begemder and Semyen, even though the rains are lighter and the water shortage more acute than in highland areas, people generally survive by cultivating drought-resistant plants, such as sorghum, rather than by the extensive use of irrigation. In the lowland country of the Gumis and Kumfel, for example,

I saw no irrigated plots, and farmers there denied that they ever irrigate their fields. The Agow of Sahalla, on the other hand, in some places have constructed elaborate systems of ditches for carrying water from streams to their fields. The most intricate and carefully dug irrigation ditches I found in the area are in the Agow village of Bīlaza in Semyen, at the mouth of the Shikina River gorge. There, far upstream from the village, water is channeled by the use of diversion dams into unlined irrigation ditches. The ditches, which are only one or two feet deep, follow the side of the valley, dropping so gradually in elevation that, when they approach the village, they are on the valley side high above the river and the cultivated fields. Farmers let irrigation water into their fields by breaching the wall of the ditch, and then, when a field has been given enough water, they seal it. A variety of crops are irrigated at Bīlaza, including cayenne pepper, chick peas, maize, barley, t'eff, bananas, and lemons. That the most extensive irrigation works in the area, those of Bīlaza, have been built by Agow people and not by Amhara seems strange, for the Amhara and not the Agow are the cultural descendants of South Arabian immigrants who used elaborate irrigation works in their homeland and presumably introduced them to Ethiopia. That the latter presumption is correct is suggested by the occurrence of numerous ruins of irrigation canals in Tigre.[13] Yet there is no evidence that the Amhara of Begemder and Semyen ever had irrigation systems much more elaborate or extensive than at the present, a situation which suggests that, as was the case in architecture, the constructional skills of the ancient Semites failed to accompany the spread of Semitic-speaking peoples southward after the fall of Axum.

WEEDING.—Some field crops, such as lentils, nug, and guaya (Lathyrus sativus), do not require weeding, for weeds are not numerous among them and are not believed to hinder their growth. Other field crops are usually weeded once during the growing season, though occasionally a crop is weeded a second time and, rarely, a third time. In weeding, men, women, and children work together. The weeding may be a community affair, and Nathaniel Pearce, a century ago, even speaks of a chief mustering his soldiers who formed into a line and, led by a woman, moved through the field singing and pulling up the weeds.[14] People sometimes simply pull up the weeds by hand, and sometimes use a dull sickle, or a hoe.

FENCING OF FIELDS.—Farmers must protect their crops not only from domestic animals, but from wild birds and quadrupeds, particularly the bush pig, wart hog, baboon, and porcupine. To assure

[13] Reale Società Geografica Italiana, 1936: 249.   [14] Pearce, 1831, I: 345–46.

the safety of their crops, farmers may fence or guard them, or they may hunt and kill the animals which raid the fields.

Gardens, which often include some perennials which are difficult to replace, are usually fenced, for they are near the house, and domestic animals are a constant threat. Fencing material for gardens includes stone, thorny brush, and other plants such as candelabra euphorbia, prickly-pear cactus, and, near former Italian installations, barbed wire. Fields, because of their size, are not usually fenced unless they are near the house or along a trail where domestic animals can get at them. Merchants and travellers particularly are none too scrupulous about keeping their animals from taking a few mouthfuls of feed at the expense of a local farmer. Thus, in open country, the trail may be bordered by piles of thorn brush to keep the voracious mules and donkeys from getting at the lentils, chick peas, and other growing plants.

GUARDING CROPS IN THE FIELD.—Some crops are not subject to frequent animal raids and so are not guarded. Other crops, such as sorghum, wheat, and barley, must be guarded in some places to assure an adequate harvest. To provide vantage points for the crop guards, farmers in many places build raised platforms, six to eight feet high, in their fields of ripening grain. A small boy is ordinarily stationed on each platform during the daytime with a sling and sometimes with a bull whip, which he cracks to frighten off birds. If there are animals in the neighborhood which raid the fields at night, a man takes over as guard. He often builds a fire in the field both for warmth and to keep animals away. He may be armed with a stick, a sling, and perhaps with tin cans which he can pound, and a rifle too, if he has one. If there are no animals nearby, the guard sits quietly by his campfire, roasting and eating grain from the field. Such night guards are so numerous in parts of the Northwest in the harvest season, that, from a favorable vantage point at night, the observer can see scattered far across the countryside the lights of many campfires built by such men keeping lonely vigil over their crops. When the guard becomes tired, he commonly sleeps on the raised platform, waking up from time to time to see whether animals are about. Early in the morning the boy returns from home to take over guard duties once more.

In some places, field platforms have small thatch shelters built on them (Fig. 43). Where there is a shelter on the platform, it usually takes up so much room that the platform can no longer serve as an observation post. In such a case, the guard must watch the field from the ground, though he uses the platform for sleeping. Near the village of Lomī Wenz in Semyen, on the other hand, I found that field guards did just the opposite, using the platform for daytime observation, but sleeping at night in greater comfort on the ground in temporary conical huts made of stacks of wild grass.

In the Gumis country, there are raised field platforms (Fig. 44) which are used not as guard stations, but as safe storage places for grain before it is threshed. In form, they are quite similar to the sun shelters found in Gumis settlements (Fig. 25) and may have developed from them.

Though it cannot be determined whether the various field platforms had a common or a multiple origin, it is clear that today in some areas they serve solely as places for storing grain out of reach of animals, in other areas solely as observation platforms, in others solely as places where guards take rest, refuge, or shelter at night, and in still others both as observation platforms and as places for rest or refuge.

HUNTING AND TRAPPING OF ANIMALS THAT RAID THE FIELDS.—Though many farmers, particularly among the Gumis and Kumfel, do nothing to kill animals that raid their fields, others are quite active, especially when crops are in the field, in trapping, hunting, and poisoning destructive predators. Mice and rats, for example, are caught in various ways, among the most common of which are these: 1) by a simple but effective trap consisting of a large flat rock balanced on edge against a stick, to which is fastened a stalk of grain as bait. As the mouse or rat eats the grain, the stick is moved and the rock falls and crushes the creature; 2) in pits whose walls gradually widen toward the bottom; these are filled with a sticky mixture of cow dung and water from which the animal is unable to extricate itself; 3) by asphyxiation in their lairs through the use of smoke. Baboons, which are troublesome in some places, are sometimes chased by men and dogs and beaten to death with clubs. Young dogs are fed roast flesh of baboon so that they will learn to like it and will be eager to help in the hunt. Bush pigs and porcupines are commonly caught in snares made of bark, vines, or wire, which are placed in openings in the hedge or at some other place where animals might enter the field. In addition to the simple traps, snares, and falls of native manufacture, traps of European manufacture are coming into use, particularly in the highland.

THE LOCUST SCOURGE.—Since antiquity, swarms of desert locusts (*Schistocerca gregaria*, Forsk.) periodically have descended on parts of Ethiopia,[15] as on other parts of the Middle East and East Africa, de-

[15] The Tropical Migratory or African Migratory Locust (*Locusta migratorica migratoroides* R. and L.) does considerable damage in the Sudan (R. C. Maxwell-

stroying crops and making agriculture precarious. The arid sections of Ethiopia, which are important breeding places, suffer most severely from the depredations of desert locusts. In Begemder and Semyen, locust infestations are frequent in the arid valley of the Tekezzay River bordering Tigre, and serious, too, in the adjacent highland regions of Semyen. In one such place in Semyen, for example, I saw fields of t'eff completely destroyed by locusts at elevations as high as 10,000 feet. Fortunately, locusts remain in the highland only during the dry season, and return to the low country after a few cold rains.[16] Sometimes entire swarms of locusts are killed in rainstorms in the highland,[17] though often only after they have inflicted serious damage to crops.

The locust scourge is viewed by some Ethiopians as punishment by God for their sins, and they make no attempt to fight the insects, though they may ask for divine mercy. William Harris, for example, said that in his time, when locusts descended on a farmer's fields, he made offerings and vows at the shrine of his guardian saint.[18] Father Francisco Alvarez in the sixteenth century was asked to help deliver an Ethiopian village from locusts; he and other Portuguese priests, Ethiopian priests, and the people of the village went into the fields carrying crosses and other religious items, and singing and crying to God for mercy. Alvarez further threatened the locusts with excommunication, an admonition which was followed shortly by the destruction of the locusts in a hail and rain storm, apparently to everyone's great surprise.[19]

PROTECTION OF CROPS AGAINST THE EVIL EYE.—Though I have not seen scarecrows in Northwest Ethiopia, similar devices, usually comprised of an ox skull or some other object mounted on a stick (Fig. 45), are found in many fields. These devices, which are reported also in Turkey[20] and are apparently in widespread use elsewhere in the world, are charms intended to protect the crop from damage from the evil eye. Among the Gumis, I observed one such charm which

---

Darling in Tothill, 1948: 404), including such nearby country as the Fung area of the Blue Nile Province. It seems likely, then, that this insect causes some damage in Ethiopia, too, particularly along the Sudan border. The Red Locust (*Nomadacris septemfasciata* Serv.) and the Brown Locust (*Locustana pardalina* Wlk.) breed in South Africa (Bodenheimer, 1951: 161) but apparently are not found in Ethiopia, though a solitary swarm of the Brown Locust did travel as far north in the Sudan as lat. 17° N. in 1937 (Tothill, 1948: 404). Among those who mention locust damage are Alvarez (1881: 67–72), Salt (Bodenheimer, 1951: 162), Plowden (1868: 30), Pearce (1831, I: 92, 108–9) and Gobat (1834: 294).

[16] Harris, 1844, II: 410.   [17] Alvarez, 1881: 69; Wylde, 1901: 292, 294.
[18] Harris, 1844, II: 410.   [19] Alvarez, 1881: 68–70.
[20] Werth, 1954: 86.

consisted of a piece of corncob and a piece of dried toadstool mounted on a stick. Sometimes, I am told, the Gumis use, for their charms, sorghum or a wild root known as "hyaena onion," which also serves as a medicinal plant [21] to promote rapid healing of wounds.

HARVESTING, THRESHING, AND WINNOWING

Harvesting is an activity of the dry season, spring-sown crops being harvested from September through February and March, and crops sown late in the rainy season being harvested principally at the end of this period. The cutting of field crops is generally done by men, though among the Gumis, Kumfel, and Agow, women share in this work. The sickle is used for harvesting most field crops, though some, such as lentils and green peas, are pulled up by hand. In harvesting sorghum, unlike most other cereals, farmers usually cut off the top of the plant with a sickle and leave the stalk in the field for animals to feed on. Only along the Sudan border, where sorghum is cultivated among cotton plants, do farmers cut down the entire stalk and then, holding it, lop off the top. This is done so that the sorghum stalks will not shade the cotton plants and hinder their growth.

After harvesting, cereals and pulses are collected in small piles and left to dry in the field for a few weeks; then they are gathered into large stacks, often eight or more feet high (Fig. 46), where they remain until the farmer has time to thresh them. The Gumis, on the other hand, commonly dry their sorghum tops on raised field platforms.

The season of threshing and winnowing, which follows the harvest, is a busy time, when men and boys work long hours; often neighboring farmers join together in this work, and their wives help by preparing large meals of flat bread, stew, and beer to sustain them. Everywhere crops are threshed in the field on a threshing circle constructed near the stacks of dry cereals and pulses. The circle is commonly ringed with stones and is generally spread with chaff and plastered with mud or cow dung and water, which, when dry, provides a hard surface ideal for threshing. Among peoples such as the Gumis and Kumfel, the plaster of the circle is made either of mud or of earth from termite mounds, for cow dung is either not available at all or it is in short supply. The threshing circle is also used widely elsewhere in Ethiopia, and is also common in the Sudan,[22] and in other parts of Africa, in the Mediterranean countries, and in other parts of the Old World.

Oxen are used for threshing large quantities of grain wherever farmers have enough animals to use for this task. In threshing with oxen, the unthreshed grain or pulses are lifted from the stack nearby

[21] Plowden, 1868: 108–9.   [22] Tothill, 1948: 284.

with pitchforks and spread over the threshing platform. Then oxen, perhaps five to eleven in number, are driven onto the platform. The jaws of the oxen are tied shut with bark or rope to keep them from eating grain. A boy or a man walks behind the oxen to keep them moving around the platform (Fig. 38). Often he sings praise-songs to them to urge them on. Meanwhile, at one side of the platform a companion starts winnowing the crop, using a pitchfork or some other type of winnowing implement.

The Gumis and Kumfel, who have few if any cattle, thresh all of their cereals by beating them with supple sticks, which are discarded at the end of the threshing season. The other peoples of Begemder and Semyen also use supple sticks for threshing, but usually only when grain or pulses are too few to make it worth using oxen. Threshing sticks are apparently widely used in Africa. J. R. Burnett says that in the Sudan threshing is usually done with a flail or spear shaft, or with an implement resembling a cricket bat.[23] S. F. Nadel [24] pictures such a "cricket bat" in use in the Nuba Hills in the Sudan. I have never seen spear shafts used for threshing in Begemder and Semyen. I have seen an implement resembling a cricket bat (Amh.: *makefkefya*), though it was not used in threshing, but for pounding grass into thatch roofs. Nowhere have I heard of men trampling out the grain themselves, though Helmer Smeds reports such a practice in Eastern Sidamo in southern Ethiopia.[25]

It should not be assumed from the above that all grains and pulses are threshed. Sometimes, for example, beans are stored in the pod and shelled as needed. Ears of maize are not usually threshed, but the kernels, when dry, are removed from the ears by hand. The Agow of Silaszī, I was told, thresh their maize with oxen, but this is exceptional and perhaps indicative of the extremes to which agricultural habit can go in Ethiopia. Sesame is cut when it is not quite mature and is tied in bunches which are stacked in the field to dry, and then the bunches are simply turned over and the seeds shaken onto a skin or a cloth.

STORAGE METHODS

SELECTION AND STORAGE OF SEED FOR PLANTING.—The Ethiopian farmer selects seed for the next year's planting at the time of threshing and winnowing. He prefers seed that is large and healthy. He may take individual seeds, or all of the seeds from a particularly fine plant, or he may set aside a large amount of seed from one field

[23] Tothill, 1948: 284.   [24] Nadel, 1947: 114.   [25] Smeds, 1955: 29.

which seems especially good, in which case he may take no seed from other fields of the same crop.

The farmer sometimes keeps his planting seed unthreshed, either on the stalk or in the pod, and sometimes he threshes and winnows it for storage. In the highland, most seed for the next year's planting is kept indoors in gourds, pots, baskets, and other small containers. Among the Kumfel and Gumis, however, farmers store much of their planting seed outdoors, on top of sun shelters, and it is usual to see heads of sorghum as well as baskets and gourds of seed heaped on top of the shelters. Insects infest much of the stored seed, and many of the samples I obtained were so badly damaged that few viable seeds were left.

STORAGE OF FOOD GRAINS AND PULSES.—People store grains and pulses intended for food either out of doors in pits, or in containers sheltered from the rain by conical thatch roofs, or indoors in containers kept either in the living house or in a special storage house.

Storage pits are used in the arid areas of the Sudan,[26] among the Eastern Galla of Harar Province,[27] and in Somaliland.[28] In Northwest Ethiopia, on the other hand, they are rather scarce and I found them in use only in the villages of Debark, Dilbīsa, and Macanna in Semyen, though they are said to have been in common use in Ethiopia a century ago,[29] and to have been carefully camouflaged to prevent their detection by invaders, though many of them were in fact discovered and plundered.[30] The apparent decline in the use of storage pits has probably resulted simply from the establishment of greater security in the country, and the substitution of means of storage that involve less labor. The people of the Kumfel village of Yīkaho, for example, say that they used storage pits during the unsettled period of the Mahdist occupation in the late 1880's to keep their grain from falling into the hands of marauders, though they have no storage pits today. Storage pits (Amh.: *gudgwad*) vary considerably in size. Coffin reports seeing some in Semyen which would hold 300 to 400 English bushels.[31] The pits I examined at Macanna village in Semyen were, however, only about three to four feet deep and two feet in diameter. Pits are lined with grass and mud or dung, and when filled with grain are covered with grass and mud. The pits may be dug near houses or in fields; at Macanna there are many individually owned pits in front of the church because the ground is easier to dig there.

[26] Tothill, 1948: 286.
[27] Brooke, 1956: 203, 207.
[28] Peck, 1942–43: 45.
[29] Pearce, 1831, I: 206–7.
[30] Pearce, 1831, I: 207.
[31] Pearce, 1831, I: 206–7.

Outdoor circular bins, covered with thatch for protection against
the rain and against animals which might steal from them, are found
in both highland and lowland Begemder and Semyen. They are, however, more numerous and more carefully constructed among the Gumis
and Kumfel, who store the bulk of their cereals in such bins. The bins
are always built near the living houses. Sometimes bins (Figs. 48 and
49) are made simply of mud and chaff plastered with cow dung. This
kind of construction is not strong enough for larger bins, which must
withstand great pressure. Thus, some of the larger bins are made of a
framework of upright poles interwoven with bamboo and plastered
over with mud and chaff. Another type is made from sorghum stalks
placed upright side by side, tied in position with bark rope, and ce-
mented together with mud and chaff. Sometimes a wide band of the
mud and chaff mixture is plastered around this kind of bin at the top
and bottom to reinforce it. In most of Begemder and Semyen outdoor
bins are built on rocks to raise them above the ground level and
to protect them against water. Among the Gumis and Kumfel, however, some outdoor bins are built on low platforms supported usually
by stilts. Stilted storage bins are also common in the southern Anglo-
Egyptian Sudan among such peoples as the Zande, Latuka, and
Mondari,[32] and among many of the peoples of the Sudan-Ethiopia
border.

The storage containers used in the house vary in size, shape, and
material of construction and generally include baskets, pots, gourds,
and larger containers. Along the motor road, tins and oil drums are
also used today by some people as storage containers. Two of the
most common large containers are the *gota* and the *gusgusha*. The
gota (Fig. 47) is a large cylinder about three feet in diameter and five
feet high. It is made of circular sections of sun-dried mud and straw
plastered with cattle dung. The circular sections fit securely one on
top of another, and the top one is usually fitted with a mud and dung
cover. When the *gota* is full, the housewife can scoop grain from it
without trouble, but when it is half empty and she can no longer reach
the grain, she may have a child climb into the container to scoop out
grain, or she may remove the upper section so that she can reach the
grain herself. Only grains grown in large quantities are stored in
gotas; around Gondar, for example, *t'eff* is usually stored in them.
The *gusgusha* is an unsectioned container made, like the *gota,* of
sun-dried mud and straw plastered with dung. *Gusgushas* are smaller
than *gotas* and are used for storing cereals and pulses grown in smaller

[32] Tothill, 1948: Figures 98, 99, and 100.

quantities. The largest of the *gusgushas* are about three feet high and about ten inches in diameter at the mouth and eighteen at the base.

THE PLACE OF THE GARDEN IN AGRICULTURE

In Oakes Ames's sense,[33] the farmers of Begemder and Semyen are primarily agriculturalists rather than horticulturalists, for their main concern and efforts are directed toward the sowing and harvesting of entire fields, in which the individuality of the plant is practically lost in the magnitude of the enterprise. Nevertheless, almost everywhere householders have small garden plots in which they cultivate plants which need individual attention, often giving them the same deliberate, careful cultivation that is characteristic of the horticulturalist.

In the highland such garden plots are found near almost every home and along streams. In the lowland regions, although some people maintain plots of maize, Amharic cabbage, squash, gourds, and beans near their homes, most establish garden plots some distance away along the banks of a stream. Whereas most fields are not fenced, gardens are, for the farmer can ill afford to lose the few plants of particular species he has in his garden, but he expects and accepts the loss of a share of his field crops to wild and domestic animals. Gardens may be fenced with thorn brush, with hedge plants such as euphorbia and bamboo, with dry stone walls, or, near large towns, with barbed wire.

Gardens in Begemder and Semyen are usually disorderly and untidy, giving the appearance of being places where plants have been concentrated without plan (Fig. 50). This appearance suggests that originally gardens were simply places in which useful plants of the forest were gathered into plots near the dwellings. Today, gardens in the middle highland of Begemder and Semyen contain domesticated plants such as spices, Amharic cabbage, potatoes, squash and gourds, maize, and perhaps a few fruit trees, but wild plants either collected in the countryside and brought home to the garden, or allowed to survive when the garden was originally cleared for planting. These wild plants include trees, basket grasses, and bamboo.

The hoe is the implement most used in cultivating the garden, though I have heard that the digging stick is occasionally used in planting seeds of squash and the plow is occasionally used to turn over the ground if the garden is a large one.

In spite of the strong preference for broadcast sowing in the fields, in the garden several methods of seeding are practiced. Maize and Amharic cabbage are broadcast, squash and gourds are planted, and

[33] Ames, 1939: 129, 132.

a few plants, for example, *gesho,* are transplanted. Manure is often applied to the garden, whereas fields generally receive little manure unless they are near the house.

Both men and women have certain jobs to do in the garden. Women usually transplant the basket grasses, for it is they who will use them; they also plant the squash, gourds, and some of the spices. Men transplant bamboo and cut it down as it is needed. Moreover, they usually sow Amharic cabbage, maize, and other plants that are broadcast, for broadcasting is the work of men. This sexual division of labor in garden care is not, however, followed universally and there are also many sporadic departures in the pattern from time to time.

Chapter VI

CULTIVATED PLANTS

Ethiopia is a center of plant diversity where *t'eff*, ensete, coffee, *ch'at*, and *nug* are believed to have first been brought into cultivation, and where there is a great variety of forms of wheat, barley, and certain other cereals, pulses, and oilseeds (see Map 5). Of the Ethiopian domesticates, until recently *t'eff* and ensete were cultivated nowhere else in the world. Just as these plants failed to spread abroad, so the Ethiopians have been slow to accept many of the introduced plants that seem to fit into their system of agriculture, and today maize and potatoes are the only important food crops of New World origin in Begemder and Semyen.

I do not plan to consider here all of the cultivated plants of Begemder and Semyen. Instead, I shall select only certain plants, especially those which were probably domesticated in Ethiopia and those which play an important part in local diet and life, and a few which are interesting to the cultural geographer for some other reason. It seems worth while to consider first the question of the position of the various cereal grains in Ethiopia and their yields, since cereal grains play an important role in Ethiopian agriculture.

THE RELATIVE IMPORTANCE OF VARIOUS CEREALS IN ETHIOPIA

The relative importance of the different cereals in Ethiopia varies not only from region to region, but locally according to altitude. Thus, *t'eff*, barley, wheat, and finger millet are the important plants of the highland, while sorghum and maize are the important food grains of the lowland.[1]

For Ethiopia as a whole, it is not altogether certain which grain occupies the highest over-all position in terms of production and acreage. Some writers accord the highest positions to sorghum and *t'eff*, though usually they do not indicate how they determined this. Perhaps the most detailed examinations of the questions of grain production in Ethiopia, Eritrea, and Somalia are those of Professors

[1] Reale Società Geografica Italiana, 1936: 249.

Raffaele Ciferri, Enrico Bartolozzi, and Guido Renzo Giglioli.[2] Ciferri and Giglioli estimated in 1939,[3] apparently on the basis of general impressions, that barley is generally the most important cultivated grain in terms of production. It is, they said, the most important grain of Christians and of less wealthy people. After barley, they held, comes *t'eff*, a luxury cereal consumed by well-to-do Christians, which receives greater care than any other cereal. After barley and *t'eff* comes sorghum, which is typical of the dry regions of Ethiopia and is thus the most important food of the Moslems who dominate these regions. Wheat, they said, is probably of less importance than sorghum, but more important than finger millet, maize, and pearl millet (*Pennisetum typhoideum*), whereas oats and rye occupy still more minor positions in Ethiopian agriculture.

To check their general impressions, Ciferri and Giglioli tabulated the grain-production figures for 1936, 1937, and 1938, obtained from various sources for about 2,000,000 hectares (one hectare equals 2.47 acres) of cultivated land located in Eritrea, northern Tigre, the Galla country, and the region of Dessie. For these two million hectares, they obtained the percentages of cultivated cereals indicated on Table 1.

TABLE 1

Cereal Production of Two Million Hectares, 1936–38

Sorghum	39.8%
Barley	21.4
T'eff	18.5
Finger millet	7.7
Wheat	5.8
Maize	5.0
Pearl millet	1.8
	100.0%

They emphasized that the figures tabulated above were for only limited regions and thus not a fair sample of the grain production of the entire country.

In 1940, approximate data of grain production were made available by the Statistical Office of the Ministry of Italian Africa for the year 1938. These were the first data dealing with cereal production of all of Italian East Africa. Professors Ciferri and Bartolozzi analyzed them and made a series of tentative conclusions, which remain, to my knowledge, the most careful consideration of cereal production for the

[2] Ciferri and Giglioli, 1939c; Ciferri and Bartolozzi, 1940.
[3] Ciferri and Giglioli, 1939c: 771–72.

Ethiopia region (Ethiopia, Eritrea, Somalia). As will be seen in Table 2, sorghum accounts for almost one-third (31.4 per cent) of the total

TABLE 2

1938 Cereal Production by Provinces in Quintals [4]

Province	Sorghum	T'eff	Barley	Wheat	Maize	Finger millet	Total
Eritrea	300,000	400,000	650,000	350,000	60,000	120,000	1,880,000
Amhara	500,000	800,000	450,000	60,000	150,000	50,000	2,010,000
Shoa	100,000	150,000	400,000	200,000	100,000	20,000	970,000
Harar	550,000	70,000	350,000	125,000	160,000	—	1,255,000
Galla and Sidamo	200,000	200,000	70,000	20,000	500,000	60,000	1,050,000
Somalia	1,000,000	—	—	—	250,000	—	1,250,000
Total	2,650,000	1,620,000	1,920,000	755,000	1,220,000	250,000	8,415,000

cereal production, barley (22.8 per cent) and *t'eff* (19.3 per cent) for about one-fifth each, while maize accounts for 14.5 per cent of the total production, wheat for 9.0 per cent, and finger millet for 3.0 per cent. It should, however, be pointed out that the production figures listed above include Somalia, which produced more sorghum than any other part of the Ethiopia region. Without the Somalia figures, and most of the area included in Somalia is not now part of the Ethiopian federation, sorghum would be displaced by barley as the most important grain in terms of production, while *t'eff* would follow sorghum.

Perhaps more interesting than the question of total cereal production is that of the relative importance of different cereals in different parts of the Ethiopia region. *T'eff* is the most important grain in the Amhara country, barley the most important grain of Eritrea and Shoa, sorghum of the Moslem region of Harar and Somalia, and maize of the southwestern section of the country.

Related to the question of grain production is that of the acreages used for the cultivation of the various cereals. Ciferri and Bartolozzi, using the estimated yields listed in Table 4 and the 1938 cereal production figures, have made an estimate of the acreages occupied by the various cereals in Ethiopia, which are listed in Table 3. As can be seen in Table 3, barley occupies by far the largest acreage in the country as a whole, sorghum occupies the second largest area, and *t'eff* the third. If we do not consider the cereal production of Somalia,

[4] Ciferri and Bartolozzi, 1940: 444. One quintal is about 220 pounds.

however, sorghum would be behind both barley and *t'eff* in acreage
occupied.

TABLE 3

Estimates of Areas of Cereal Production by Provinces in 1938, in Hectares [5]

Province	Sorghum	*T'eff*	Barley	Wheat	Maize	Finger millet	Total
Eritrea	20,000	36,360	92,860	8,750	6,000	10,910	174,880
Amhara	33,330	72,730	64,290	15,000	15,000	4,550	204,900
Shoa	6,670	13,640	57,140	50,000	10,000	1,820	139,270
Harar	36,670	6,360	50,000	31,250	16,000	—	140,280
Galla and Sidamo	13,330	18,180	10,000	4,375	50,000	5,460	101,345
Somalia	66,670	—	—	—	25,000	—	91,670
Total	176,670	147,270	274,290	109,375	122,000	22,740	852,345

Neither the 1939 estimates of Ciferri and Giglioli nor the 1938 cereal
production figures of the Statistical Office of the Ministry of Italian
Africa are more than very rough approximations. Still, it will probably be many years before Ethiopian statistics on agricultural production will be reliable and we can only give general impressions of
the importance of various cereals in the country. Moreover, we must
be very careful to make clear whether by "importance" we mean area
occupied or quantity of grain produced. Further, we must always
bear in mind the section of the country with which we are dealing
as well as the altitudinal zone.

YIELDS AND GENERAL USES OF CEREAL GRAINS

The estimates of yields of cereal grains in Ethiopia, listed in Table
4, show that small-seeded grains generally yield substantially more

TABLE 4

Estimated Yields of Cereals in Italian East Africa [6]
Quintals per Hectare

Sorghum	14–15
T'eff	10–12
Barley	7–8
Wheat	3–5
Maize	9–10
Finger millet	10–12

[5] Figures from Ciferri and Bartolozzi, 1940: 504.
[6] Figures from Ciferri and Giglioli, 1939c: 772.

per hectare than wheat and barley, a fact which may help explain their continued importance in the country. The estimates of sorghum yields (14–15 quintals per hectare) are above the 1948–52 estimates for the Sudan (7), the Near East as a whole (10), and the United States (12). Barley yields (7–8 quintals per hectare) and wheat yields (3–5), however, are below those of comparable regions such as Iran (average for 1948–52: barley 10, wheat 9) and Turkey (barley 11, wheat 10), as well as the average for the United States (barley 14, wheat 11).

There is considerable variation from place to place in the Northwest in the use of the various cereals, according to their availability and other factors. Despite this, four of the common cereals, wheat, barley, sorghum, and maize, tend to have the same range of uses: roasting of heads over the fire, the parching of grain, the making of various kinds of porridge, as ingredients in unfermented flat bread (Amh.: *kĭtta*), in beer, and, except among the Gumis and Kumfel, in fermented flat bread (Amh.: *injera*), raised bread, and the hard bread balls which are commonly carried by travellers. The other cereals, including *t'eff*, finger millet, and rye, on the other hand, have more restricted uses, which will be considered later.

FOOD PLANTS

Ensete

DESCRIPTION AND USES.—The *Ensete edule* (formerly *Musa ensete*) (Fig. 51) is a banana-like plant, sometimes called the "false banana," which is native to Ethiopia and to certain sections of the Sudan and the Great Lakes area of East Africa. Though it has recently been widely distributed around the world as an ornamental, it is cultivated for food only in Ethiopia. The cultivated plant, which is common in the south of Ethiopia rather than the north, reaches heights of from about 17 to 43 feet at maturity; then, when the plant is from three to six years of age, it flowers, bears fruit, and dies.[7] The cultivated plant, however, does not depend on seeds for reproduction, for people everywhere reproduce it vegetatively by digging up and planting lateral shoots.

The genus *Ensete* itself, if we accept the recent decision of E. E. Cheesman (1947, 1948) to separate it from the genus *Musa* and to raise it to generic rank, differs from *Musa* in significant ways. It has, for example, its greatest development in Africa,[8] whereas *Musa* has

[7] Smeds, 1955: 16.

[8] It is found in various sections of Ethiopia, north as well as south, in the Nuba Mountains of Kordofan, the Ruwenzoris (Wylde, 1901: 106–7; Smeds, 1955: 15), and

no species native to Africa. The genera differ also in their characteristic habitat. Many species of *Ensete* grow in highlands where the climate is cool, whereas *Musa* has its commonest habitat in rainforest
country.[9] In Ethiopia, the cultivated *Ensete edule* occurs at from about
5,000 to 10,000 feet. In the Gughé Mountains of southern Ethiopia,
Ensete edule grows at higher elevations than any other crop except
barley,[10] in situations where it must withstand seasonal frosts.

The principal source of food is the ensete plant itself, particularly
the false stem and the young shoots, which are boiled and eaten as a
vegetable, or pounded, buried, fermented, and made into a sort of
"bread." The ensete "bread" I sampled near Jimma was a stringy,
grey-brown, doughy flat loaf about an inch thick. The bread was delivered to me wrapped in a green ensete leaf tied with ensete fiber.
Inside the green leaf was another, a golden-brown dried leaf in which
the bread had been baked. The ensete bread smelled a bit like tomato
pizza, and tasted sour and not very different from *injera,* the flat grain-
bread of northern Ethiopia. The fruit of the *Ensete edule* is leathery,
has little pulp, and contains about four seeds, each about one centi-
meter or more in diameter. The fruit itself is not commonly eaten,
though in some places the seeds are boiled and fed to children.[11] Hugh
Scott mentions that the pith of the inflorescence stalk is also cooked,
though no one else reports this use.

Though the use of ensete for food has attracted far more attention
among foreigners, its use as a wrapping and construction material is
geographically far more widespread. The leaves commonly serve as a
wrapping material and for thatch and coverings, the leaf stems for
woven containers and mats and, after shredding, as mattress filler, and
the fiber is used for rope or thread.[12]

IMPORTANCE IN SOUTHERN HIGHLAND ETHIOPIA.—The most important present-day ensete cultivation is among Cushitic-speaking groups
of the southern part of the Ethiopian Plateau, though there are also
islands of ensete cultivation in the central part of the Plateau. Some
writers believe that there has been a recession of ensete culture [13] as
a result of the spread of the influence of the Amhara southward, for
the Amhara generally despise the ensete as food.[14] It is interesting in
this connection to note that in Eastern Sidamo, ensete farmers today

---

in the Immatong Hills of the southeastern Sudan (Tothill, 1948: 58), though it
extends to India, Burma, Southern China, Siam, the Philippine Islands, Java, and
New Guinea (E. E. Cheesman, 1947: 98, 100).

[9] E. E. Cheesman, 1947: 98–99.　　　[10] Scott, 1952: 131.　　　[11] Scott, 1952: 23.

[12] Though I heard of the use of ensete fiber for rope at Jimma, I did not hear of
its use for thread, though this is mentioned by Smeds (1955: 25).

[13] Stiehler, 1948: 266.　　　[14] Harris, 1844, II: 399; Smeds, 1955: 38.

cultivate barley, usually in small amounts, to give as rent to their Amhara landlords,[15] who will not accept ensete.

In some regions, such as the Jimma area, the ensete is simply one of a number of food plants, each of which is important to the local people. In other regions, however, ensete is so important that it almost completely overshadows other food plants, and forms a monoculture. The circular-shaped, closely-fenced plantations characteristic of the areas of ensete monoculture in southern Ethiopia are so distinctive and conspicuous a part of the cultural landscape that some writers have described ensete monoculture as one of the three main economic systems of Ethiopia, the other two being nomadic cattle-herding and seed-plow culture.[16]

It has been argued with considerable validity that ensete cultivation is superior to north Ethiopian grain agriculture in maintaining the fertility of the soil because manures are extensively used in the ensete areas of the south,[17] whereas they are not important and often not used at all in grain areas of the north. Moreover, because the Amhara have looked down on the ensete as food, because the ensete itself is too bulky to transport long distances and requires time to prepare for eating, and because an ensete plantation is difficult to destroy quickly and thoroughly, the ensete raisers have been more secure against northern invaders than they would have been if they had cultivated fields of grain,[18] which could easily have been harvested and carried off. A thick, almost impenetrable plantation of ensete serves, too, as excellent protection for men, cattle, and settlement. All of these factors have contributed to make the regions of ensete monoculture among the most densely populated rural sections of Ethiopia, with estimates ranging from about 180 to 450 people per square mile.[19]

NUTRITIONAL VALUE.—Because regions of ensete cultivation have fairly dense populations and ensete eaters appear to be in excellent health, it has been suggested that ensete has high value as a food.[20] An analysis of the nutritional value of ensete bread,[21] one of the principal forms in which ensete is eaten, indicates, on the other hand, that the bread is not well balanced as a food, but comparable to other starchy tropical products such as manioc flour. In the areas of ensete monoculture, such as Eastern Sidamo, where the natives appear to be in good physical condition, they in fact obtain their protein from other foods such as milk, meat, and legumes.[22] Comparative nutritional

---

[15] Smeds, 1955: 29.   [16] Smeds, 1955: 3, 35.   [17] Smeds, 1955: 38.
[18] Stiehler, 1948: 266.   [19] Smeds, 1955: 34.   [20] Smeds, 1955: 39.
[21] Copertini, 1938: 445–46.

[22] Smeds (1955: 39) indicates that milk is important in the diet of the ensete eaters of Eastern Sidamo though meat "is not much appreciated" (Smeds, 1955: 34).

studies of people living under different economic conditions and using different food in Ethiopia would be extremely useful. There doubtless are considerable differences among pastoralists, people who practice ensete monoculture, people, like the residents of Jiren near Jimma, who use ensete along with other root crops, grains, legumes, and animal products, and the grain farmers of northern Ethiopia among whom root crop cultivation is not important at all.

DISTRIBUTION AND USE IN BEGEMDER AND SEMYEN.—The early Portuguese travellers, as well as Charles Jacques Poncet and James Bruce, do not seem to have noticed ensete cultivation in the mountainous Semyen region. Walter Plowden, however, brought attention to an abundant growth of (cultivated?) ensete in a valley apparently located on the west side of Bwa-īt mountain a century ago. He said that many small villages there were almost hidden by forests of ensete.[23] Similarly, Th. v. Heuglin reported cultivated ensete in the Woina-Thale and on the Belleghes River in Semyen [24] at about the same time. On our mule trip in Semyen, we passed very close to the places mentioned by Heuglin and Plowden, but did not see cultivated ensete.

Not having actually seen cultivated ensete in Semyen, I have had to rely entirely on what local people told me about it. I am presenting this information here because it is in greater detail than anything I have read about ensete in Semyen and serves to locate villages where it is used.

At Derasgie my informant, Ato Alemo Kidaney Marīam, who knew the ensete from neighboring villages, spoke of two forms, the *enset* and the *gunaguna,* as being different though related plants. The *enset,* he said, is reproduced from segments of the root, which is dug up and cut into pieces; it neither flowers, bears fruit, nor puts out offshoots. It dies eventually of a shortage of water or is killed by wild animals. If this is true, the *enset* of Semyen is entirely dependent on man for reproduction. The *gunaguna,* which can be readily distinguished, said my informant, from the *enset* by its leaves which are reddish on the bottom, is found wild, bears seed, and dies. People sometimes go into the country to dig up young *gunaguna* plants and transplant them near their homes, but they do not reproduce them vegetatively. In the Agow country at Sahalla the people do not know *enset,* but have heard of *gunaguna* which is grown either from seed or from young transplanted plants, but is not reproduced by cuttings.

The information given me, if true, suggests that we may be deal-

---

Stiehler lists vegetables (cabbage), lentils, and meat as important supplements to ensete bread (1948: 265).

[23] Plowden, 1868: 395.   [24] Dove, 1890: 22.

ing with different types of the *Ensete* in Semyen: one, the *gunaguna*, which is a local wild plant and can flower, fruit, and survive in a wild state, and the other, the *enset,* which may have been introduced from a warmer climate and which cannot fruit in Semyen. Major William Harris, in 1844, described two plants found in Shoa Province which were called there *ensete* and *koba,* both of which were planted for their leaves.[25] Moreover, he added, the only noticeable difference is that the stem and middle rib of the leaf of the *koba* are red but in the *ensete* they are both light green. Helmer Smeds has spoken of a similar distinction, for he writes that the *koba* variety differs from the *Ensete edule* in the red to purple color of the back of its leaf.[26] One traveller reported that along the valley of the Gumara River near Lake T'ana the wild ensete which grew there and had carmine leaf panicles was called *guma-guma* by the local people to distinguish it from the edible *Ensete.*[27] That the natives of Shoa distinguish two types of ensete, as do those along Lake T'ana, seems to lend credence to the view that in Semyen, where a similar distinction is made, we may be dealing with different types, whether races or varieties, of the plant.

Perhaps equally curious is the fact that in Shoa and in Semyen the green-leaved ensete is called *enset* or *ensete,* whereas the other form with red on the underside of its leaves is called by other names: *guma-guma* along Lake T'ana, *gunaguna* in Semyen, and *koba* in Shoa.[28] Smeds gives *inset* as the Sidamo word for *Ensete edule, kojo* as Amharic, and *gunaguna* as Tigrinya;[29] thus, the word *inset* or *enset*

[25] Harris, 1844, II: 399.   [26] Smeds, 1955: 18.

[27] Hayes, 1905: 92.

[28] There is considerable confusion in the literature about the names used by the various Ethiopian peoples for ensete. Smeds says that the ensete is called *inset* in Sidamo, *hutta* in the Kulla language of Kaffa, *uarki* in Galla, *kojo* in Amharic, and *gunaguna* in Tigrinya. He adds that *worket* has been given as the Gurage name for ensete, but Leslau (1950: 148) gives the word *äsät* as the Gurage name for ensete. In Begemder and Semyen, the wild ensete is referred to by the Amhara as *gunaguna* and the cultivated ensete is usually referred to simply as *enset.* We can see from the above that there are terms for the ensete which are used by more than one linguistic group and that in one area more than one name may be used for different types of the plant, but a careful study of all these names must be made before we can be certain exactly how each of the names is used from place to place. Professor Wolf Leslau tells me that the problem of names used for ensete is a very complicated one among the Gurage, for they use different names to refer to ensete at various stages of growth and with different qualities of one sort or another. This abundance of names shows the regard the Gurage have for the ensete and the care with which they follow its development and observe the differences among plants. A similar situation is found among some of the Nilotic peoples whose lives are so centered on their cattle that their languages are filled with words used to refer to the differences among their animals.

[29] Smeds, 1955: 18.

may have been applied to a cultivated form of ensete introduced to the Shoa and to the Begemder and Semyen Amhara from the Sidamo country,[30] and the old words *gunaguna* (Tigrinya, and Begemder and Semyen Amharic) and *koba, kojo,* or *k'otch'o* (Shoa Amharic) continued in use for the local wild ensete.

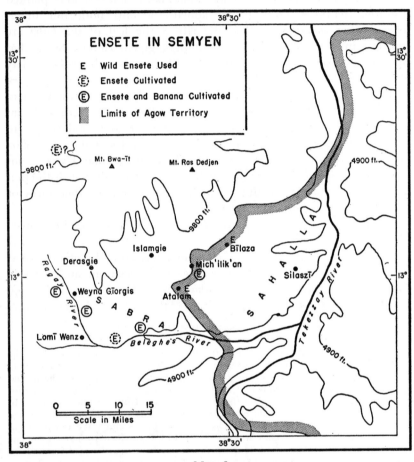

MAP 6

As shown on the accompanying map (Map 6), on which are plotted data on ensete use and cultivation in Semyen, the plant, surprisingly, is cultivated more among the Amhara than among the Agow. Some Agow in Sahalla say that they have never seen cultivated ensete among

[30] Smeds (1955: 15) has said that no wild ensetes are found in eastern Sidamo, so we may have to look elsewhere for the place of ensete domestication.

their people, though it is grown there by people who have intermarried with the Amhara and are considered to be mixed people. Moreover, say the Agow of Sahalla, the Agow living in the regions to the east of the Tekezzay River do not cultivate ensete either.

At Derasgie at an elevation of about 10,000 feet ensete does not grow, though it is said to be cultivated at nearby Weyna Gīorgis along the Ragay River, as well as in the Sabra region and in the villages of Kotk'ara, Kīvaīva, and Akirma. In these villages, ensete is said to be grown around the houses, the *gunaguna* from seed or young transplanted wild plants, the *enset* from cuttings. The *enset* is irrigated in the dry season, though the *gunaguna* is said not to be usually watered. Curiously, though the leaves are said to be used as wrapping material or woven into rain capes (Amh.: *gessa*) and mats, the plant is not used for food except in times of food shortage. Then it is said to be uprooted and the edible parts cooked in porridge with grain flour, cayenne pepper, salt, and butter. I have not heard of the people of Semyen burying and fermenting ensete pulp and baking it into a "bread," as is done in southern Ethiopia. Ensete transplanting and harvesting is said to be entirely in the hands of the men, a situation reminiscent of southern Ethiopian ensete-hoe areas where men apparently do most of the work.[31] Ensete is not traded from the lowland into neighboring highland regions, such as Derasgie, for even in times of crop failure there is usually enough barley to tide the people over. At Atalam village, whose people are considered to be mixed Agow-Amhara, the leaves of wild ensete are used to wrap bread for baking. At the village of Mich'ilik'an, between Timbahoch and Owchara, where the people also are mixed Agow-Amhara, *gunaguna* is said to be grown from seed irrigated. It is used for wrapping bread, but not as a scarcity food. No ensete is cultivated by the Agow of Silaszī village. At Bīlaza, another Agow village, wild ensete leaves are used for baking, but the plant is not used for food, even in times of food shortage.

Another curious aspect of ensete distribution in Semyen is that in most places where ensete is cultivated or used, so is the true banana (*Musa sapientum*, Amh.: *muz*; see Map 6), though in Ethiopia as a whole the areas of ensete cultivation and those of banana cultivation seem to be unrelated.[32]

Though W. Stiehler located two present-day areas of ensete cultivation near Gondar, I could find little basis for this. It is true only that ensete grows occasionally in gardens and around churches, as at Weuleka village, but it is not common in the area. G. Rohlfs said

[31] Stiehler, 1948: 261.   [32] Stiehler, 1948: 267.

in the last century that ensete occurred around Gondar in a wild state,[33] and James Bruce said earlier that it grew well at Gondar,[34] though he gave no indication that he spoke of cultivated ensete or that it was used for food there. According to Arthur Hayes, another traveller named Stecker spoke of the ornamental ensete growing, apparently wild, along the Gumara River east of Lake T'ana [35] and said that the natives called it *guma-guma* to distinguish it from the edible ensete, though it is not clear to me whether Stecker meant that the edible, cultivated ensete was also found there. Arthur Hayes, in a note, said that ensete was grown in gardens as an ornamental plant and that its stalk was used as food by the natives, but he seemed to be referring to Ethiopia in a general sense rather than to the Gumara River region.

The only other references to ensete I have found for the T'ana region point to the southern shores of Lake T'ana which are part of Godjam Province. James Bruce, for example, spoke of thick plantations of ensete growing south of Lake T'ana [36] in Godjam where in his time it was the main food of the Agow-speaking people. Ensete was sold for food in the market as well as "a manufacture of the leaf of that plant, painted with different colours like Mosaic work." [37] Arthur Hayes [38] has quoted a statement by Stecker in which the latter refers to ensete plantations and apparently wild ensete, too, on Zegie Peninsula at the south end of Lake T'ana. In 1903, when Hayes visited the area, only a few plants remained.

At Debre Tabor, I was told that the leaves of *gunaguna* are used to wrap bread (Amh.: *dabo*) for baking and to separate the cakes of flat bread (Amh.: *injera*) when it is stacked on a basket to be served for eating. I am not certain whether the *gunaguna* referred to is cultivated or not.

THE ANTIQUITY OF ENSETE CULTIVATION IN ETHIOPIA.—James Bruce [39] thought that the ensete may have been a cultivated food plant of ancient Egypt which eventually was displaced by cereals. This idea has been revived recently by a botanist, Vivi Laurent-Täckholm, who has argued that the ensete was known to the ancient Egyptians and was probably cultivated by them as a food plant. In support of this, she has noted that there is a similarity in form between the ensete and a common plant design on pottery found at Naqada in Upper Egypt, and dating from the Middle Predynastic Period.[40] The plant of

---

[33] Dove, 1890: 22.   [34] Bruce, 1790, V: 37.
[35] Hayes, 1905: 92.   [36] Bruce, 1790, III: 584, V: 36–37.
[37] Bruce, 1790, III: 589.   [38] Hayes, 1905: 159.
[39] Bruce, 1790, V: 40–41.   [40] Laurent-Täckholm, 1951.

Naqada, she has argued, was pictured on the pottery in a scene of daily life because it was important to people, most likely as a food plant. In addition, Mrs. Laurent-Täckholm has pointed out, there is a hieroglyphic sign which has been called by Egyptologists "The Plant of the South" and which may represent the ensete. This sign is "characterized by a pendant top and usually 2 pairs of basal leaves," and frequently in sculpture it is shown with a somewhat swollen base.[41] The principal objections to the interesting suggestion of Mrs. Laurent-Täckholm have been these: 1) that both the plant design on the Naqada pottery and the hieroglyph "Plant of the South" actually represent plants other than ensete, 2) that even if they do represent ensete, this proves only that people had knowledge of the plant, not that they cultivated it, 3) that the ensete could not have survived under the climatic conditions and in the marshy riverine habitat postulated for it in ancient Egypt, and 4) that no remains of the ensete plant have been found in Egyptian ruins. With respect to the first objection, it is true that the pottery design is most generally interpreted by Egyptologists as representing an aloe, and that the hieroglyph is interpreted as representing a *Juncus* or *Scirpus,* though these interpretations may, of course, be incorrect. With respect to the second objection, it may be argued that the occurrence of the pottery design in scenes of daily life suggests that the plant was important locally. With respect to the third objection, it has been argued that the climate of Egypt in ancient times, like that of the present, was suitable for ensete cultivation. Though, for example, ensete is unknown as a cultivated plant in Egypt today, it was successfully introduced to Egyptian gardens in the last century. It has to be protected from strong winds, but it did very well, attained great size, and flowered and fruited. It is more questionable whether the marshy conditions which prevailed along the Nile Valley, and in which the "Plant of Naqada" is pictured, were a suitable habitat for the ensete, which in Ethiopia is not a marsh plant, but a plant of moist, well-drained locations. With respect to the fourth objection, Laurent-Täckholm and Drar have suggested the possibility that certain Predynastic fibers, whose identity has not yet finally been settled, are actually from the ensete,[42] though the evidence presented so far is not convincing. Despite the above objections to the suggestion that ensete may have been cultivated in ancient Egypt, it must be acknowledged that the possibility remains, and that ensete seeds and fiber may be somewhere

[41] Laurent-Täckholm and Drar, 1954: 537–38.
[42] Laurent-Täckholm and Drar, 1954: 538–41.

preserved and awaiting discovery. Should such cultivation eventually be established, there would be raised all sorts of further interesting questions about ancient contacts between Egypt and Ethiopia.

The history of the domestication of ensete in Ethiopia and the spread of ensete cultivation there are equally a mystery. The plant was not mentioned by the author of the *Periplus* in the first century A.D. or by Cosmas in talking of the Axumite dominions in the sixth century. Apparently Europeans first heard of it from the Portuguese who visited Ethiopia in the sixteenth and seventeenth centuries.[43] James Bruce reported a tradition in Ethiopia that the ensete was brought by the Galla northward from Enarea to Maitsha, then to Goutto, the Agow, and Damot.[44] This local tradition was discounted by W. Stiehler who considered the isolated areas of ensete cultivation in northern Ethiopia to be remnants of a once wider area of ensete cultivation [45] which he supposed to go back in time to the period when Negroid groups occupied the Ethiopian highlands. This notion that ensete cultivation is of great antiquity is discussed by Helmer Smeds. He acknowledges that the plant is looked upon as having magical qualities, that it is grown around churches, and that the seeds have been used as tribute by subjugated peoples. These things may indicate considerable age for ensete cultivation.

CONCLUSIONS.—It seems that the best arguments for W. Stiehler's assumption that the Semyen area of ensete cultivation is the remnant of a culture which once was geographically more extensive are the following: 1) some of the Agow-speaking peoples, considered to be the ancient, pre-Semitic inhabitants of northern Ethiopia, who live in Godjam and along the south shore of Lake T'ana, have had plantations of ensete which in some places were the basis of subsistence; 2) the Amhara, who are relatively recent invaders, on the other hand, reject the plant as food; 3) in such a rough, mountainous, and inaccessible region as Semyen, conservative habits might lead to plants such as ensete being cultivated today, whereas elsewhere they may have been abandoned as a result of the acceptance of the Semitic prejudice against them; 4) the ensete occurs occasionally as a cultivated plant around churches.

The last argument is perhaps the most untrustworthy of the four, for the trees and other plants commonly found within church compounds in Ethiopia are sometimes recent introductions like, for example, the eucalyptus, or sometimes remnants of the former natural vegetation cover, like the native juniper, or wild plants which are

---

[43] See, for example, Beckingham and Huntingford, 1954: 47.
[44] Bruce, 1790, III: 584.   [45] Stiehler, 1948: 266.

still found in the countryside. Since wild ensete has been reported from various places in northern Ethiopia, it does not seem strange that it should be found in church compounds, too. Such occurrences do not seem to indicate necessarily that ensete was formerly cultivated nearby, though this is admittedly a possibility.

The first and third arguments, that the Agow of Godjam cultivated ensete and that it is found in inaccessible regions of Semyen, are more plausible. There are, however, serious objections to these arguments. First, it would seem that if the ancient Agow peoples cultivated the ensete fairly generally in the north, it would still be found among the most conservative Agow groups.[46] This is not the case, however, for neither the Christian Agow of Sahalla nor the K'amant, who have kept their ancient religion, cultivate the ensete. Even in Semyen the ensete is used and cultivated more among the Amhara than among the Agow, a situation which lends no support to the supposition that the Semyen ensete region is the remnant of an earlier, more widespread cultivation.

Careful study of the ensete, its cultivation and use, is needed before we can state with any degree of certainty what the origin and early distribution of ensete cultivation may have been. It seems that the supposition of a large-scale recession of ensete cultivation in the north is questionable.[47] Indeed, the uses of wild and cultivated ensete in Semyen—as a fiber plant and as a scarcity food—may indicate that the wild plant was early and widely used in Ethiopia for its fiber and planted or transplanted at home for convenience. Certainly its leaves are extremely useful as a wrapping material and the value of the leaves of the wild plant for this would have been apparent. Perhaps ensete first gained its position as an important food plant in southern Ethiopia and then southern types of the plant spread northward where today they are known as *enset* to distinguish them from the wild or semicultivated local varieties.

T'eff

T'eff (*Eragrostis teff*) is one of the interesting curiosities among the domestic plants of Ethiopia. It is a tiny-seeded grass (Fig. 45) which grows from about one and one-half to three feet in height, and al-

[46] One might even expect to find ensete cultivated by remnant, pre-Agow Negroid groups in northern Ethiopia, such as the Barīa, Cunama, and Gumis, but these groups nowhere seem to live at elevations high enough for ensete cultivation.

[47] Smeds (1955: 38) says that today "the picture of a continuing regress of the cultivation of *Ensete edule* given by Stiehler may be a little exaggerated" and points out that Amhara who live among ensete eaters have begun to use the plant for food.

though in northern Ethiopia it is an important cereal, it is cultivated nowhere else in the world as a food plant. It seems curious that
the Ethiopians should have domesticated this grass, for the seeds are
small, their average dimensions being about one by one and one-half
millimeters. Whereas one hundred normal seeds of soft wheat weigh
about five grams, one hundred t'eff seeds weigh only one twenty-fifth
of a gram; [48] thus, a hundred average grains of soft wheat are equal
in weight to about 12,500 t'eff seeds, a ratio of 125 t'eff seeds to every
grain of wheat!

HISTORY OF DOMESTICATION.—About 43 per cent of the species in
the genus Eragrostis are African, and Africa is believed to be the center
of its evolution.[49] The closest wild relative of t'eff is Eragrostis pilosa,
which has a wide distribution in the hot and temperate regions of
both hemispheres. The characteristics of t'eff are so similar to those of
Eragrostis pilosa that it has been claimed that t'eff should be considered a variety or subspecies of E. pilosa rather than a true species.[50]
The seeds of Eragrostis pilosa, as well as the seeds of other wild species
of Eragrostis, are collected for food in times of scarcity in parts of
Africa other than Ethiopia, including west tropical Africa [51] and the
eastern Sudan,[52] a situation which suggests that t'eff, too, may originally have been used only when people were forced to it.

Grains of a species of Eragrostis were discovered in Egypt in bricks
from the pyramid of Dassur, which is believed to have been built
before 3000 B.C., and in other bricks believed to date from 1400 to
1300 B.C. Some writers claim that the seed discovered is that of
Eragrostis teff which, they say, was probably cultivated in ancient
Egypt.[53] Other writers believe the seed in question is that of the wild
Eragrostis pilosa, which is common in Egypt and may have been
gathered for use in making bricks.[54] The latter explanation seems to
be more likely in the absence of other evidence.

Arabic references to a grain called tahf indicate that in South
Arabia a wild plant resembling t'eff (perhaps Eragrostis pilosa) was
used in times of food scarcity as early as the ninth century.[55] Because
of this, it has been suggested that the Semites, arriving in Ethiopia
from South Arabia, may have applied the name for their wild scarcity
food to the related domesticated cereal which was already cultivated
by the pre-Semitic inhabitants of Ethiopia.

[48] Ciferri and Baldrati, 1940: 170.
[49] Ciferri and Baldrati, 1939: 11; Ciferri and Baldrati, 1940: 171.
[50] Ciferri and Baldrati, 1940: 171.   [51] Dalziel, 1937: 528.
[52] Haudricourt, 1941: 129.   [53] Ciferri and Baldrati, 1939: 30.
[54] Haudricourt, 1941: 129–30.
[55] Haudricourt, 1941: 130; Abd Allah ibn Ahmad, 1840–42, II: 163–64.

If an Ethiopian origin of *t'eff* is accepted, and this appears to be
reasonable, it seems likely that its domestication took place somewhere
in the northern section of the highland, for not only does Ethiopian
legend point to the north as the homeland of *t'eff*,[56] but in the past,
and in general today, it is more important and more highly valued
there than in the south.

W. Stiehler has suggested that *t'eff* probably originated in the area
that was to come under Axumite dominion (Serae, Shire, Tigre) where
it probably had been taken into cultivation by the Cushitic-speaking
Agow or even by earlier inhabitants. He believes, further, that after
the Semitic conquest of the Axum area, *t'eff* may have remained for
a long time the food of the lower classes, and that it was probably
accepted by the upper classes only gradually, after the acculturation
of Semitic and Cushitic peoples. Stiehler relates the spread of *t'eff*
southward to the last expansion of Amharic people for, he says, before
then it was either entirely absent in some places in the south, as at
Harar, or it played only an unimportant role. The diffusion of *t'eff*
cultivation was apparently in the hands of merchants, southward-
moving groups of Amharicized settlers, and soldiers from the north
stationed in the south.[57] Today, *t'eff* is gaining importance among
many of the Galla and Sidamo people of the south, though many
writers continue to emphasize that it is a grain of Christian Ethiopians.[58]

European knowledge of *t'eff* dates from the time of sixteenth-century
Portuguese contacts with Ethiopia, though its first scientific description was not made until the late eighteenth century when James Bruce
brought some seed back to Europe with him. The cultivation of *t'eff*
for fodder has been attempted abroad many times, but perhaps the
most important effort to distribute the seed around the world for use
as a fodder plant was that undertaken by the staff of the Royal
Botanical Gardens at Kew, who, starting about 1886, distributed *t'eff*
seed to botanical gardens in India and in the British colonies in the
Americas, Asia, Australia, and South Africa.[59] *T'eff* proved quite successful as a hay crop in the summer rain areas of South Africa because of the ease with which it dries; as a result, it is very important in
the Union today and is deemed one of the best plant acquisitions in
the last half of the nineteenth century.[60]

[56] Stiehler, 1948: 274.   [57] Stiehler, 1948: 274.
[58] Stiehler, 1948: 274; Ciferri and Baldrati, 1940: 171.
[59] The correspondence between officials at Kew and the British Foreign Office
and people living in Ethiopia to obtain *t'eff* seed and knowledge of conditions of
its cultivation is included in Kew, Royal Gardens, 1887.
[60] Ciferri and Baldrati, 1940: 173–74; Van de Wall and Alvord, 1954: 20–21.

DISTRIBUTION AND TYPES IN NORTHWEST ETHIOPIA.—*T'eff* is the preferred grain food of the people of the middle highland of Begemder and Semyen, and everywhere between elevations of 5,000 and 8,000 feet [61] it is an important crop. Although the zones of optimal yield for *t'eff* and wheat correspond, 5,300 to 7,300 feet,[62] *t'eff* has been so serious a competitor for wheat as to displace the center of wheat cultivation upward to between 8,000 and 8,700 feet. *T'eff* is usually planted on soils of medium to light texture because yields are higher on them than on heavy soils.

It has been reported that for commercial purposes three kinds of *t'eff* are distinguished, according to the dominant color of the seeds: white, grey, and red.[63] In the markets of Begemder and Semyen, however, I found *t'eff* usually referred to either as *nech'* (white) or *t'ik'ur* (dark). The *t'ik'ur t'effs* were red, violet, or red-violet, but never black. Sometimes in the markets these types are referred to as *k'ai t'eff* ("red *t'eff*"). In every batch of white *t'eff* there are red seeds and in every batch of red *t'eff* there are white seeds. Several varieties of *t'eff* have been distinguished by botanists, but there is such difference in type from village to village that it seems likely that a wealth of new forms remains undiscovered. In one village alone, for example, I found that the people have distinct names for ten different kinds of *t'eff*.[64]

CARE OF *T'eff*.—*T'eff* receives better care than perhaps any other

[61] Writers do not agree on these limits of *t'eff* cultivation in Ethiopia. Professor Roberto Almagià (Reale Società Geografica Italiana, 1936: 249) says that *t'eff* grows well from 1,000 to 3,000 meters (3,400 to 10,000 feet); Ciferri and Baldrati (1940: 173) say that *t'eff* is ordinarily cultivated between 1,300 and 2,300 meters, rarely to 2,600 meters (4,300 to 7,500 feet; rarely to 8,700 feet). A review of Russian work on Ethiopian agriculture says that *t'eff* is found at 2,600 meters (8,700 feet), but that its highest limit is 3,000 meters (10,000 feet). I shall use here the figures 5,000 to 8,000 feet as comprising the area in which *t'eff* is important, though I observed it growing as high as 9,000 feet. Stiehler (1948: 269) states that the lower limit of *t'eff* is at 1,300 to 1,500 meters (4,300 to 5,000 feet) and the upper limit at 2,400 to 2,600 meters (8,000 to 8,700 feet) which is rarely exceeded.

[62] Stiehler, 1948: 274–75.

[63] Ciferri and Baldrati, 1939: 20; these authors, however, are not certain of the origin of the grey *t'eff* and seem to think that it does not come from distinct grey-seeded varieties.

[64] Some people have pleasant stories to explain the origin of the names for their local types of *t'eff*. At Weuleka village near Gondar, for example, there is a type of *t'eff* called *azen bekantu*, which means "sadness for nothing," and people give this explanation for this strange name: Once there was a farmer who sowed a field of *t'eff*. Every morning he went to the field to see how his *t'eff* was doing. Finally, he recognized that the soil in his field was not good enough for the *t'eff* to grow and he went away sorrowing. Months later, he returned to his field and was surprised to see that it was filled with fine *t'eff* which he called *azen bekantu*, "sadness for nothing."

cereal in Ethiopia: the preparation of fields for *t'eff* is better, the weeding more thorough, and the harvest carried out more carefully. It has been said, in fact, that *t'eff* is probably the only cereal to receive careful attention in Ethiopia.[65] Farmers harvest it, unlike most cereals, before the seeds have reached complete maturity, for at maturity many seeds fall to the ground and would thus be lost.[66]

T'eff YIELDS.—*T'eff* yields in good years from forty to one to as much as forty-eight to one, and in bad years twenty to one.[67] As has been indicated previously, *t'eff* yields per acre are high—about 850 to 1,100 pounds of grain per acre—higher than yields of wheat and barley, comparable with yields of finger millet, and somewhat lower than yields of sorghum and pearl millet.

T'eff AS A FOOD.—T'eff is favored over all the other cereals available for making *injera,* the fermented flat bread which is a staple food for most of the peoples of the Northwest. Most Amhara like *t'eff* so well for this purpose, in fact, that, though they live at elevations too high or too low for its cultivation, they still import as much as they can afford for making *injera.* Though most *t'eff* is used in making *injera,* it is also sometimes used in making the unfermented flat bread, *kitta,* and as an ingredient in raised bread, *dabo,* and the hard bread balls, *dabo kollo,* which travellers commonly carry with them. *T'eff* is used in porridge and beer on rare occasions, but I have never heard of its being eaten roasted or parched.

Many Europeans in Ethiopia have doubted that *t'eff* has much value nutritionally. Analyses of *t'eff* seeds, however, have shown that they contain remarkable amounts of iron, and that in other respects they compare well in food value with wheat, rice, and maize.[68] Moreover, *t'eff* has an additional advantage over wheat because in milling it gives a return in flour of 99 per cent, whereas wheat gives a return of only 60 to 80 per cent.[69] In addition, *t'eff* has two other considerable advantages over wheat and other Ethiopian cereals: It is apparently free of troublesome parasites, and it can be stored for many years without spoiling.[70] A serious deficiency of *t'eff,* on the other hand, is the absence of glutin, rendering it unsuitable for making European-type raised bread. This shortcoming troubled Italian agronomists who hoped that *t'eff* might be useful in making bread for the Italian colonists who were expected to settle in Ethiopia. Experiments in

[65] Ciferri and Baldrati, 1940: 171–72. [66] Ciferri and Baldrati, 1940: 173.
[67] Ciferri and Baldrati, 1939: 47.
[68] Ciferri and Baldrati, 1939: 52; Ciferri and Baldrati, 1940: 174; Interdepartmental Committee on Nutrition for National Defense, 1959: 36, 82, Table 6 following p. 46.
[69] Ciferri and Baldrati, 1939: 54. [70] Ciferri and Baldrati, 1940: 175.

mixing *t'eff* flour with the flours of other grains in making bread were unsuccessful, but it was suggested that *t'eff* seeds could, as a last resort, be used in soups as a substitute for rice. A further hindrance, perhaps, to the use of *t'eff* by Europeans is that some types, especially the red-seeded ones, have an odor that is unpleasant if one is not accustomed to it. Because of these deficiencies, the conclusion of Raffaele Ciferri and Isaia Baldrati, that *t'eff* will probably remain an important food only to the natives of Ethiopia, seems reasonable.

Wheat

As shown previously (Table 2), much less wheat is grown in Ethiopia than *t'eff,* sorghum, barley, and maize. Despite this and despite the fact that Ethiopia contains an insignificant portion of the world's wheat acreage, the Ethiopian Plateau contains a great variety of forms of hard, 28-chromosome wheat and is considered to be the center of evolution of hard wheat.[71] Nicolai Vavilov, whose studies brought the first recognition of Ethiopia's position in the development of the 28-chromosome wheats, says that not only does Ethiopia have the greatest number of varieties of wheat, but that botanical, physiological, and genetic studies show that the Ethiopian wheats should actually be divided into separate botanical species.[72] Of the soft, 42-chromosome wheats, neither spelt (*Triticum spelta*) nor Indian dwarf wheat (*T. sphaerococcum*) seems to be cultivated in Ethiopia, though *Triticum vulgare* and *T. compactum* are.[73]

Within Ethiopia, the 28-chromosome hard wheats are estimated to account for 90 per cent of the total wheat production and the 42-chromosome soft wheats for only 10 per cent. The hard wheats include *Triticum durum* (macaroni wheat) and *T. turgidum* (rivet or cone wheat) which account for 75 per cent of total production, *T. dicoccum* (emmer wheat) which accounts for 10 per cent, and *T. polonicum* (Polish wheat), 5 per cent. The soft wheats *T. vulgare* (bread wheat) and *T. compactum* (club wheat) together account for 10 per cent, with *T. vulgare* by far more widespread, more abundant, and in greater variety. Not only are hard or emmer-type wheats more important in production, but most of them grow at almost all elevations within the range of wheat (4,900 to 11,500 feet), whereas soft or bread wheats are cultivated only at medium elevations between 7,200 and 9,800 feet.[74]

Even more curious than the minor importance of soft wheats are the

[71] Ciferri and Giglioli, 1939e: 229; Ciferri and Giglioli, 1939a: 248.
[72] Vavilov, 1949: 38–39.   [73] Ciferri and Giglioli, 1939c: 765.
[74] Ciferri and Giglioli, 1939e: 234, 260.

facts that the greatest abundance of soft varieties is found in Eritrea, that in the Ethiopian section of the plateau the cultivation of soft wheat is concentrated around Harar, Addis Ababa, and Axum, and that in the south and west of the plateau soft wheats constitute only from 0.1 to 5 per cent of cultivated wheats.[75] The concentration of soft wheats largely in areas such as Axum, Harar, and Eritrea, where Semitic influence has been strongest, may indicate that these wheats were introduced to the Ethiopian Plateau relatively late.

The people of Begemder and Semyen distinguish between emmer wheat (*adja*) and other wheats as a group (Amh.: *sinde*), as well as among races of wheat. Generally two broad groups of wheat other than emmer are distinguished on the basis of the color of their seed: *nech'* (white) and *t'ik'ur* (dark) or *k'aī* (red), though there are many local types of wheat to which villagers give specific names. People grow more of the white-seeded forms of wheat, which they prefer. Wheat serves all the common uses of grain, in flat bread, porridge, beer, for parching, etc., and it is the favored grain in making the raised bread *dabo,* which is made occasionally but is not a staple food.

Barley

Ethiopia is considered to be an important center of barley domes-tication [76] and barley (Amh.: *gebs*) is one of the major cereal grains. The optimum zone of barley cultivation is from about 6,000 to 12,000 feet, according to Russian studies, with an upper limit of about 13,000 feet (4,000 meters).[77] Barley is of minor importance below 6,500 feet on the plateau, but above that it gradually increases in importance until above 8,000 feet it is the main cultivated plant.

In Begemder and Semyen, there are both many-rowed and two-rowed forms of barley, the latter being closely related to wild barleys. Farmers distinguish between white and dark-seeded forms, large and small-seeded ones, and early and late-maturing ones. Barley is usually sown in May or June and harvested in October or November, though early-maturing forms are already harvested in late August or early September. The early-maturing forms are particularly valuable be-cause they provide food at a time when the previous year's grain sup-ply is low and before other crops are ready for harvest. Often a second crop is sown after the first is harvested, the farmer either taking ad-vantage of late rains or raising the barley in irrigated plots.

Everywhere the people of highland Begemder and Semyen prefer

[75] Ciferri and Giglioli, 1939c: 767–68.   [76] Vavilov, 1926: 170–71.
[77] *Bollettino* della R. Società Geografica Italiana, 1937: 310; Stiehler, 1948: 268.

wheat over barley for raised bread, and *t'eff* over barley for fermented
flat bread, though in the high mountain areas most people cannot
afford much *t'eff*, and barley is commonly substituted for it. As a malt
grain, on the other hand, barley is unsurpassed by any other cereal,
and it is generally used for this purpose wherever it can be obtained,
except among the Gumis, who substitute sorghum and maize.

Sorghum

Sorghum (*Sorghum vulgare*) is by far the most important cereal
cultivated in the hot, arid lowland sections of the Northwest, as in
most other lowland areas of the Ethiopia region. In the highland, on
the other hand, though some types are found as high as 8,000 feet,
sorghum is simply one cereal among many. It serves the common
range of cereal uses, and in addition, like maize, the seed is popped,
and the stalks are chewed as a confection and are used as a construction material.

The majority of the cultivated species of sorghum are African, with
three centers of diversity: west tropical Africa, southeast Africa, and
northeast Africa.[78] Begemder and Semyen is part of the northeast
African center of diversity and contains such variety that in one village there are sorghum types, distinguished by their seed color, size,
or by other qualities, which are often unknown twenty miles away.
Everywhere, however, the sorghum plants are tall, averaging perhaps
seven feet in height at maturity, and have red, yellow, or white seeds.
The Hametsh of Camcamba and the Kumfel of Yīkaho have only one
sorghum variety, with white seed, called *gissa* in Hametsh and *bavarī*
in Kumfel. This is said to be the same type known in the Sudan as
juheyla. The Gumis of Bodella have two varieties of sorghum: a white-
seeded type called *kwontch* and a red-seeded type called *dirkīna*. The
Gumis commonly mix the seed of these two types in sowing. In the
Agow village of Silaszī, the people distinguish three types of sorghum:
two whitish-yellow, and one a quick-maturing red-seeded type which
is not planted until the middle of the rainy season. Among the Amhara
the general word for sorghum is *mashilla*, although they also dif-
ferentiate and name several types. Around Gondar, the Amhara
usually distinguish three principal types: a red-seeded type known as
zengada, and two white-seeded types known as *bulley mashilla* and
wareyta mashilla. The white-seeded types are preferred because their
seeds make better beer and fermented flat bread. A fourth type of
sorghum grown in the highland is called *tobbīa*. This type has reddish
seed, which is said not to be eaten by birds. Despite the existence of a

[78] Snowden, 1936: 21.

great variety of sorghum types, in the marketplaces of Begemder and Semyen sorghum seed is usually referred to simply as *nech'* (white) or *k'aī* (red), the finer distinctions being of no importance there.

In addition to the types of sorghum mentioned above, there is a special form known in Amharic as *tinkish,* which is grown for its sweet stalk which is preferred over the stalks of other sorghums as a confection. The Gumis plant sweet-stalked sorghum (Gumis: *gīampa*) near their houses in one section of their maize fields, cutting it green for use as a sweet, though permitting some plants to mature for seed. The Kumfel of Yīkaho, on the other hand, sow sweet sorghum (Kumfel: *kansī*) seed mixed with grain sorghum, cutting some of the sweet sorghum for use before the grain sorghum is harvested, while permitting other sweet sorghum plants to mature in the field.

Finger Millet

Finger millet (*Eleusine coracana*) is the only one of the lesser millets which is important in Ethiopia. It is used by most of the groups in Begemder and Semyen and is known by several names: in Amharic, *dagussa;* in Kumfel, *dagussey;* in Hametsh, *dagutcha;* and in Gumis, *tanka.* This plant, whose small, round, red seeds look remarkably like those of Amharic cabbage (*Brassica juncea?*), is cultivated at altitudes up to 7,500 feet,[79] though it is generally more important in the arid lowland regions. It is, for example, an important food crop along the Sudan border, though curiously it is not known by the Agow of Sahalla.

A common use of finger millet is for making beer, especially that beer which is distilled into the liquor *arak'i.* Finger millet also commonly serves as an ingredient in unfermented and fermented flat bread. It is rarely used in porridge or raised bread, and is not roasted or parched and eaten.

Pearl Millet

Pearl millet (*Pennisetum typhoideum*) is a cereal of the arid regions of Eritrea and Tigre. I did not see it cultivated anywhere in Begemder and Semyen, although some people know it by name: in Tigrinya, *bultuk,* and in Sudan Arabic, *dukhn.* Though it is a valuable crop because it matures rapidly (in about sixty days), is drought-resistant, and is extremely productive,[80] the highlanders of Tigre Province do not cultivate it, but look on it as a curiosity and call it

---

[79] The upper limit of finger millet cultivation in Ethiopia according to Russian studies (*Bollettino* della R. Società Geografica Italiana, 1937: 309) is about 7,800 feet.

[80] Ciferri and Giglioli, 1939c: 772; Chiovenda, 1928: 546.

"the slaves' finger millet" because it is cultivated by the Barīa, a Negroid people living in the lowland.[81]

Oats

While some observers report that oats (*Avena* sp.) are cultivated here and there on poor soils in northern Ethiopia for horses and mules,[82] others deny having seen cultivated oats there at all.[83] In the Northwest, I saw none cultivated, though wild oats (*Avena*) commonly grow in fields of wheat and barley, and some Ethiopians have seen and like European oats. Generally, if the farmer has time, he weeds the wild oats out of his grain field. If he has no time for weeding, however, he harvests the oats along with the main crop, and then either uses them unintentionally or separates them in winnowing. In the latter case, the oat seeds may be fed to chickens or may simply be thrown away.

Contrary to the general practice, however, there are some partial steps toward the domestication of the oat in highland Semyen. The first of these steps occurs sometimes when a field is fallowed and an abundant volunteer crop of oats springs up; the oats are harvested with the sickle and stored to be used as fodder. In two Semyen settlements, Islamgie and Derasgie, I found a further step toward domestication. There, oats growing among the barley mature at about the same time as the barley, and they are harvested and threshed along with it. In the final basket-winnowing process, the oat seeds are separated from the barley seeds, and some women store them, especially in time of failure of the barley crop. Later, the oats are mixed with the barley again and used in making beer or fermented flat bread. Oats are never used alone for food, however, and are never sown separately. Only the heavier oat seeds, which are not separated in the basket winnowing, are thus unintentionally sown with the barley seed for the next year's crop.

Rye

Rye (*Secale cereale*) is known in Amharic as *senaf k'olo*, which means lazy or sluggish parched grain. This, in fact, describes its principal use as *k'olo* or parched grain, though in some places it is used for other things, too. Rye is grown usually only in the cold highland, though in some places it extends into the middle highland. In the hot low country, however, many inhabitants do not know the plant. Even where it is most used, it is a minor crop grown in small quantities.

[81] Parkyns, 1868: 180.   [82] Plowden, 1868: 155; Harris, 1844, II: 397.
[83] Pearce, 1831, I: 205; Wylde, 1901: 277.

FIG. 1 (*above*).—Looking toward the village of Macanna (elevation about 11,500 feet) from the west side of Mt. Ras Dedjen. The houses of the village are almost indistinguishable from the plowed fields that surround them.

FIG. 2 (*left*).—A thicket of a bamboo along the Metemma trail in the hot lowland.

FIG. 3.—Tall grass along the trail in the hot lowland in the dry season.

FIG 4.—Dry forest in the lowland south of Metemma at the height of the dry season in February. Note the termite mound at the center of the photograph.

FIG. 5.—Debre Tabor (8,500 feet) as seen from a hill nearby. The eucalyptus trees growing in the town itself give it a wooded appearance. The brush on the hillslope in the foreground is cut and burned whenever the land is to be farmed.

FIG. 6.—Lobelias and other plants growing near the crest of Mt. Ras Dedjen (15,000 feet).

FIG. 7.—The castle of Fasiladas at Gondar. This castle, which was built in the early seventeenth century, was one of the first of the Gondar castles.

FIG. 8.—The castle of King Bekafa to the left and the castle of the Empress Mentuab and of her son, Īyasu 2nd. These castles were built at Gondar in the eighteenth century.

FIG. 9 (*left*).—"The bridge of Fasil" across the Megech' River south of Gondar.

FIG. 10 (*below left*).—Group of priests, choir-men-scribes, and boy deacons outside of the church of Debre Tabor Īyesus.

FIG. 11 (*below*).—Christian clergymen in Gondar.

Fig. 12 (*above left*).—Gerasmatch Gebre Mariam of Derasgie with two retainers: a typical minor official.

Fig. 13 (*above*).—A Falasha couple of Weuleka village near Gondar. The man is a weaver, his wife a potter, and one of their sons is a blacksmith.

Fig. 14 (*left*).—Womber Muluna Mersha (right), high priest of the K'amant people of Ch'ilga, with members of his family.

FIG. 15.—A group of Agow men of Kilashoa village, Sahalla.

FIG. 16.—Looking across the dry lowland of the Agow toward the gorge of the Shikina River and the highland of Beyeda which is occupied by the Amhara.

FIG. 17.—A Kumfel family group in the village of Yīkaho.

FIG. 18.—A Kumfel mother and daughter of the village of Yīkaho. The thatch-roofed chicken coop raised on stilts is characteristic of Kumfel settlements.

FIGS. 19 AND 20.—Wayt'o fisherman-farmer of Godja village and his wife.

FIG. 21.—Wayt'o fisherman in his balsa in Lake T'ana.

FIGS. 22 AND 23 (*both above*).—Shifrī Ananī, a Gumis man of Bodella village. Note his peppercorn hair.

Fig. 24.—Gumis children near Metemma.   Fig. 25.—Goats resting under a sun shelter in the Gumis village of Bodella. Baskets and other goods are stored on top of the sun shelter.

Fig. 26 (*above*).—A raised goat house in the Kumfel village of Camcamba. In the background is a thatch-roofed sun shelter supported by a circle of poles. Such shelters, as well as flat-topped sun shelters, are used by the Kumfel.

Fig. 27 (*right*).—Gumis women with gourds and baskets in nets suspended from their carrying sticks. Iron-tipped sticks (*gumba*) such as that held by the woman in the foreground are frequently carried by Gumis women when walking.

Fig. 28 (*right*).—Gumis mother and child, Bodella village. The bands tied around her arms and the pattern of scars are characteristic of Gumis women.

Fig. 29 (*below*).—Women in the highland at Debre Tabor carrying home earthen jugs of water.

Fig. 30 (*below right*).—Agow village of Mavīan in Sahalla perched high in the hills far from the nearest water supply. The straw piled on top of the acacia tree in the foreground is used as fodder and is kept in the tree to keep it out of reach of the animals.

Fig. 31 (*right*).—Gumis women dipping water with a gourd from a pit dug in a dry stream bed in February, at the height of the dry season.

Figs. 32 and 33 (*below*).—Houses in early stages of construction.

Fig. 34 (*above left*).—Two-story stone house of a priest at Wogeda Īyesus near Debre Tabor. For the floor plan of this house see Sketch 2.

Fig. 35 (*above*).—Plowing a field near Marīam Deber along the edge of a gully. Note the plowman using his whip.

Fig. 36 (*left*).—Man in Weuleka village carrying the beam of his plow to the field.

FIG. 37 (*below left*).—A plowed field with large boulders in Wogeda Īyesus village near Debre Tabor.

FIG. 38 (*below*).—A boy of Derasgie throwing grain into the center of the threshing circle so that the oxen may trample it.

FIGS. 39 AND 40 (*above*).—Gumis men of
Bodella village using the winnowing scoop
and the brush to winnow sorghum.

FIG. 41 (*right*).—Area being cleared for planting in the Gumis country. The piled brush is
ready for firing.

Fig. 42 (*above*).—Field of sorghum in the Gumis village of Bodella. Farmers cultivate around the tree stumps.

Fig. 43 (*right*).—A Kumfel field platform with a small thatch shelter built on it near Zenda Gīorgis.

Fig. 44 (*above*).—Platform in a Gumis field in Bodella village with sorghum piled on it awaiting threshing. The sorghum is interplanted wtih gourds and cotton.

Fig. 45 (*right*).—An ox skull mounted on a stick in a field of young *t'eff* to protect the crop from the evil eye.

FIG. 46 (*above*).—Stacking green peas and horse beans in a pile for drying at Mecane Birhan, near Derasgie.

FIG. 47 (*left*).—A new sectioned storage bin (*gota*) drying in the sun.

FIG. 48 (*right*).—Two thatch-roofed storage containers (foreground) in Gelshiu village near Ch'ilga.

FIG. 49 (*below*).—Outdoor storage bins under construction in the Gumis village of Bodella. When completed, these bins will have thatch roofs to keep out the rain.

FIG. 50 (*below right*).—Garden of a Christian *debtera* in Marīam Deber village near Gondar. In the foreground are squash and potatoes, in the center maize and Amharic cabbage, in the left background is a castor oil plant, and in the center background is the *missana* tree.

Fig. 51.—The Ensete.

Fig. 52.—Agow man of Silaszī village in Sahalla in his cotton field, which is located in the lowland along the Tekezzay River, hours away from home.

Fig. 53.—Gumis women and a man picking cotton in February. Note the cut stalks of sorghum scattered among the cotton plants.

FIG. 54 (*above*).—Gumis man of Metemma village looking over gourds which are soaking in a stream.

FIG. 55 (*right*).—Typical ox of Northwest Ethiopia. Note the pronounced dewlap and the hump.

Fig. 56.—Goat in the Gumis village of Bodella.

Fig. 57.—Amhara goats at Debark in Semyen.

Fig. 58.—Gumis sheep in the village of Bodella. Gumis sheep have no noticeable fleece, though highland sheep do.

Fig. 59.—Amhara sheep at Debark in Semyen.

Fig. 60.—An Ethiopian donkey. This animal, unlike most pack donkeys, is provided with both a sheepskin and a burlap bag filled with straw to protect its back.

Fig. 61.—An Ethiopian mule in Gondar. Note the European-type stirrups and the cloth pad over the saddle.

Fig. 62.—A woman of Teiwodiros Ketema in K'wara milking a cow in the early morning. A boy is holding the calf nearby while the cow is being milked. The back legs of the cow are tied because it is restive.

Fig. 63.—A calf skin stuffed with straw, to which the cow is brought at milking time, if her own calf has died.

Fig. 64.—An Amhara girl making butter in a gourd suspended from a tripod.

Fig. 65 (*above*).—An Amhara girl rocking a pottery jug in making butter.

Fig. 66 (*above right*).—A *warka* tree (*Ficus vasta*) near Ch'ilga. In the lower branches of this tree are several plaited beehives placed there so that bees will enter them.

Fig. 67 (*right*).—A cylindrical clay beehive in Agow village of Mavian in Sahalla. The grass weighted with stones on top of the hive protects it from the rain.

Fig. 68 (*right*).—Sprouted barley spread out on a skin in the sun. The beer pot in the background is being smoked over a small fire.

Fig. 69 (*below*).—A cake of grain cooking on a metal plate over the fire. The cake will be broken up and used in making beer.

Fig. 70 (*below right*).—A tanner's wife in the Gondar market trimming baskets with leather.

Fig. 71 (*above left*).—A tanner trampling on an oxhide to soften it.

Fig. 72 (*above*).—A Gondar silversmith at work before his charcoal fire.

Fig. 73 (*left*).—A Falasha blacksmith at work. The young man in the background is working a pair of bellows to increase the heat of the charcoal fire.

FIG. 74 (left).—A Falasha potter about to remove her pots from the fire, just after the firing.

FIG. 75 (below).—The first weekly market at Gondar after the long Lenten fast. This market attracts thousands more people than most weekly markets at Gondar.

Fig. 76.—People travelling to the Gondar market over the main motor road from the north.

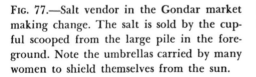

Fig. 77.—Salt vendor in the Gondar market making change. The salt is sold by the cupful scooped from the large pile in the foreground. Note the umbrellas carried by many women to shield themselves from the sun.

Fig. 78.—Trader in the Debre Tabor weekly market sawing a salt brick into smaller pieces.

FIG. 79 (*above*).—Woman selling cotton by weight in the daily Gondar market. She balances stones against the cotton. Such stones are said to weigh a certain number of Maria Theresa dollars.

FIG. 80 (*above right*).—Yemen Arab trader with his wives and mule in front of his house. Such Arab traders know Ethiopia better than any other foreigners.

FIG. 81 (*right*).—A woman carrying a load of wood to the weekly market at Gondar.

FIG. 82 (*above left*).—The wood section of the daily market at Debre Tabor. Eucalyptus trees are growing in the background among the houses.

FIG. 83 (*above*).—A woman carrying home dried cakes of cattle dung she has collected for fuel in Semyen at an elevation of 10,000 feet. At such heights the shortage of wood for fuel is most acute.

FIG. 84 (*left*).—Trees growing within the compound of the church of Derasgie Mariam in Semyen, where they are protected from fuel-short housewives.

I have heard that sometimes they are sown broadcast, which again shows how strong the idea of broadcasting is in Northwest Ethiopia. Potatoes are harvested by turning over the ground with the plow after other crops growing with them have been cut. They are stored in large, mud-covered baskets inside the house away from the heat. They are washed, skinned, and cooked whole or quartered in stew. Children sometimes throw whole potatoes into the fire to bake but adults do not usually do this.

I have seen the sweet potato (*Ipomoea batatas*), another New World plant, grown in only two gardens in Begemder and Semyen. It appears to be a recent introduction, perhaps from southern Ethiopia where it is widely cultivated. The sweet potato is known in Amharic as *ye sukwar dinitch*, and in Begemder and Semyen it is eaten either boiled or fried. Most people consider it too sweet for stew. I have not seen yams, coco-yams, the Galla potato (*Coleus edulis*), or manioc cultivated in Begemder and Semyen, although all of these plants except manioc are common in the southern part of the Ethiopian Plateau.

Squash

Squash (*Cucurbita pepo* and *Cucurbita maxima;* Amh.: *dubba;* Kumfel: *duvi;* Gumis: *paītua*) is among the few vegetables used by the Amhara. It does well everywhere at elevations up to about 8,000 feet. Sometimes squash seed is planted in the garden to protect it from domestic animals, but sometimes it is broadcast or planted among field crops, especially among sorghum and maize. Squash is usually cooked in stew (*wot'*). Its seeds are sometimes parched on the fire and eaten, and sometimes they are cooked and eaten or added to stew.

SPICE PLANTS AND STIMULANTS

Spices

Since Ethiopians season most of their food so heavily that few Europeans can stand its fiery taste, no account of Ethiopian cultivated plants would be complete without mentioning the many spice plants.

The most important spice in the local diet and the one most universally cultivated is cayenne pepper (*Capsicum frutescens;* Amh.: *berberei*), a New World plant which seems to have been introduced to Ethiopia at the end of the sixteenth or the beginning of the seventeenth century.[89] In Begemder and Semyen, I found cayenne pepper cultivated everywhere except at elevations above 9,000 feet. People who live in regions too high for the cultivation of cayenne pepper buy it in the

[89] Chiovenda, 1912: 30.

marketplace, for it is an essential element of the Ethiopian diet.

Cayenne pepper seed is usually broadcast in gardens near the houses or along a stream, or in fields, often under shady trees, though sometimes seedlings are grown in a seedbed and transplanted. Everywhere the plant requires irrigation and it is commonly fertilized with dung. The fruit is picked mature in January, February, or March, usually starting in the second year of its growth. Women then dry the fruits in the sun, pound them in a mortar, and sift them to remove the seeds from the powdered seed pod. Then the powder is ground still finer on a special spice grinding stone.

Cayenne pepper is mixed with ground mustard seed and other spices to make a sauce, *dilih,* which is kept in a gourd or in a pot in the house. The *dilih* is used daily in stews of various kinds. Besides its primary use in stews, cayenne pepper is added to other foods and is so essential as an ingredient in Ethiopian cooking that travellers frequently carry it with them.

In Begemder and Semyen, people also use cone pepper (*Capsicum conoides*) which is cultivated only in the lowlands and is more pungent than cayenne pepper. Cone pepper in Amharic is *shīrba* or *shīrba berberei* and in Kumfel *sairba.* Ethiopians are often mildly amused at the inability of Europeans to eat their highly spiced food, but even they sometimes break out in sweat when eating food spiced with particularly strong *shīrba berberei.*

Amharic cabbage or leaf mustard (*Brassica juncea?*) is widely cultivated in Begemder and Semyen and is known to the Agow as *hamira,* to the Kumfel as *amlī,* and to the Amhara as *gomen.* It is grown for its leaves which are used in stew, and for its seeds which are used in the hot sauce *dilih.* Some people cultivate it around their houses, and others in gardens or in maize fields. The small red seed of Amharic cabbage is broadcast when the rains begin, and the leaves are pulled from the plant as needed. When the plant is mature it is cut down with a sickle and the seeds are removed either by hand or by threshing with a stick. Some farmers do not reseed their plots of Amharic cabbage, but allow some plants to mature and to reseed the field or garden naturally.

Black mustard (*Brassica nigra*) is called *sonafitch* in Amharic and *sonafitchī* in Kumfel. It grows wherever Amharic cabbage is found. In Debre Tabor, I found that black mustard seed is sown mixed with Amharic cabbage seed and harvested at the same time as cabbage, the cabbage being placed in one pile for threshing and the mustard in another. Elsewhere, farmers sometimes sow mustard and sometimes let it propagate itself; often they consider it to be a wild plant. Mustard is usually harvested by women because they are the cooks and make the sauces in which it is used. Farmers told me that they do not eat the leaves of black mustard because it is too strong, but Emilio Chiovenda reported that mustard leaves are eaten.[90]

Other spices found in the markets of Begemder and Semyen, but not all cultivated there, are the Korarima cardomom (*Aframomum corarima;* Amh.: *kororīma*) which has been an article of export from East Africa to the Levant at least since the beginning of the Christian era,[91] coriander (*Coriandrum sativum;* Amh.: *dimbilal*), basil (*Ocymum basilicum;* Amh.: *zaccacavī*), black pepper (*Piper nigrum;* Amh.: *k'ondo berberei*), ginger (*Zingiber officinale;* Amh.: *jinjibil*), *Carum copticum,* black cumin (*Nigella sativa;* Amh.: *azmud* or *avosseda*), and fenugreek (*Trigonella foenum graecum;* Amh.: *avīsh*). The odor of powdered fenugreek mingled with that of cayenne pepper constitutes one of the characteristic odors of the Ethiopian household and of the women who grind the spices and prepare the food. Garlic (*Allium sativum;* Amh.: *nech' shinkurt*) and shallots (*Allium ascalonicum;* Amh.: *shinkurt*) are found in every market and are widely used in cooking. Imported turmeric (Amh.: *erd*) is also widely used in cooking.

Coffee

Ethiopia is believed to be the place of origin of Arabian coffee (*Coffea arabica* L.), the word "coffee" being derived, according to one theory, from "Kaffa," an important coffee-producing district in the south. Today, coffee is the most important Ethiopian export by value, accounting for a little more than half of the Federation's exports in 1956. Most Ethiopian coffee is grown in the highland regions of the south, especially in the provinces of Kaffa-Jimma on the Ethiopian Plateau, and Harar on the Somali Plateau.[92] Though an occasional Moslem of Begemder and Semyen cultivates a few coffee plants in his garden, there is no commercial cultivation of coffee in the province except in the Dera region along the southeastern shore of Lake T'ana, where cultivation is reported to be carried on on a small scale. There is, however, considerable production of coffee just south of the lake on Zegie Peninsula in Godjam Province. Some of this coffee is shipped northward overland by pack train or across the lake by balsa; the market town of Delgī, on the west shore of the lake, is an important destination of the balsa traffic in coffee.

Coffee is very expensive in Northwest Ethiopia, especially in view of the standard of living. In early 1954, for example, green coffee beans

[90] Chiovenda, 1912: 23.   [91] Burkill, 1935, I: 60.
[92] For an account of Ethiopian coffee production, see Sylvain, 1958.

sold for about fifty cents U.S. per pound, and shortly thereafter rose even higher, to eighty cents U.S. per pound, following a jump in world coffee prices. Despite its high cost, almost everyone drinks coffee, and it has remained an important trade item everywhere in the Northwest, where it is known to all groups as *buna*.

Despite the fact that Arabian coffee originated in Ethiopia and that coffee is everywhere a popular drink today, it has come into general use in Christian areas only in recent times. A century ago, for example, one writer reported that coffee was not as a rule drunk by Christians.[93] The missionary Krapf, indeed, was not even permitted to prepare coffee in the houses of Christians, nor would they supply him with vessels for making it, lest they be made unclean.[94] William Harris observed further that coffee was forbidden to Christians on pain of exclusion from the church.[95] The prejudice against coffee and the sanctions applied against those who used it derived from the fact that it was regarded as a Moslem drink,[96] for Ethiopian Christians often have had a negative reaction to things Moslem. The prejudice against coffee was held not only by the Christians, but by the K'amant as well,[97] for they also consider the Moslems to be their enemies. It was probably because both Christians and K'amant rejected coffee that Charles Jacques Poncet, who visited Gondar and northern Ethiopia in the late seventeenth century, said that it was little valued in the country and even concluded that it was not used there.[98] Today, unlike the past, there are few remnants of the ancient prejudice against coffee, except among the K'amant, who still do not permit their priests to drink it.

Ch'at

Ch'at (*Catha edulis*) is a perennial shrub of the family Celastraceae, which grows in the middle highland. Its leaves, which have stimulating and reputedly strengthening properties, are chewed by Moslems. Most writers believe that *ch'at* was first domesticated in Ethiopia, but Moslems in South Arabia have been cultivating and using the plant for a long time, perhaps initially because there was no specific Koranic prohibition against it. In Yemen a century ago it was considered as important a crop as coffee, and today it is still grown there and its leaves are chewed daily by a high percentage of men.[99] *Ch'at* is also

---

[93] Dove, 1890: 22.
[94] Foster, 1949: 106, 155.
[95] Harris, 1844, III: 179.
[96] Pearce, 1831, II: 13.
[97] Rassam, 1869, I: 209.
[98] Foster, 1949: 106, 155.
[99] Candolle, 1885: 134; Simmons *et al.*, 1954: 327.

widely used in Somaliland and Kenya, though not in the Sudan.[100] It has even come into limited use in Europe, where druggists in Lyons, France, after discovering that *ch'at* has a quality which enables the patient to tolerate more caffeine, made of *ch'at* extract some pills which they called "New Abyssinian Tonic." [101]

In Ethiopia, since Moslems are the primary consumers of *ch'at*, production is concentrated in the Moslem sections of the country. Though it is generally a garden plant which is sold only in small quantities in the marketplace, it is produced commercially on a large scale in the Harar area. Harar *ch'at*, in fact, is transported to Aden by air. This is the only instance known to me of the regular use of air transport for an Ethiopian agricultural export, and it is possible only because of the high price *ch'at* commands in the Aden market. Among the Moslems in Ethiopia, *ch'at* is widely chewed by ordinary people because of its stimulating effect, and by holy men for inspiration. In Addīs Alem, the Moslem quarter of Gondar, it is estimated that most people over fifteen chew *ch'at*. At Islamgie village in Semyen, all of the adults chew *ch'at*, but priests take more than others. It is interesting to note, however, that among the Wayt'o, only Moslem holy men chew *ch'at*, and then only on their Friday sabbath and at other times of prayer. Ethiopian Christians of the Northwest say that many Arab Moslems take *ch'at* for its supposed aphrodisiac qualities, a use reported also for Harar. In southern Ethiopia, *ch'at* leaves, besides being chewed as a stimulant, are used as an astringent medicine, to dispel sleep, and are put in water or milk to make a bitter beverage.[102] The continued use of large amounts of *ch'at* is said to be the cause of the frequency of heart ailment in Harar,[103] to dull the intellectual faculties, lead to schizophrenic behavior, and encourage the development of deficiency and infectious diseases. On the other hand, *ch'at* leaves contain significant amounts of calcium, iron, niacin, ascorbic acid, and beta-carotene, the latter two of which are generally deficient in the Ethiopian diet.[104]

In Begemder and Semyen, neither the Amhara, Falasha, Kumfel, nor Gumis normally cultivate *ch'at* or use it, although an occasional Christian will grow *ch'at* as a cash crop for sale to Moslems, and Christians in Debre Tabor sometimes cultivate *ch'at* and use it in mead as a substitute for *gesho* (*Rhamnus prinoides*). Also, Christians who are

---

[100] Kirk, 1946: 135.

[101] Azaïs and Chambard, 1931: 13.

[102] Harris, 1844, II: 107.

[103] Azaïs and Chambard, 1931: 13.

[104] Except for the footnoted sentence above, this paragraph is based on Interdepartmental Committee on Nutrition for National Defense, 1959: 99–100.

possessed by Moslem evil spirits (*zar*) may take *ch'at* to appease the spirits and to get them to leave, which seems to emphasize the fact that *ch'at* consumption is viewed as an Islamic habit.

Gesho

Everywhere in highland Begemder and Semyen, people use the leaves of the shrub *gesho* (*Rhamnus prinoides*), as we use hops, to give a slightly bitter taste to their beer, mead, and the distilled liquor *arak'i*. Apparently the plant will not grow in the lowland along the Sudan border, and the Kumfel and Gumis usually make their beer without it, much to the displeasure of Amhara visitors from the highland. Sometimes, however, the Kumfel and Gumis buy *gesho* brought from the highland for use in beer, and the Kumfel, like the highlanders, sometimes use a substitute, the leaves of *girowa*.

The planting and care of *gesho* are usually in the hands of men, who plant the seed in small patches near streams. At the end of one year the young plants are dug up and transplanted in the garden, usually along its margins, the men taking care that it is watered for the first year after transplanting. The women usually pick the leaves of *gesho*, for the brewing of beer is their work.

Tobacco

Though it is used by most of the Moslem and pagan peoples of Ethiopia, tobacco (*Nicotiana tabacum* and *Nicotiana rustica;* Amh. and K'amant: *timboho;* Agow: *timbah;* Gumis: *timbaka*) is generally avoided by the Amhara, Falasha, and K'amant, who regard the use of it as a Moslem habit. Indeed, one of the common replies of an Amhara, when asked whether he smokes, is "No, I am a Christian." Though I do not know what the sanctions against the use of tobacco are today, in the last century Christians were not permitted to enter a church if they had been smoking tobacco, which was regarded as a sin.[105] The Emperor Johannes even went so far as to cut off the lips of a person who had been smoking tobacco, and to remove his nose if he had been snuffing.[106] These punishments nevertheless were less severe than those imposed in the past by rulers of other lands, such as the Sultan of Turkey and the Grand Duke of Muscovy, when fighting the use of tobacco among their people. Even as late as a generation ago, Moslems of the Wahabi sect of Saudi Arabia are reported to have executed men for using tobacco,[107] which was contrary to their strict

[105] Pearce, 1831, I: 335; Harris, 1844, III: 179.   [106] Rey, 1935: 67.
[107] Harrison, 1924: 222.

beliefs. The Amhara of Northwest Ethiopia support their rejection of tobacco with the legend that once, long ago, when a heathen who had opposed Christianity all his life died, a tobacco plant sprang up from his grave.[108] In fact, the use of tobacco was probably rejected by Christian Ethiopians, as was the drinking of coffee for a long time and the use of camel flesh today, simply as a negative reaction to Moslem habit. It is clear that the belief was not introduced to Ethiopian Christians from the Copts of Egypt, for they use tobacco freely. Indeed, a century ago, the Egyptian *Abuna* who headed the Ethiopian church was so incensed at the ban on tobacco that he threatened to break every one of the pipes over the heads of the priests if he could not teach the Ethiopians that the use of tobacco was not sinful.[109]

Despite the fact that Christians regard the use of tobacco as a Moslem habit, not all Moslems use it. In the Jabarti village of Islamgie in Semyen, for example, most people avoid tobacco because, they say, its use is forbidden by the Koran! Nor do the Wayt'o people of Lake T'ana use tobacco, though they are Moslems and sometimes cultivate it for sale to the Jabartis and Arabs.

Moreover, the traditional rejection of tobacco among the Christians is weakening and today tobacco smoking is slowly gaining popularity among them. Some young men who have been educated in Addis Ababa have taken up the habit there and continued it when they have returned to the Northwest. In other cases, the habit has been introduced by migrants or former slaves from central and southern Ethiopia, where the use of tobacco is more acceptable. Thus, at Debre Tabor, there are freed Galla slaves who smoke tobacco in water pipes, and throughout the region there are policemen from other parts of Ethiopia who have been stationed in the Northwest by the government and who have continued to smoke, serving thereby as agents in introducing the habit. Moreover, some non-smoking Amhara and K'amant farmers have begun to cultivate tobacco for commercial purposes, and other Amhara in Debre Tabor have begun to use green tobacco leaves as an animal medicine and as a substitute for *gesho* in making beer.

It will be interesting to see what happens to the use of tobacco among the Gumis who have recently been converted to Ethiopian Christianity, for the Gumis are perhaps the most inveterate tobacco users in Northwest Ethiopia, using snuff and chewing tobacco in

[108] Rey (1935: 67) was told a similar story in which the villain was identified as the heretic Arius. Similar legends sprang up about tobacco elsewhere in Christendom as well as in the Islamic world at an earlier date (Ortiz, 1947: 231–32).

[109] Pearce, 1831, II: 78.

addition to smoking regular pipes and water pipes made of gourds. It seems that everyone in a Gumis village, including men, women, and children, is either smoking or would like to be smoking and it is a common sight to see a cluster of vociferous little children impatiently awaiting their turns on their mother's pipe. Among the Gumis, the planting and care of tobacco is entirely in the hands of the men who sow tobacco seed broadcast in August near the banks of streams. It is neither irrigated nor weeded. When mature, the tobacco plant is cut down by men using sickles. They then strip the leaves from the plants and dry them on stones in the field for a week or two. After the leaves are dry the men carry them home and crush them in a mortar. The crushed tobacco is sprinkled with water and then rolled into a large, oval-shaped ball. The ball, which weighs several pounds, is hung from roof beams inside the house. When tobacco is needed the ball is taken down and pieces of the strong tobacco are broken off.

The Grape

The growing of grapes (*Vitis vinifera*) is believed to be ancient in Ethiopia.[110] Not only was it common when the Portuguese arrived,[111] but it may have been done at ancient Axum for there are representations of grape clusters and leaves on an altar stone at the foot of one of the monoliths there.[112]

Despite its antiquity in Ethiopia, the grape does not appear ever to have been important generally, though the middle highland, in Amharic *weyna dega* or "grape highland," is said to have been named after the grape, which in Amharic is *weyn*. The grape vine has, it is true, been cultivated extensively at various times in a few places such as along the east shore of Lake T'ana at Imfraz,[113] in the districts of Dreeda and Karoota (Korata?)[114] on the southeastern shore of the lake, in Dembya, and around Axum.[115] Nevertheless, the people were not fond of wine in the past [116] and the vine was either planted as a curiosity [117] or, more usually, was grown by priests and monks to get grapes for sacramental purposes.

Unfortunately, we cannot be altogether certain just how priests prepare their grapes for communion, for this is a closely guarded secret known only to them. James Bruce said that bruised grapes were served to communicants by spoon, seeds and all, though he thought

[110] Dove, 1890: 21; Chiovenda, 1912: 36.
[111] Alvarez, 1881: 411–12; Chiovenda, 1912: 35.
[112] Wylde, 1901: 154.   [113] Pearce, 1831, I: 237.   [114] Bruce, 1790, III: 335.
[115] Beckingham and Huntingford, 1954: 48.   [116] Bruce, 1790, III: 335.
[117] Harris, 1844, II: 407.

he detected another taste besides that of the grapes.[118] Other writers [119] have said that priests make a wine from raisins for sacramental purposes. Some priests in Begemder and Semyen today admit that they use only raisins for making their communion wine, but others insist that they make wine from fresh grapes.

To make raisin wine, according to Francisco Alvarez' sixteenth-century account, priests take raisins, soak them in water for ten days until they swell, then dry, crush and press them through a cloth, the resulting juice being the "wine" which is used in communion.[120] A priest of Wogeda Īyesus church near Debre Tabor told me that when making grape wine for communion, he first crushes the grapes and strains them through a cloth to remove their seeds and skins. Then he adds water to the juice and ferments it for about a year in a large pot like those used for making mead.

Although sacramental wine is commonly used by Amhara Christians, some of the other groups who are not Christian, such as the Falasha, Jabartis, Gumis, and K'amant, do not use it. The Falasha, indeed, believe that Amhara priests add human blood to their sacramental wine. The K'amant use beer rather than wine for sacramental purposes. The Kumfel, on the other hand, use sacramental wine made by the Amhara priests who staff their churches. The Wayt'o, although they are Moslems, drink wine made by their priests for the feast of Arefa.

There are suggestions that the making of wine (and the cultivation of grapes?) may have been first practiced in Ethiopia for sacramental purposes, and that the use of wine has been spread southward by Christian priests and monks. These suggestions include the fact that the non-Amharic and non-Christian groups mentioned above do not use wine in their religious services, that Christian priests bring grapes into the Kumfel country for sacramental purposes, that among the Amhara the process of wine making is a secret of the priests, and that people generally do not like wine.

It is interesting that wine has never become popular in Ethiopia. It may simply be that people prefer the taste of beer and mead to that of wine, or possibly that the extra work involved in making wine has not been considered worth the trouble. It may even be that the lack of suitable storage containers has kept wine from assuming a more important position in the country, for the Ethiopians have neither

[118] Bruce, 1790, III: 334.
[119] Beckingham and Huntingford, 1954: 48; Chiovenda, 1912: 35; Alvarez, 1881: 411–12.
[120] Alvarez, 1881: 411–12.

glazed pots, wooden casks, glass bottles, nor leakproof leather bags, and wine will keep no more than a month [121] in their unglazed earthen jars.

OIL AND FIBER PLANTS AND GOURDS

Nug

Nug (*Guizotia abyssinica*) is an annual, yellow-flowered composita cultivated for its small, elongated, black oilseed. In India it yields per acre about 300 to 400 pounds of seeds, which have an oil content of 40 to 50 per cent.[122] In Ethiopia it is typically a crop of middle altitudes, from about 4,200 to 8,000 feet, and is known among the peoples of Begemder and Semyen as *nug* in Amharic, *lungwa* in K'amant, *nuwa* in Agow, *leungh'ewī* in Kumfel, and *belungwa* in Hametsh. Nearly all botanists agree that the center of origin of *nug* is the Ethiopian Plateau,[123] for not only are four of the five species of *Guizotia* found in Ethiopia, but *Guizotia abyssinica* itself is reported growing wild in Ethiopia [124] and it is cultivated widely there today and apparently has been since antiquity.

Today *Guizotia abyssinica* is also cultivated in many other tropical and temperate regions, always under conditions of moderate rainfall. In India, particularly along the west coast near Bombay, it is a widespread and important oil plant. Whether *nug* was carried to India by the Portuguese who found it in Ethiopia, or whether it had spread to India in Axumite times or earlier, we cannot say.

The oil of *Guizotia abyssinica*, known to Europeans as "Niger oil," "Niger seed oil," or "Kersani oil," is clear, yellow, and edible. The Italians in Ethiopia and Eritrea consider it an inferior substitute for olive oil. In India, because of its low price, it is used to adulterate sesame and castor oils.[125] The seed has been imported to the coastal cities of East Africa from India, and to England from both India and Africa.

When the Italians conquered Ethiopia they apparently encouraged Ethiopian farmers to cultivate *nug* as a cash crop, and a few small pressing plants were established for extracting *nug* oil. In 1953, one of these plants was still operating in Gondar under the direction of an Italian, and south of Gondar in K'olediba there was a small, Arab-run, ox-powered pressing plant. Many farmers grow small plots of *nug* for sale, but because of considerable price fluctuations from year to

---

[121] Pearce, 1831, I: 236.
[123] Candussio, 1941: 348.
[125] Watt, 1890, IV: 187; Engler, 1895, Theil B: 495.

[122] Aïyer, 1947: 211.
[124] Engler, 1895, Theil B: 494.

year they have been discouraged from expanding their plantings. In December and January, just after the *nug* harvest, a quintal of *nug* may sell for as little as $4.80 U.S., whereas later in the year the price rises to ten or eleven dollars. To operate a pressing plant profitably, enough *nug* seed must be purchased at the time of low prices to keep the machines operating for the entire year. Export duties on *nug* oil and the small and uncertain source of supply have further combined to inhibit expansion.

Nug oil is used in most households in Northwest Ethiopia and it is the work of the women to extract the oil from the seed. To do this the housewife first parches the seed and crushes it in a wooden mortar, then grinds it still finer on a grinding stone. She mixes the ground seed with water and boils it for several hours, stirring it from time to time to help the oil rise to the surface. Finally she pours off the oil into a container in which it is stored.

In Northwest Ethiopia, the most common use of *nug* oil is in cooking, for it is a common ingredient in stew and it is used to grease the frying plate, called in Amharic *magogo,* on which the fermented flat bread *injera* is cooked. *Nug* is especially important on fast days as a substitute for butter, which along with other animal foods is forbidden then. *Nug* seed is sometimes crushed and made into a non-alcoholic drink called *chilka,* made of one part honey, five parts water, and one part crushed *nug* seed. In addition to its use in food, *nug* oil is sometimes burned in lamps and *nug* seed is mixed with the sap of euphorbia to make a mouse poison, the mice being attracted by the *nug* seed.

Flax

In Northwest Ethiopia, flax (*Linum usitatissimum*) is cultivated at altitudes of from 5,000 to 10,000 feet. Flax is usually sown broadcast from April to June and harvested from October to December; sometimes it is planted in the same field with barley, in which case the barley is harvested first.

Although flax was cultivated for both fiber and oil in ancient Egypt and southwestern Asia, in Ethiopia it is cultivated exclusively for its seed. Flaxseed, which is known in Amharic as *telba,* is usually cooked in stew. Sometimes it is crushed and, in the same way as *nug,* is mixed with honey and water to make the drink *chilka.*

Sesame

Sesame (*Sesamum indicum*), a plant of great antiquity in the Middle East, is a characteristic food plant of the hot lowland areas of North-

west Ethiopia below about 5,000 feet in elevation. It is traded to the
highland and is found in many of the markets there. It is known to
the Amhara, K'amant, and Agow as *salīt*, to the Kumfel as *salītī*,
to the Gumis as *gīzkwa*, and to the Hametsh as *kifa*. Sesame is commonly grown among other crops, either planted in fields of cotton or
on the edge of sorghum fields or sown mixed with sorghum seed or
with sorghum and haricot beans. Occasionally, too, sesame is grown
alone. After being cut with sickles, the mature plants are stood in the
field to dry for several days and then the seeds are shaken onto a
threshing platform or onto skins or blankets.

Sesame seed is eaten raw, parched, and cooked, is added to stew,
made into the drink *chilka,* and is crushed and added to bread dough.
Gumis women sometimes use sesame oil as a hair dressing. I have never
heard of sesame oil being burned in lamps, perhaps because it is very
expensive.

Castor-Oil Plant

The castor-oil plant (*Ricinus communis*), a native of tropical
Africa, was cultivated in Pharaonic Egypt where it was a source of
oil long before the olive.[126] It has probably also been cultivated in
Ethiopia since great antiquity, though it usually occupies only a minor
position among the plants of the middle highland, where it is most
common. The castor-oil plant (Amh.: *gulo*) is often simply a volunteer on better soils along the edges of the garden or near the house.
Sometimes farmers plant the seed of such volunteer plants in a seedbed and later transplant the seedlings into the garden. At other times,
they dig up young wild plants and bring them home to plant in the
garden. In a few places such as one area near Lake T'ana, small fields
of castor-oil plants are raised commercially; some of the seed is even
shipped by merchants to Asmara.

In Northwest Ethiopia I did not hear of castor-oil seed being pressed
and the oil extracted, a procedure which is widespread elsewhere in
the Old World. Castor-oil seeds, which are harvested from December
to February, are used to soften leather and to clean the frying plate
used for cooking the flat bread *injera,* and are burned for light.

Castor-oil seeds are considered a poor substitute for the other oil
seeds commonly used to clean the frying plate. When the seeds are
burned for light, they are pierced and strung on a piece of wood or
grass, making a beaded stick longer than a pencil. People light these
sticks in the fire and carry them about the house to light their way.
The sticks are not put upright in holders as candles are, nor are they

[126] Burkill, 1935, II: 1907.

ordinarily used outside of the house. At wedding feasts, two or three of these sticks are sometimes tied together and used to light the wedding hall. In the northern Sudan, the leaves of the castor-oil plant are placed on the scalp to relieve headaches,[127] and the seeds are swallowed by women to cause sterility. I did not hear of such uses in Northwest Ethiopia.

Safflower

Safflower (*Carthamus tinctorius*), whose flowers provide the red safflower dye of commerce, is cultivated in Ethiopia not as a dye plant, but for its seed. It is called in Amharic *suf* and in Kumfel *sufī*, words related to the Arabic word *safra*, which means "yellow." Everywhere at altitudes of from 4,000 to 8,000 feet, where safflower is grown, its white, hairy-tufted seed is of minor importance as a food. It is sometimes parched and eaten by travellers, or crushed and used to grease the frying plate, or it is ground, mixed with honey and water, and drunk. Safflower oil is commonly added to stew and is burned in lamps.

Because of the striking resemblance of safflower seed and sunflower seed, the latter, a New World introduction rare in Northwest Ethiopia, is called in Amharic *ye arab suf* ("foreign safflower").[128]

Cotton

The cotton of Northwest Ethiopia, a short-staple variety, is a perennial shrub (*Gossypium* spp.).[129] Though some is cultivated south of Gondar near Lake T'ana, the bulk of the cotton of Northwest Ethiopia is found in lowland regions, especially along the Sudan border and along the Tekezzay River and its tributaries.

Cotton is of greater commercial importance along the Sudan border than anywhere else in the Northwest. In January and February, at the time of cotton harvest, hundreds of traders with caravans of donkeys arrive in the Gumis villages from Gondar, Alefa, K'wara, and the Sudan. The traders camp in and near the villages, buying cotton from the local people as they harvest it. The merchants pack the cot-

[127] Halim, 1939: 35.

[128] The word "Arab" in Ethiopia also has come to mean "foreign" or "imported." See Leslau, 1949b.

[129] The cotton seed I collected in Ethiopia has not yet been grown and classified. According to G. Edward Nicholson (1958), who collected seed extensively in Ethiopia, especially in the south, southwest, northeast, and east of the country, Ethiopian cotton types include *Gossypium hirsutum* var. *punctatum*, *G. barbadense*, and *G. herbaceum* var. *acerifolium*. For a discussion of Ethiopian cottons see Nicholson, 1958, and for a consideration of Ethiopian cotton and cotton textile production, see Nicholson, 1956.

ton into woven fiber containers which they load two to a donkey. A container of cotton sells in Gondar, ten to twelve days away, for about twice the lowland price.

The Sudan border groups, the Gumis and Kumfel, sow cotton seed broadcast when the rains begin in June and cover the seed by scraping soil over it with the hoe. Though people weed their cotton once in the season, they neither irrigate nor fertilize it, though animals grazing in the fields contribute their droppings. Cotton is generally inter-planted with sorghum, which matures before the cotton and is cut down completely to provide as much sunlight as possible.

In harvesting the cotton along the Sudan border, men and women work together (Fig. 53). Sometimes a man will also enlist the aid of his neighbors and, in turn, will help them with their harvest. The harvested cotton is stored near the houses in large, raised outdoor con-tainers. It is sometimes carried there by donkeys, sometimes by men who wrap it in cloaks which they carry on their heads, and some-times by women who carry it in baskets suspended from each end of a carrying stick. Since the border people treat cotton as a perennial, they harvest a crop from a planting each year for five years. Then they abandon the planting, though if the cotton revives temporarily the farmer will harvest it once again.

In Sahalla, the Agow cultivate small, unirrigated fields of cotton along the Tekezzay River and its tributaries (Fig. 52). Agow cotton fields are usually community affairs with various families of a village owning sections of a field. The poorer families often have such small plots that their needs for cotton are not met by their harvest. In such cases they must buy additional cotton from wealthier families or in the market.

The Agow cotton fields are low in the valley of the Tekezzay and its tributaries, rather than near the villages which are on higher ground. Because of their fear of malaria, the Agow usually visit their fields only for sowing and harvesting the cotton. In most places, farmers surround their fields with thorn branches to keep out wild animals and then leave them unguarded and uncared for. In some places, however, they hire poor men to guard and cultivate the cotton fields during the dry season, in return for which they receive a share of the crop. To get a supply of food such men take turns each week going to the village which may be a few hours away.

Gourds

Gourds (*Lagenaria vulgaris*) are found at elevations up to about 8,000 feet in fields, on the edges of gardens, or around the houses where often they climb over the thatch roofs. In the highland above about 6,000 feet only one type of gourd grows, known in Amharic simply as *k'il,* but around Lake T'ana and in the lowland, a large type of gourd, called in Amharic *ye bahir k'il,* "lake or sea gourd," is also grown. Because large gourds are in demand throughout the highland, they are carried to highland markets from the Lake T'ana region and other places where they grow.

In highland regions, though gourds are in widespread use as milk containers and cups, they are far less numerous than pottery vessels. Along the Sudan border, on the contrary, gourds are ubiquitous and of great variety, serving as water and grain containers, as beer pitchers, drinking cups, and bowls for water pipes.

Before gourds can be used, they must be soaked in water to loosen the bitter flesh inside them. Thus, after they are harvested they are taken to a nearby stream where they are cut open and soaked in the water for several days (Fig. 54). The inside of the gourd is then washed by hand and is dried for a few days before it is used.

FRUITS AND FRUIT TREES

Even though Ethiopia is not far from the Mediterranean and Persian centers of stone fruit domestication, tree crops play an insignificant role there. This situation is due not only to the indifference of the people to tree cultivation and to their ignorance of the methods of tree culture, but to the difficulties encountered in changing from winter to summer rain in introducing many European and southwest Asian trees to Ethiopia.

Among the few kinds of fruit trees cultivated in Ethiopia are the peach (*Prunus persica;* Amh.: *kwok*), the orange (*Citrus aurantium;* Amh.: *burtikan*), the citron (*Citrus medica*), the lemon (*Citrus limonum*), the shaddock (*Citrus decumana*), and the pomegranate (*Punica granatum*). Fruit trees do not occur in orchards, but as individuals or small groups in gardens or around homes and churches. Most of the cultivated fruits are consumed at home, though lemons are sold in many markets of the country.

The Olive

The wild oleaster (*Olea chrysophylla*) is found in the middle highland of Northwest Ethiopia as in other highland regions of East and South Africa. The true olive tree (*Olea europaea*), on the other hand, does not occur wild or cultivated in the Northwest. Indeed, I have never seen the olive grown by native people anywhere in Ethiopia. Even the fruit of the oleaster is apparently not used in the country.[130] The Italians have tried to acclimatize the European olive tree on the Ethiopian Plateau and to graft the European olive to the oleaster, but such attempts have largely failed.[131] The failure of the true olive to spread to Ethiopia may thus be due more to the difficulty involved in passing from winter to summer rain country than to the characteristic indifference of Ethiopians to tree culture.

The Fig

Ficus Carica, which yields the fig of commerce, is, like the true olive tree, not cultivated in Northwest Ethiopia. The wild fig tree (*Ficus Sycomorus*), like other wild fig trees of the Middle East and Southern Asia, is, however, important in legal and ceremonial functions. Thus, in the sixteenth century Francisco Alvarez reported that in front of the gate of the Ethiopian king's enclosure was a large sycamore fig tree under which were some masonry platforms and stone chairs said to belong to the judges of the king's court.[132] In Gondar even today there is an enormous fig tree outside the wall surrounding the ancient castles. Under this tree sit officials and important spectators to view the *mascal* ceremony in September. The tree also serves as an outdoor court where disputants meet to settle their difficulties. Elsewhere in Ethiopia the sycamore fig has been described as a holy tree which was planted over the graves of important men, and to which people then made offerings.[133] Another wild fig tree, the *shoala* (*Ficus Sur,* Forsk.), is important in times of food scarcity when its fruit and inner bark are eaten.[134]

A few banana plants (*Musa sapientum*), known in Amharic as *muz*, are cultivated here and there in lowland regions of Northwest Ethiopia, but the fruit very seldom is found in highland markets. The plantain is unknown in Ethiopia.

[130] There is a statement by James Bruce that olive oil is used in baptism (1790, III: 334) and that the king of Ethiopia was anointed "with plain oil of olives, which being poured upon the crown of his head, he rubs into his long hair indecently enough with both his hands, pretty much as his soldiers do with theirs when they get access to plenty of butter" (Bruce, 1790, III: 263). In his "Short History of Gondar" Balambaras Mengistu Taïye mentions the use of the flower of the oleaster in the anointment oil used formerly by the kings of Gondar (Taïye, 1944 [Eth.]: 12), but says nothing of the use of olive oil or of olives themselves. The author of the *Periplus* mentions a little olive oil being imported to Axum (Schoff, 1912: 24). The olive oil referred to by Bruce may have been imported or, what is more likely, it may have been another type of oil to which the flowers of the oleaster were added.

[131] Bent, 1893: 88; Chiovenda, 1912: 11; Istituto Agricola Coloniale, 1937: 28; Nistri, 1937: 35.

[132] Alvarez, 1881: 82.   [133] Harris, 1844, II: 401, III: 48–49.

[134] Harris, 1844, II: 401; Chiovenda, 1928: 554.

Chapter VII

ANIMAL HUSBANDRY

In most parts of Northwest Ethiopia, there are numerous useful domestic animals, such as cattle, sheep, goats, mules, horses, donkeys, chickens, and dogs, and animal husbandry plays an important part in the economy. Animals serve for traction, packing, riding, as scavengers, and as village guards; they provide milk, meat, and eggs for food, wool and hair for fiber, and hides and skins, bones, tendons, urine, and dung for construction and other uses. Though most animal products are consumed at home, hides and skins constitute one of the important exports of the region. The importance of domestic animals in Ethiopia is well illustrated by the fact that, in the past, tribute was sometimes paid in animals to conquerors and rulers,[1] the assessment being determined by the number of animals a man owned,[2] and that even today in some places taxes are levied on the basis of a set amount for each animal or for each pair of plowing oxen.

Perhaps as interesting as the importance of animal husbandry and animal products in Northwest Ethiopia is the role that culture has played in the use of the animal resource. Thus, as in the "cattle-complex area" of East Africa, a man's wealth may be judged by the number of herd animals, particularly cattle, that he possesses. This has led people to regard cattle as symbols of prestige and to emphasize the increase in the numbers of their animals rather than to maximize their economic utility. An even more striking effect of culture is the role that group attitudes, preferences, and prejudices have had in the development of a system of animal husbandry in which certain animals occupy important and useful positions while others are rejected or used to only a limited degree.

DOMESTIC ANIMALS AND ATTITUDES TOWARD THEM

CATTLE.—In Northwest Ethiopia, there are numerous cattle in the middle highland and smaller numbers in other altitude zones. They

[1] Perham, 1948: 191–92; Bruce, 1790, II: 9; Plowden, 1868: 137–38.
[2] Perham, 1948: 192.

are rare in the disease-ridden Sudan border country, which separates
the Ethiopian and Nilotic centers of cattle herding. In the border
country, for example, the Kumfel have only a few cattle and the
Gumis have none, except for an occasional animal which they purchase for slaughter. The Gumis are, in fact, so unfamiliar with cattle
that they are somewhat afraid of them. On the conversion of a reputed 2,000 Gumis to Ethiopian Christianity at Matavīa village in
1954, for example, the Gumis slaughtered the cattle provided for
their baptismal feast by shooting them, an act which amused the
Amhara present because it wasted precious bullets which could have
been saved by simply cutting the animals' throats.

Like many peoples of East Africa, the cattle-keeping groups of
Northwest Ethiopia value their cattle very highly. Since a man's
wealth is often measured by the size of his herds, he is loath to kill
his cattle but, on the contrary, makes every effort to increase their
numbers. Traditionally,[3] when the number of a man's cattle reached
one thousand, he bathed in milk before the people of the neighborhood, and then slaughtered an animal and provided a feast for the
group that had assembled to watch. By this traditional act of conspicuous consumption of milk and beef on a lavish scale out of reach
of ordinary men, the wealthy man confirmed his status.

The cattle of Northwest Ethiopia are medium-sized animals of the
shorthorned Zebu type, with humps and a pronounced dewlap (Fig.
55). Usually they are brown or black or mixtures of either or both of
these colors with white. This type of cattle is believed to have arrived
in Ethiopia from India by way of Arabia, but the manner in which
it arrived and the date have not been established. I did not see long-
horned humped cattle in Northwest Ethiopia, though such animals,
the "sanga" or "Galla" cattle, which are believed to be descended from
a longhorn Zebu and Hamitic longhorn cross,[4] are found among the
Ethiopian Galla.[5] Sanga cattle have apparently long been rare in the
Northwest, for when James Bruce saw some there in the eighteenth
century, he believed their enormous horns to be a malformation resulting from disease.[6]

Though dwarf cattle are found in West Africa and in the Nuba
Mountains,[7] I found no evidence of their existence in Northwest
Ethiopia. It is true, however, that the oxen of the lowland Agow of
Sahalla are noticeably smaller than those of the highland Amhara,

---

[3] This tradition is still mentioned in the Northwest, but Father Lobo (1789:
69–70) encountered it already in the seventeenth century.

[4] Bisschop, 1936: 864.   [5] Harris, 1844, II: 419.
[6] Salt, 1814: 258.   [7] Nadel, 1947: 60.

though it is not known whether these animals, like the dwarfs of West Africa, are more resistant to disease than the larger animals of the highland.

GOATS AND SHEEP.—The goats of Northwest Ethiopia are small black and white, or brown and white animals. Mature males have sizable curved horns, though the nannies have only short horns. Goats (Figs. 56 and 57) are hardier than the other herd animals, and are found everywhere from the highest mountains to the lowest valleys.

Sheep, which usually run in herds with goats, are of the fat-tailed variety, though the tails are not as large as those of sheep elsewhere in the Middle East. Sheep (Figs. 58 and 59) are found among all tribes and in all of the altitudinal zones, though in some places, such as the Gondar area, they are few in number, and in others, such as the high mountain regions, they are especially numerous. In the highland, sheep have long fleeces, but along the Sudan border they have short hair.

HORSES, MULES, AND DONKEYS.—In the sixteenth century, when the Galla first moved from the eastern lowland of Ethiopia into the plateau, apparently under pressure from the Somali, they had few if any horses, and they fought on foot. However, they soon acquired horses and became skilled in their use, and by the mid-sixteenth century, because of their increased mobility and their traditional nomadic daring, they conquered large parts of the highland, menacing the very existence of the Abyssinian state. At first, the horses of the Galla were inferior to those of the Amhara, but in time the Galla developed better animals which they trained to withstand fatigue. By the nineteenth century, the Galla had excellent, spirited horses and in far greater numbers than did the Amhara.[8] Whereas among the Amhara only chiefs had good horses, among the Galla even poor men commonly had fine animals. That the excellence of Galla horses was recognized is indicated by the considerable northward trade of horses from the Galla country a century ago.[9] The ultimate defeat of the Galla cavalry, which for centuries terrorized the Amhara armies, was due not to the quality of their horses or horsemanship, but to their lack of political cohesion and their contempt for firearms. The latter was so strong that the Galla fought against Amhara armies, including hundreds of musketeers, armed only with lances,[10] until their final subjugation.

Today, the Galla are still Ethiopia's best horse breeders, and most of them prefer the horse to the mule in every respect. The Amhara, on the other hand, prefer the mule both for riding and for general

[8] Plowden, 1868: 151–52. [9] Plowden, 1868: 154. [10] Plowden, 1868: 304.

transportation; in the Amhara country, mules more commonly serve as riding animals and are more expensive than horses. The Amhara, nevertheless, recognize that horses can run faster than mules and have always used them in battle. Indeed, great men and warriors in Ethiopia were generally better known by the names of their horses than by their own, for the Ethiopian foot soldier commonly took the name of a horse as the war cry which he shouted in battle.[11] In the Northwest today, only men of wealth possess riding mules and horses, for a first-class riding mule may cost as much as sixty dollars U.S., a sum beyond the reach of the average Ethiopian. Thus, riding mules and horses are prestige animals which are painstakingly groomed and ridden with pride. Indeed, one of the most impressive sights in the area is that of an important man riding on his lively, fast-stepping mule, accompanied by his gunbearer and flanked by a retinue of servants and followers. Women, on the other hand, do not usually ride mules or horses unless they belong to upper-class families.

The mules and horses of Northwest Ethiopia are very small by European standards, generally only four and one-half to five feet high (Fig. 61), and local people still speak with appreciation of the huge army mules the Italians brought with them when they invaded the country. Local donkeys are usually gray and extremely small (Fig. 60), though donkeys from some places, such as Debre Tabor, are a bit larger and stronger than the average. In breeding larger mules, the people of the Northwest commonly use male donkeys imported from Sennar, long-legged, graceful animals which are considerably taller than the common Ethiopian donkey.

CHICKENS.—Though chickens are one of the most widespread domestic animals in Africa, prohibitions against eating their flesh and eggs exist in large parts of the continent.[12] The prohibitions have a bewildering diversity, not only from group to group, but according to the sex, age, and state of health of the person, as well as, in the case of eggs, according to the method of preparation. The origin of these prohibitions has not been satisfactorily explained, but since the one against eggs is more widespread, it may have developed first and then, by extension, the prohibition may have been applied to chickens. The fact that the most common explanation advanced by Africans for the avoidance of eggs is that they cause sterility or impotence, suggests that the avoidance may have developed from fear lest eating the fertility symbol, the egg, would inhibit fertility in humans.

In Ethiopia, prohibitions against using chickens and eggs as food have been found among many groups, though with the spread of

[11] Plowden, 1868: 159.   [12] Lagercrantz, 1950: 39–44.

Amhara and Western influence they are breaking down somewhat. The Galla, for example, did not eat chickens or eggs in the past, though today some do.[13] The Somali,[14] Danakil,[15] and Adaiel,[16] too, were prejudiced against chickens in the past and either did not keep them or, if they did, abhorred their flesh. Today, noble Somali still will not eat either poultry or eggs, though they are probably less strict about this than formerly.[17] In Eastern Sidamo in south central Ethiopia, the statement that the keeping of fowl is a specialty of the Amhara [18] suggests that the native people may still have prohibitions against them. Likewise, the Janjero of southern Ethiopia eat neither fowl nor eggs,[19] and in Kaffa women might not eat chickens in former days under pain of being enslaved, though men were allowed to eat them.[20] Among the Amhara, and among all the peoples of Northwest Ethiopia, chickens are found running loose in almost every house compound. Though they are neglected and little valued as compared to herd animals, their meat and eggs are everywhere relished and used in stew. Except for the tradition among the Amhara that only men, not women, may kill chickens,[21] there are no hints that there ever were restrictions against the slaughter or use of chickens and eggs as food in the Northwest, except, as against all animal products, at times of fasting.

PIGS.—It is not known how widely domestic pigs (*Sus*) had diffused in Africa south of the Sahara in pre-European times. It is generally assumed, however, that the pig did not reach West Africa until the Portuguese carried it there on their voyages of discovery in the fifteenth century. On the other side of the continent, though, pigs had been kept in Egypt since predynastic times [22] and had early spread up the Nile to Nubia. Pig keeping persisted among the Nubians at least until the twelfth century when their kingdoms were overrun by Moslems from Egypt. The intolerance of the Moslem conquerors is aptly illustrated by their first acts after the capitulation of the Nubian Christians at Ibrīm in 1173, when they immediately jailed and tortured the priests and killed the pigs.[23] Though early data are lacking, pigs may have spread from Nubia still farther up the Nile, for they are found today in Sennar,[24] among the pagan people of the Nuba

[13] Paulitschke, 1893: 157, 229; Huntingford, 1955: 28.
[14] Paulitschke, 1893: 157; Salt, 1814: 179.
[15] Paulitschke, 1893: 157; Salt, 1814: 179.   [16] Salt, 1814: 179.
[17] I. M. Lewis, 1955: 74.   [18] Smeds, 1955: 32.
[19] Huntingford, 1955: 138.   [20] Huntingford, 1955: 109.
[21] Addis Ababa, University College, 1953: 17.   [22] L. B. Jensen, 1953: 99.
[23] Budge, 1928, I: 105.
[24] Bruce, 1790, IV: 421; Hartmann, 1883: 31; Hahn, 1896: 217; Sauer, 1952: 35.

Mountains,[25] and among various groups along the Sudan-Ethiopia border. Thus, R. E. Cheesman reported that people of the Gumis tribe living around Hulgizi near the Blue Nile in Godjam had tame black pigs running loose in their villages.[26] The Maban people who live farther south near Kurmuk also have black domestic pigs.[27] Still farther south around the Jokau River, a tributary of the Sobat, the Koma, another group of border tribes, some of whom formerly lived in the Ethiopian highland, keep domestic pigs and permit them to wander about the forest feeding on roots and the fruits of trees.[28]

Despite the possibility that pigs had spread to the western borders of Ethiopia in pre-European times, there is no proof that they were ever kept elsewhere in the country. Philipp Paulitschke, it is true, stated that the domestic pig had been found among the Galla people and that it was displaced with the spread of Islam,[29] but he gave no specific evidence or reference, and his statement is supported by no other observer. Indeed, the peoples of Ethiopia, including those of the Northwest, despise the flesh of pigs, and the only domestic pigs found in the country today are kept for consumption by European residents. A strange aspect of the prejudice against pork in the Northwest is that it is held by Christians and pagan Cushites such as the K'amant as well as by Moslems and Jews. The antipathy to pork may, then, have its roots deep in the traditions of the Cushitic-speaking peoples of northeast Africa, and may have been introduced into the region at an early date by Cushitic-speaking peoples rather than with Judaism, Christianity,[30] or Islam, which came later. Whatever the origin of the Ethiopian prejudice against pork, it is clear that the Ethiopians of the highland, like the Moslems of the Sudan, have put pressure on the peoples of the Sudan-Ethiopia border to abandon pig keeping, though they have not been altogether successful.

Though the true pig (*Sus*) is not found in a wild state in Northwest Ethiopia, both the bush pig (*Potamochoerus*) and the wart hog (*Phaecochoerus*) are. The bush pig is known in Amharic by the same name, *assama*, as the domestic pig, but it is never tamed, as it is elsewhere in Africa. Ethiopians will not hunt either the bush pig or the wart hog for food, because they regard the flesh of both to be unclean. James Bruce said, for example, that after he had killed "five boars,"

[25] Crowfoot, 1925: 125; Nadel, 1947: 60.   [26] R. E. Cheesman, 1936: 371.
[27] According to a personal communication with Miss Frances Turk of the American Mission at El Obeid in the Sudan.
[28] Corfield, 1938: 151.   [29] Paulitschke, 1893: 228–29.
[30] Since pork is eaten by Christian Copts in Egypt (L. B. Jensen, 1953: 99) today, it does not seem likely that they had anything to do with the introduction of pig prejudice into Ethiopia.

he did not dare risk eating their flesh lest he offend the local people.[31] Similarly, when Nathaniel Pearce shared the meat of "a hog" with an Ethiopian boy, another companion refused to eat, and even made another fire over which to broil his deer, lest it be defiled.[32] Curiously, however, the strictures against eating the flesh of the wart hog are sometimes overlooked by the peoples of Northwest Ethiopia, because this flesh is believed to be of medicinal value; similar lapses occur elsewhere in the area of pork avoidance, which stretches from Morocco to Mindanao.

CAMELS.—In Northeast Africa, camels are kept principally in the arid lowland regions bordering the Red Sea and the Indian Ocean. The zone of camel keeping is narrow in Eritrea, where the Ethiopian Plateau is close to the coast, but widens considerably in the Somali country to the south, before ending in the Northern Territory of Kenya. Though the regions farther south in East Africa do not appear to be suitable for camel keeping, there have nevertheless been a few attempts to introduce and use the camel there: in Zanzibar at various times in the past,[33] in the steppe regions of Tanganyika after the first world war as pack animals,[34] and in the unsuccessful campaign led by Barreto against the legendary Monomotapa in 1569.[35] Though these efforts all appear to have failed, the Germans were successful in introducing the camel to the arid regions of Southwest Africa, where it served, among other things, as a riding animal for the police.[36]

In Ethiopia itself, the plateau is not suitable for camel keeping, and camels which are brought there do not thrive, and usually do not long survive.[37] Among the best examples of the unsuitability of the highland for camels is that of the column of British troops which invaded Italian-held Ethiopia from the Sudan in January, 1941. Although the British recognized the risk involved in bringing camels into the highland, they were unable to obtain mules in sufficient numbers for the campaign.[38] Long columns of camels were, therefore, driven through the hard, scrub and thorn border country and into the cool plateau of Godjam. The animals died in such numbers on the trek that, to find the way, it is said that "a compass was not needed; one could orient the column by the stink of dead camels." [39] When, finally, in early May, the column entered Addis Ababa, the last fifty

---

[31] Bruce, 1790, III: 146. [32] Pearce, 1831, II: 178.
[33] Hahn, 1896: 234. [34] Boettger, 1958: 222.
[35] Hahn, 1896: 234. [36] Brehm, 1920, 13: 51; Boettger, 1958: 222.
[37] Harris, 1844, II: 73–74; Hahn, 1896: 233; Paulitschke, 1893: 223.
[38] Steer, 1942: 142–43; Allen, 1943: 38.
[39] British Ministry of Information, 1942: 62.

exhausted camels were slaughtered on the hills nearby; the remains of fifteen thousand others marked the trail back to the Sudan.[40]

Because of the risk involved in bringing camels into the plateau, camel caravans rarely enter the highland of Begemder and Semyen from the Sudan. Travellers usually exchange their camels in the lowland for horses, mules, and donkeys. Thus, Charles Jacques Poncet's group in the late seventeenth century left their animals at the village of Girana, at the edge of the plateau,[41] while others have left their camels at Wehinī,[42] or even at Metemma,[43] from two to six days away from the middle elevations of the plateau.

Though no study has been made to determine exactly why the dromedary does not do well in highland Ethiopia, it is known that it is a sensitive creature which has difficulty whenever it moves out of its arid habitat. William Harris attributed the inability of camels to survive in the highland to the severity of the climate and to the steepness of the Ethiopian mountains.[44] Charles Jacques Poncet said, on the other hand, that camels die in the highland because they are poisoned by unfamiliar herbs.[45] W. E. D. Allen, writing of the loss of camels in the British Abyssinian campaign of 1941, maintained that the thin air of the plateau, the cold, the rain, and the lush grass proved fatal.[46]

Even the hot Sudan borderlands of Northwest Ethiopia are not suited to the camel. G. L. Steer, for example, wrote of the hard going in the rough border country where "camels stooped and slithered and broke their legs and groaned themselves dead." [47] Sir Samuel Baker, travelling along the Atbara River in the Sudan during the July rainy period, said that his camels had great difficulty in proceeding, for their feet sank deep into the mud which formed sticky clods which almost disabled them.[48] Moreover, Baker noted, biting flies tormented the camels constantly during the rainy period so that they were driven almost mad.[49] I was told that in the border country, as well as in the highland, camels are frequently poisoned by plants which inflame their stomachs and which they do not learn to avoid. All of these difficulties and dangers serve to exclude camels from both the highland and the Sudan border country of Northwest Ethiopia. Any attempt to propagate them there would certainly lead to the same failure that met the earlier efforts to introduce them to Spain and the United States.

The people of the lowland Moslem tribes of Ethiopia relish both

[40] British Ministry of Information, 1942: 67.
[42] Dove, 1890: 12.
[45] Foster, 1949: 110.
[48] Baker, 1867: 107.
[43] Hayes, 1905: 46–47.
[46] Allen, 1943: 38.
[49] Baker, 1867: 527.
[41] Foster, 1949: 112–13.
[44] Harris, 1844, I: 325.
[47] Steer, 1942: 143.

the milk and meat of camels. Christian Ethiopians, on the contrary, have had a prejudice against using the milk of camels and the eating of their flesh.[50] Mansfield Parkyns described his experience: "The camel is to all an object of horror. Following to the letter the commands of Moses, they refuse to eat animals which do not chew the cud, and those which have not cloven hoofs. . . . I remember one man whom I brought with me into the Mussulman country made objections on being offered camels meat. 'Am I a Mussulman?' said he. 'No,' I replied, 'nor am I either'; at the same time putting into my mouth a huge piece of fat and an onion. The poor fellow, though hungry, resisted." [51]

In the past, Christian highlanders sometimes have maintained their prejudices against the camel for a while after conquering and settling among Moslem camel herders. Thus, the ruling class of the Mansa, a tribe of cultivators living thirty miles northwest of Massawa, kept the prohibition against using camels' milk and meat a century ago when they were Christians, though most of them have since accepted Islam and no longer observe this prohibition.[52] The ruling caste of another group of tribes, the Tigre-speaking Beit Asgade, who live in Eritrea north of Keren, have similarly become Moslems in the last century, and use camels' milk and meat today. Indeed, one of the reasons suggested for their conversion to Islam is that, as nomads, they had to use camels' milk, which was forbidden them by Christian prejudice.[53] This reason, whether or not it is true, nevertheless calls attention to the fact that Christians regard the drinking of camels' milk to be a symbol of Islam.

As interesting as the contrasts within the Ethiopia region in the use of the milk and flesh of camels, are the differences in the use of camels as riding animals. The Danakil and Somali tribesmen of the eastern lowland of Ethiopia, despite the fact that their camels are well built and robust, traditionally have used them for packing, but not for riding.[54] Indeed, the Somali consider it a shame to ride a camel,[55] though in an emergency the sick and injured do ride.[56] To the north among the Habab of lowland Eritrea, on the contrary, people

[50] Parkyns, 1868: 291–92; Reale Società Geografica Italiana, 1936: 256.
[51] Parkyns, 1868: 291–92.   [52] Trimingham, 1952: 162–63.
[53] Trimingham, 1952: 161.
[54] Paulitschke, 1893: 223–24; Ratzel, 1897: 488. The Turkana of East Africa, who have obtained camels in fairly recent times, do not use them for transport of any kind (Gulliver and Gulliver, 1953: 60).
[55] Haggenmacher, 1876: 34.
[56] I. M. Lewis, 1955: 67; Personal communication, Clarke Brooke, Portland State College.

ride camels,[57] apparently without prejudice, as do the camel herders of the Sudan and other parts of the Middle East. That the camel is not ridden in most of coastal Ethiopia, nor the donkey in the highland, are interesting and curious facts, especially in view of the use of both animals for this purpose elsewhere in the Middle East. It may be that the Ethiopians' failure to ride these animals results from their introduction to the region at a time before the habit of riding them became established, and that the Ethiopians, while taking over the riding of the horse when it was introduced, have never extended the riding habit to the animals introduced earlier.

It has been Ethiopia's blessing that camels do not long survive in the highland and that the warlike lowland tribes to the east do not ride them, for, because of this, camel nomads have not been as potent a menace to the highlands as one might otherwise expect. Unlike Egypt, which has time and time again suffered the incursions of camel-mounted raiders, Ethiopia has been largely free of this form of invasion.

CIVET CATS.—The civet cat (*Viverra civetta*) is not a domestic animal but is captured wild and kept in cages. From time to time, a secretion from its anal glands is scraped off and marketed to be used as a perfume base. Civet has for millennia found its way from Ethiopia into foreign markets and it is even today one of the minor exports of the country.

Traditionally, civet has been a production of southern Ethiopia among the Galla and Sidamo [58] and in such regions as Kaffa, Jimma, Enarea, Guma, Gera, and Wanbera.[59] In the past, some civet was produced in the Northwest, for Charles Jacques Poncet reported at the end of the seventeenth century that people around Ch'ilga sold civet in the marketplace, and that Imfraz, a district just north of Lake T'ana, was famous for its trade in civet and slaves.[60] At Imfraz, merchants kept as many as three hundred civet cats, fed them meat and milk, and scraped the civet from their bodies once a week and kept it in oxhorns which were well stopped. It is not clear why civet cats should have been kept in such numbers in Poncet's time and not since. I found no civet at all in the markets of Begemder and Semyen, nor did I hear any reports of civet cats being kept in Northwest Ethiopia.

BREEDING OF LIVESTOCK

The mating of livestock in Northwest Ethiopia is generally haphazard. Though male and female animals are commonly placed in

[57] Castaldi, 1936: 214, 216, 219.
[58] Bruce, 1790, III: 385; Pearce, 1831, II: 9; Parkyns, 1868: 405; Cerulli, 1956: 120.
[59] Beckingham and Huntingford, 1954: 52.   [60] Foster, 1949: 113, 136.

proximity and encouraged to mate, more often than not they are left to their own designs. It is especially strange that, despite the fact that milking animals give only small amounts of milk and that dairy products are important in local diet, people do not attempt to breed animals to provide more milk. With mule breeding, however, greater care is often taken. In some places, for example, local mares are mated with the tall, handsome male donkeys which are imported from Sennar in the Sudan solely for breeding purposes. Sennar donkeys find their way into Begemder and Semyen mainly from Tessenei and Kassala by way of the Eritrean market town of Om Ager, just north of the Setīt (Tekezzay) River, which is regularly visited by highland merchants. In the past, some Sennar donkeys came to Begemder and Semyen by way of Metemma, though few, if any, come that way today. Because of their high price, five or six times the price of a good Ethiopian donkey, Sennar donkeys are not owned by many people. The man who is fortunate enough to have one commonly rents out the animal for stud, the fee being paid in cash, feed, or both. Because they are valuable and susceptible to illness in the highland, Sennar donkeys, like prized horses and mules, are sometimes stabled within the house from about mid-September to mid-December, immediately after the rains, when they are most susceptible to illness.

Within Begemder and Semyen there are a few places especially noted for the high quality of the donkeys, mules, or horses produced there. Debre Tabor donkeys, for example, are renowned for their size and strength. The Woggera district north of Gondar is famed for its horses and mules, which find their way into markets throughout the region. The superiority of these animals probably results from an abundance of feed and the salubrity of the climate in the regions where they are raised, as well, perhaps, as from greater attention given to animal breeding in these places.

Daily Care and Feeding of Animals

In the highland, herd animals usually graze during the day in uncultivated areas near the family compound, under the care of boys and young men. Cattle, donkeys, pack horses, and mules run in one herd, and goats and sheep in another. If several families live near one another, they sometimes pool their herds and the boys take turns watching them. At night the herd animals are driven inside the thorn-fenced family compounds for protection from hyenas and other predators.[61] In many places, to further restrict their movements, cattle are kept in corrals made of stone or of brush and thorn. Donkeys,

---

[61] I have not heard of hyenas being hunted to minimize the loss of livestock or, as among the Ruwala Bedouin (Musil, 1928: 20), to obtain hyena flesh for food.

pack horses, and mules are generally kept at night in a circular thatch-roofed hut of their own. Goats and sheep often have a similar hut with walls of stone [62] or wattle, but sometimes they are kept in a section of the house which serves as a stable.

Riding horses and mules are stabled in the living house at night, and where disease is prevalent they may be kept indoors throughout the year except when they are being ridden.[63] Because such horses and mules are penned up night and day, they get little exercise and, though they become fat and sleek through careful feeding and grooming, traditionally they have been no match in battle for the Galla war horses, which were lean, muscular, and active.[64]

Among the Gumis, goats and sheep are the only common herd animals. When occasionally a Gumis buys an ox in the highland for meat, he simply keeps it tied near the house until it is slaughtered. During most of the year Gumis children watch the flocks of sheep and goats, but in the harvest season and immediately afterwards the animals are permitted to graze unattended. They are, however, always housed at night in circular, wattle-walled, thatch-roofed shelters which are raised a few feet above the ground on stilts, strange-looking structures used also by the Kumfel nearby and found among many peoples of the southeastern Sudan but seldom in highland Ethiopia.

Of all the domestic animals of Northwest Ethiopia only chickens, which have little prestige value, are placed in the care of women and girls. Chickens are free to run about the compound during the day, but at night they are usually kept in a hut near the living house. In a Falasha hamlet in Weuleka village, I found that a low, hollow mound made of stones and earth served as chicken coop, though I did not see such coops elsewhere. Among the Kumfel, there are thatch-roofed coops raised on stilts (Fig. 18), which the chickens enter by means of portable ramps.

The highly valued riding horses and mules are given better treatment than any other of the domestic animals. Often, definite efforts are made to keep them supplied throughout the year with good feed such as fresh grass, chaff, and grain, and salt is provided as often as possible. Moreover, Ethiopians in various places have been reported

[62] In Mariam Deber village south of Gondar, the people live in wattle-walled homes, but sometimes build their goat houses of stone because, they say, the goats would kick down wattle walls.

[63] Walter Plowden noted that the southern Galla even made wooden platforms for their horses to stand on during the rainy season to keep them out of the mud and excreta, whereas the Wollo Galla and Amhara laid a bed of fitted stones for the same purpose (Plowden, 1868: 158).

[64] Plowden, 1868: 157.

to give their horses or mules additional special feed such as barley flour mixed with honey, barley flour mixed with flaxseed and *nug,* maize, sorghum, bread made of *t'eff* and barley, honey and meat balls, mead, milk, butter, and even boiled chickens and the blood of oxen.[65]

In sharp contrast, most other domestic animals are left to their own resources as far as getting food is concerned. During the summer rainy season, there is abundant green grass in the fallowed fields and in the countryside and the animals grow sleek and fat. Then, following the rainy season, come the grain harvests lasting from October to January, and the animals can get sufficient feed from the stubble in the fields and from the chaff left after threshing. But when these chaff supplies are exhausted, there develops a shortage of feed, for the Ethiopians plant no pasture, cultivate no feed crops, and store no fodder for their animals. The animals must survive as best they can on the dry grasses available. The latter half of the dry season is a lean time, particularly for the cattle, which gradually but persistently lose weight until, when at last the rains begin again, they are in a weakened and gaunt state with noticeably protruding ribs. Farmers feed salt and bits of grain or bread to the cattle at this time, but these bits are simply appetizers to encourage them to eat the sere, impalatable grass in the fields.

Even chickens, which Westerners might expect to be fed, are ordinarily expected to scavenge their own food and only occasionally are given feed. A hen and her new brood, it is true, are fed barley or other grain and flat bread, but this is only a temporary measure.

THE USE OF SALT IN FEEDING DOMESTIC ANIMALS.—The herdsmen of Northwest Ethiopia regard salt as a valuable item in the diet of their domestic animals, for it is believed to stimulate their appetites for food and water, and thus indirectly help in keeping them well-nourished and healthy. Whenever possible, salt is supplied to the animals at natural salt deposits to which they are driven from time to time. In the Amora Gedel region, for example, cattle are driven to local salt springs; on the boundary of the Gondar and Ch'ilga *awradjas,* Amhara and K'amant herdsmen let their animals feed on the salty mud of the Goang River; and in lowland Sahalla people drive their animals to nearby streams where there is salty mud for them to lick.

If sufficient salt for the animals is not available from free natural sources, people often purchase salt for them in local marketplaces from supplies that are transported in brick form (Fig. 78) from the Danakil Depression and that are sold for human consumption as well. In the market, salt bricks are sometimes sawed into small sizes and

[65] Plowden, 1868: 155–58; Pearce, 1831, I: 341–42.

sold directly, and sometimes they are crushed and the salt sold by the cupful or by similar measures (Fig. 77).

Because purchased salt is expensive, it is generally fed regularly only to valuable animals such as cattle, riding horses, and mules: in the rainy season to encourage them to eat the lush green grasses which abound at that time, and in the dry season to stimulate their appetite for the impalatable dry grasses that then constitute the only forage available. Less valuable animals tend to be fed salt only at particular times when it is deemed necessary: to encourage ewes and female goats to give more milk to their young, to encourage ailing animals to eat, and to help fatten or bloat an animal before taking it to market. Salt may be fed directly to animals by hand, wrapped in leaves, or by letting them lick a brick, or it may be fed in water, grain, flat bread, porridge, or balls of flour called *imbulbul*.

GELDING

Gelding is practiced in Northwest Africa for all domestic animals except dogs, though there are differences from place to place in the animals commonly gelded. People geld their animals for various reasons: horses, mules, donkeys, and bulls so that they may grow larger and stronger; rams, male goats, and roosters so that they may become heavier and sell for a better price; tom cats (which are rarely gelded) so that they will become good mousers and will not stray far from home.

Usually the owner of an animal gelds it himself, but occasionally he hires a native doctor to minimize the danger of mortality in gelding valuable bulls, mules, and horses. Gelding is commonly done in one of two ways: by making an incision to remove the testicles, or by severing the seminal passages above the testicles by pressure or blows without breaking the skin. I have not heard in Northwest Ethiopia of the practices described by S. F. Nadel for the Nuba: [66] biting through the testicles and squeezing them to pulp between the hands or grinding them between stones.

The simplest, least dangerous, and most widespread method of gelding practiced in the Northwest is that of severing the seminal passages above the testicles by blows. Generally, this method is followed for bulls, rams, and male goats, whereas incision castration is used for horses, mules, donkeys, and roosters. To sever the seminal passages of a bull, the beast is first tied by its horns and thrown to the ground. Then its four legs are tied together with the back legs pulled forward. Then the testicles are drawn backwards, placed over

[66] Nadel, 1947: 60.

the yoke of a plow, and passed between two sticks, the lower of which rests on the yoke. Using a smooth round or oval-shaped stone, a man beats the stick above the pouch until the passages on the inside, but not the skin, are broken. The bull is then fed forcibly, while he is still tied on the ground, with butter and beer or other liquids. The butter is given to the animal to "cool his stomach and heart" and the beer to encourage him to pass urine and blood. When sheep and goats are gelded by this method, they are sometimes tied, though, if strong men are doing the work, they are not. The plow yoke is placed on the ground and the men either pound the skin above the testicles with a rock or press down on the skin heavily with their fingers to break the passages. Sheep and goats are not given butter, beer, or liquid after the operation, nor are they given special care. Young bulls, on the other hand, are watched carefully for a week or so afterwards and are allowed to graze and to eat well until they recover.

The incision castration practiced on mules, horses, donkeys, and roosters is a delicate operation in which a sharp, native razor or an imported straight razor is used. In this operation the pouch is slit at its upper end and the testicles are pulled out by hand while the animal lies tied on the ground. After the operation, the incision is cauterized with a red-hot iron and cold butter is smeared over it. Often, an animal bleeds so much that ground moist leaves are applied to the wound to stop the bleeding. Sometimes the incision is sewed closed with thread, but other times it is left open to enable the blood to escape readily and to lessen the danger of infection. After castration, the animal is commonly confined to a corral and given special feed until, after a few weeks, it is well again.

ANIMAL AILMENTS AND THEIR TREATMENT

Although the animal diseases of Northwest Ethiopia have not been studied in detail, it is readily apparent even from cursory observation and inquiry that there are striking differences in their nature and severity from highland to lowland. Europeans who have travelled in Ethiopia only during the dry season or during the rainy season only in the highland, tend to minimize the dangers of the low country for domestic animals. Ethiopian highlanders, on the contrary, have had long and costly experience with the low country and they are wary of it; they regard it as disease-ridden and unsafe for most domestic animals, a place to be avoided, particularly in the rainy season.

Of all the common domestic animals, horses and mules are in greatest danger in the low country, as is shown by the experiences of R. E. Cheesman, Sir Samuel Baker, and others. Cheesman, on a journey to the Sudan border town of Metemma in late September, had nineteen out of twenty-two mules sicken and die, though they were in the lowland for less than two weeks altogether. Cheesman was able to transport his goods only because he had fifteen donkeys in the caravan, none of which, fortunately, were affected, though there are places where even donkeys cannot live.[67] The disease that caused the death of Cheesman's mules, and that also affects horses and donkeys, is known to the local people as *nigma* and to Europeans as horse sickness, but its origin and cure were not known in Cheesman's time and, to my knowledge, they are not known even today. Sir Samuel Baker, who visited Metemma before the rains began in late April, 1862, observed that there were no good horses in the market there, for there was an epidemic in the region that was fatal to them. Further, he reported that the dead and decaying bodies of a half-dozen donkeys, three or four camels, and a number of horses lay in and around a small stream nearby. Shortly after he left Metemma, Baker's own horse was taken ill, fell down, and soon died of horse sickness. Baker described the illness of the horse as starting with an inflammation of the bowels that he thought might have been caused by eating poisonous plants together with young herbs;[68] the symptoms are identical to those of an illness which caused the death of two of my donkeys on a dry-season trip to Metemma in 1954.

Besides the illnesses of horses, mules, and donkeys, there are diseases of cattle which apparently have kept these animals from increasing in numbers among the Gumis and other peoples along the border between Northwest Ethiopia and the Sudan. Even in some lower sections of the plateau, cattle keeping is hindered by disease as, for example, on Dek Island in Lake T'ana where R. E. Cheesman saw both dead animals and skeletons in the fields, and observed that cattle used for plowing have to be replaced constantly because of the unhealthiness of the island.[69]

There have also been a number of unconfirmed reports that the tsetse fly (*Glossina*), dreaded carrier of the trypanosome which causes sleeping sickness, is found along the Sudan borderlands of Northwest Ethiopia and in the valleys of the Blue Nile and Tekezzay rivers. Though it is true that the tsetse fly has been diffused widely in Africa since the arrival of the Europeans, most writers doubt that it has yet reached Northwest Ethiopia. In the Sudan, however, there has been a surprising increase of trypanosomiasis outside of the areas where the tsetse fly is found, a situation which has led to the suggestion that

[67] R. E. Cheesman, 1936: 10.   [68] Baker: 1867: 502, 517, 521.
[69] R. E. Cheesman, 1936: 127.

other biting flies, such as the *Tabanidae,* may be responsible for transmitting the trypanosomes.[70] If there is merit in this suggestion, it is possible that sleeping sickness is also present in the Sudan border region of Northwest Ethiopia, for there are reports of biting Tabanid flies occurring there.

Apart from their role in carrying diseases, flies can be extremely troublesome to animals, either because they bite or simply because they settle on the animals in such great numbers. Sir Samuel Baker spoke of the "seroot fly" which worried the animals almost to death with its bites.[71] James Bruce reported a similar situation in which numerous flies appeared which made all the cattle stop feeding and run wildly about the plain until, worn out with fatigue, fright, and hunger, they died.[72]

The same combination of charms and practical medicine that is applied in the prevention and treatment of human illness is used for animals. It is common, for example, to see around the necks of horses, mules, and donkeys strips of goatskin which serve as charms to protect them against evil spirits; such strips are placed around the necks of these animals at the beginning of the Ethiopian new year in September and remain until eventually they fall off. Moreover, there are said to be local spirits who demand sacrifices from those who trespass on their dominions. Travelling merchants commonly make sacrifices to such spirits either before starting on a trip or along the way.

One of the most common needs for practical medicine is on crosscountry treks, for the backs of mules, donkeys, and horses are inadequately protected against the movements of their loads, and often develop raw and bleeding friction wounds. If sufficient pack animals are available, merchants normally rotate them in load-carrying so that the sores will have a chance to heal and all of the animals will have a chance to rest. Usually sores heal more or less satisfactorily after several days, but many older animals have large areas of scar tissue on their backs which open up readily when they are under a load. Usually friction wounds are covered with flies, but only if the flies prove extremely troublesome for the animal, or if the muleteer has pity, will he cover the wounds with leaves. In time, the leaves fall or brush from the wound, but they provide an immediate, temporary relief to the animal. Often the friction wounds become so badly infected that the animal is in danger of losing his life, in which case the common treatment is to cauterize the wound with a red-hot iron, after the diseased flesh has been cut away. A similar treatment is ap-

[70] D. J. Lewis, 1949; P. A. Buxton, 1948: 18.   [71] Baker, 1867: 184.
[72] Bruce, 1790, I: 388.

plied to infections of the foot, in which the Ethiopians first extract the matter by boring and "then pour in, over a red-hot iron, honey, goat's fat, and oil," and then cover the wound with a piece of cloth.[73]

TRANSHUMANCE

There are no nomads in Northwest Ethiopia, but here and there herdsmen migrate seasonally with their cattle, though other domestic animals are not usually involved in such migrations. In some places the cattle migration occurs in the rainy season and in others in the dry season. In Marīam Deber village south of Gondar, for example, there is a rainy season migration in which all cattle except plow oxen, aged animals, and a few milking cows and their calves are sent into the cold highland (*dega*) in order to avoid mud and flies. This movement from the village of Marīam Deber involves small distances, usually only two to six hours away from the village. The people of Marīam Deber make arrangements for grazing before the rainy season begins, paying the village chief in the grazing area a fee for the season of about three dollars (Ethiopian) for each hundred cattle. Perhaps because of the cost, sheep and goats are left behind in the home village. While in the high country, cattle are generally cared for by boys and young men who camp out. Usually they obtain a weekly supply of food from home, though wealthy men who have many cattle and who watch over their animals personally take their wives with them to the highland, build small huts, and set up temporary residence there. Rainy season movements of cattle from muddy, low-lying country to higher and drier country are common, too, among the people living around the north end of Lake T'ana, many of whom drive their cattle through Dembya into the higher country north of Gondar. This migration involves distances of one, two, or more days away from home. Because of this, the herdsmen do not usually take their wives with them, though sometimes they take their daughters along to cook and to perform the necessary tasks around the temporary huts which they build.

When cattle migrate in the dry season it is not to avoid mud, but to obtain pasturage and water. At the height of the dry season, for example, there is a movement of animals from the plateau near Ch'ilga into the low country to the west to enable the cattle to feed on the green grass that grows along the banks of the ponded streams there. In the Agow village of Silaszī in Semyen, dairy cattle and calves under a year old, as well as a bull or two, are kept in the village during the rainy season, but are sent to graze along the Tekezzay River during

[73] Plowden, 1868: 158.

the dry season, from January to June. The other cattle as well as the sheep and goats are kept throughout the year in stream valleys an hour or more from the village, for the village is perched well up on a hillside, far from water.

Use of Animals and Animal Products

Packing, Riding, and Plowing.—Donkeys, mules, horses, men, and women bear the loads in Northwest Ethiopia. Of the domestic animals, the sturdy, willing and long-suffering donkey is clearly superior to both the mule and the horse as a pack animal, for not only are donkeys more resistant to the diseases of the low country, but they are more economical and efficient to use. Whereas a pack horse or mule costs about twenty-eight dollars U.S. and carries a load of seventy-five to one hundred pounds, a donkey costs seven dollars U.S. and carries a load of fifty pounds. Moreover, because of its lighter load, the donkey requires less equipment than the pack mule or horse. A simple sheep-skin, for example, is enough to protect the back of a pack donkey (Fig. 60), while a special pack saddle is needed for the pack mule or horse.

In Northwest Ethiopia, mules and horses are the principal riding animals, whereas donkeys, despite their great strength and endurance, are not generally ridden. Even the long-legged Sennar riding donkey, which is imported to Ethiopia, is used only for breeding mules. The one time I saw a donkey ridden was in the village of Matavia near the Sudan border, but this was exceptional and apparently in imitation of Sudanese Arabs who have and commonly use riding donkeys.

Oxen are the plow animals everywhere in the area. Where they are few in number, poor people sometimes use horses and mules for plowing, and in one unusual case, when all the cattle of a district had died, even donkeys were used to pull the plow. Despite their importance in plowing, however, oxen are not ridden or used as pack animals in Northwest Ethiopia, though in some parts of the country and among various East and South African tribes and among the Baggara Arabs of the Sudan, oxen are either saddled and ridden, used for pack animals, or both. There is evidence that cattle were once more commonly used for transport in Ethiopia, and that the practice has declined in recent generations. W. Stiehler argues unconvincingly that this decline resulted from the introduction of the plow, because, he says, plowing is a far more important use of oxen than packing.[74]

Although the ox-drawn wheeled vehicle was used in Mesopotamia

[74] Stiehler, 1948: 260. For an excellent review of the literature pertaining to the riding of oxen in Ethiopia see Lindblom, 1931.

by 3000 B.C. and had reached Egypt before 1500 B.C.,[75] it was not diffused to Ethiopia, nor has any evidence of other native wheeled
vehicles ever been discovered there. Today, it is true, a few horse-
drawn carts are used in the market section of Gondar, but invariably
their wheels and axles have been salvaged from European-made motor
vehicles. Similarly, the wheels and axles of the two-wheeled, horse-
drawn *garrīs*, which are used as taxis in Asmara, Addis Ababa, Jimma,
and certain other large Ethiopian towns, though not in Gondar, are
taken from European vehicles. In Diredawa, where there are camel-
drawn carts, their wheels and axles are also foreign made.

Riding Equipment.—The Ethiopian saddle consists simply of a
wooden frame with a high wooden pommel and cantle which are
covered with leather. A removable quilt-like pad is fitted over the
frame to provide a seat for the rider. The traditional Ethiopian stirrup
is a toe ring suspended from a leather strap that is attached to the
frame, and through which the barefoot rider puts his big toe or first
few toes. Most upper-class Ethiopians, however, now use European-
type stirrups because they wear shoes. The saddle girth, a narrow
leather strap, is loosely cinched and often a rider when mounting has
someone hold the opposite stirrup firmly to keep the saddle from
slipping off the animal's back.[76] In riding downhill, the saddle often
slides far forward onto the animal's shoulder and in riding uphill it
commonly slides backward until the rider is sitting on the animal's
rump. A sheepskin is placed on the back of the mule or horse before
the saddle is put on but, even with this protection, the animal's back
is usually rubbed raw after a few days of riding.

The Ethiopian bit, which is made of iron, is mounted in a bridle
that also has a ring that passes around the animal's lower jaw. The
bit presses against the roof of the animal's mouth and when used hard
causes it to bleed. After having been broken to the native bit, Ethiopian horses do not respond readily to the American bit.

DUNG AND URINE.—In much of the Northwest, women and girls
collect cattle dung and carry it home in baskets (Fig. 83), for it is an
important cooking fuel and is used as a plaster to cover sun-dried
containers, wattle walls, threshing circles, and other things. Moreover,
in some places it is also scattered as fertilizer in the garden or in
nearby fields.

Though generally the droppings of horses, mules, and donkeys are
not used, in a few places they, too, are collected and either used for
fuel or as fertilizer in the garden. The Agow of Silaszī even use mule

[75] Childe, 1954: 3, 15.
[76] Ethiopians, unlike Americans, mount from the right side of the animal.

and donkey droppings in making grain containers for, they claim, such containers do not crack as readily as those in which cattle dung is used. Though I did not see anyone collect the droppings of sheep and goats, I was told that near Gondar they are sometimes gathered and used in the garden as fertilizer. Human droppings, on the other hand, are left to decay where they fall and are not consciously used for manuring or for any other purpose, though W. Stiehler has reported such use in the Konso country in southern Ethiopia.[77]

So far as I can determine, the only type of urine used is that of cattle which is employed in softening hides and skins.

HIDES, SKINS, BONES, AND HAIR.—The hides and skins of cattle, sheep, and goats serve a variety of uses in the household, in agriculture, and elsewhere, and their tendons commonly provide thread for sewing the hides and skins. On the other hand, the hides, skins, and tendons of donkeys, horses, and mules are not used at all, apparently because the prejudice against the flesh of these animals has been extended to these products. The bones of these animals are not used either, though the bones of sheep, goats, and cattle are commonly cooked in stew, the marrow being eaten or serving as a leather softener. Though there are few bone implements except the ox-rib scraper of the potter, there is apparently no prejudice against using the bones of animals whose flesh is edible.

Though generally the hair of goats is not clipped, in the Guna region and in parts of Semyen sheep are sheared and the wool is used either in weaving cloth or as pillow stuffing. The feeling against using the flesh, hides, skins, and tendons of donkeys, horses, and mules fortunately has not been extended to their hair. The tail hairs of horses and mules, for example, are commonly clipped and made into flicks, called *ch'ira* in Amharic, which are in general use in Ethiopia and the northern Sudan. Tail hairs of horses and mules, and sometimes mane hairs, are also used in making beer strainers (Amh.: *wontuft*), in decorating baskets, and in making braided string and rope. Though donkey hair is not used in most places, in highland Semyen it, too, is sometimes made into braided rope.

Though I have not seen the horns of goats or sheep used in the Northwest, cattle horns are used by horn craftsmen for making drinking cups for mead and distilled liquor.

MEAT AS A FOOD.—Meat is a favorite food of the people of Northwest Ethiopia. Because cattle are valued highly, they slaughter only old animals and therefore do not get as much beef as chicken, goat, and sheep flesh. Meat is eaten fresh, usually in stew, but it is not

[77] Stiehler, 1948: 261.

preserved in any form, either by smoking, salting, or pickling. It is true that meat which cannot be consumed immediately is sometimes tied on beams in the house and exposed to the smoke of an open fire and eaten bit by bit until it is all gone, but, since the meat is usually eaten within a few days, it cannot properly be considered smoked.

BLOODLETTING AND EATING THE FLESH OF A LIVING ANIMAL.—The practice of bleeding cattle to obtain blood for drinking is common among the Nilotic tribes and among many peoples of East Africa, though in Ethiopia it has been reported only among the Galla.[78] Sture Lagercrantz points out, however, that even among the Galla the practice is not general, but is restricted to the southern Galla tribes.[79] In northern Ethiopia, the one report of the practice was by Henry Salt, who, in the last century, saw a Galla chief drink a hornful of warm blood taken from the neck of a cow.[80] In the Northwest, the practice is not followed today, and I have seen no reports of it occurring there in the past.

Though they do not bleed cattle for food, the people of northern Ethiopia have an even stranger custom, that of cutting away the living flesh of a cow for food. Though I have not personally observed the practice, and doubt that it is widespread today, it has been reported many times in the past,[81] though apparently only on restricted occasions. Mansfield Parkyns, for example, was told that it was practiced by men who were driving home cattle which they had stolen or taken in raids; in such cases, the men either had to go hungry, slaughter an animal and either leave most of the flesh or carry it along, or simply cut a steak from the living animal.[82] The latter procedure was in many ways preferable, because the men satisfied their hunger and still had a live though scarred animal. A similar practice occurs among the Rguibat Moors of the western Sahara who in times of famine are said to remove fat from the hump of a living camel and then sew up the resulting wound.[83]

MILKING AND DAIRY ACTIVITIES.—Northwest Ethiopia lies well within the milking zone of Africa, that two-thirds of the continent in which milk is used as food, and it is important in the diet of most peoples in the area. It is true that the Negro Gumis of the Sudan border, like many peoples of rainforest West and Central Africa,[84] do not commonly milk their animals, though they have milkable sheep and goats. They do not, however, have any prejudice against using milk as a

---

[78] Baumann, Thurnwald, and Westermann, 1940: 238.
[79] Lagercrantz, 1950: 54.   [80] Hotten, 1868: 45.
[81] Bruce, 1790, III: 142–43; Salt, 1814: 295; Parkyns, 1868: 204–5.
[82] Parkyns, 1868: 204–5.   [83] Briggs, 1958: 135.   [84] Simoons, 1954: 61–62.

food, for they allow their children to drink the milk of goats in the field and they sometimes purchase boiled butter which they drink, add to stew, or use as a hair pomade.

In Northwest Ethiopia, cows' milk provides the bulk of the milk supply and is preferred over the milk of all other domestic animals. Indeed, in those sections of the highland where cattle are numerous, most people use only cows' milk, for they do not consider it worth the effort to milk goats or sheep. Even in such sections, however, some poor people and young shepherds use goats' milk, the former driven to it by poverty, the latter drinking it for refreshment when they are in the field. Moreover, in some lowland areas, contrary to the general pattern, goats' milk is the principal milk used, though in other parts of the lowland, such as the cattle-poor Kumfel country, people do without milk rather than milk their goats, a practice they regard as undignified. Nevertheless, even those who disdain goats' milk as food will often use it as a cough medicine, or make it into butter which serves either as a hair pomade or as a base for medicine.

Though many smile at the idea of milking sheep, in a few places some poor people milk their sheep to obtain food for their children. I was told, moreover, that in highland Semyen shepherds occasionally drink sheep milk in the field, and that among the Sahalla Agow adults sometimes consume the milk from their sheep.

Though donkeys were milked in dynastic Egypt and in ancient Mesopotamia,[85] the use of donkeys' milk is rare today and is restricted principally to cosmetics, medicine, and magic.[86] In Northwest Ethiopia, people regard the milk of donkeys, like their flesh, to be unclean, and inquiries about the use of donkeys' milk frequently provoke amused smiles or guffaws of laughter. Nevertheless, though most people deny ever using donkeys' milk, in some places they admit using it as a cough medicine, though the person to whom it is given is not told what it is, lest he refuse to take it. This use has also been reported from the northern Sudan,[87] and elsewhere. Another rare use of donkeys' milk is in ceremonies of exorcism when the evil spirit (zar) possessing a man demands donkeys' milk as a bribe for leaving his body; this demand does not deny the unclean status of donkeys' milk, for patients in the ceremonies of exorcism commonly eat all sorts of filth which would ordinarily be repulsive to them. Mares' milk, like donkeys' milk, is regarded as unclean and is apparently never used.

Little is known about the way in which the milking habit spread into those areas of the Old World, such as Negro Africa and East Asia, where strong prejudices against milk existed. Perhaps the most

[85] Forde, 1949: 453. [86] Sauer, 1952: 93. [87] Halim, 1939: 30.

conspicuous means of spreading the use of milk has been through the migrations and conquests by milking peoples. On the other hand, subtle changes in attitudes toward milk must have taken place by more gradual processes, too. The fact that in Northwest Ethiopia types of milk and butter which are disdained as food are sometimes used as medicines and cosmetics suggests that milk and dairy products may have spread first as medicinals and cosmetics and only later came to be important in the diet. In the acceptance of dairy products as food, children may have played an important role, for they are curious about new foods and they enjoy greater freedom from societal pressures to conform with the existing foodways.

Milking of Cows: Sexual Division of Labor, Yields, Techniques, and Vessels.—No single sexual division of labor in milking cows is followed throughout Northwest Ethiopia. In the Gondar area, for example, milking is the work of men and boys, whereas among the Agow of Sahalla, men are sometimes assisted by women, in Debre Tabor and among the Kumfel milking is done by both men and women, and in some parts of highland Semyen and elsewhere it is considered the work of women.

Ethiopian cows give very little milk; normally at one milking it takes the milk of two cows to fill a gourd holding three liters. During the rainy season, however, one cow may give as much as two liters per milking, and in the dry season less than one liter. Cows are usually milked twice a day: in the early morning before they go to the pasture and in the evening when they have returned home. A cow is milked in the presence of its calf, which is usually allowed to drink for a minute or two to start the milk flowing before a boy or woman removes the calf and holds it, despite its vigorous protests, alongside the cow. Should a calf die, its skin is dried and stuffed with straw (Fig. 63) and brought to the cow to nuzzle in order to encourage the giving of milk. The cow is sometimes also given a little salt to stimulate it to give milk when its calf has died. Many an Ethiopian cow is skittish and difficult to milk; commonly the back legs of such an animal are tied loosely with a leather thong (Fig. 62) to prevent it from kicking. When an animal is especially troublesome, a leather thong or rope may also be tied around its horns and held by a man to keep it under control.

There are two common types of milk containers in use in Northwest Ethiopia: [88] a milking gourd (*gereyra* in Amharic) and a woven grass container (*quacha* in Amharic) which is of the same shape as the milk-

[88] G. W. B. Huntingford (1955: 25) says that the Galla are not permitted to put milk into vessels of pottery, but I have heard of no such prohibition in Northwest Ethiopia.

ing gourd and, like it, has a capacity of two or three liters. The milking gourd usually has a woven grass ring attached to its base so that it can be set down without toppling over. The top of the gourd is cut off to be used as a lid; to insure a close fit, a woven grass edging is made on both the rim of the lid and the rim of the gourd. Rim edgings are commonly made of cow hair interwoven with grass, and then a cow-hair string is added connecting the lid and gourd in order to prevent their becoming separated. So that the gourd may more readily be carried, a leather strap is usually tied to it to form a handle. Sometimes a gourd is decorated with cowrie shells, though I cannot say whether these are for decoration alone or whether they also have a magical function. The woven grass container, *quacha*, is usually smeared on the inside with butter or milk or smoked until it becomes reasonably leakproof. In addition, both types of milk containers are smoked every third or fourth day either by holding them over a fire or by dropping into them smoking bits of wood: *avalo, zigita (Carissa edulis?),* or *kaga (Rosa abyssinica),* though they are washed with water only occasionally.

Manufacture, Use, and Sale of Dairy Products.—Before drinking milk, the people of Northwest Ethiopia usually first permit it to sour. Some of the sour milk, instead of being drunk directly, is spiced with cayenne pepper and added as a sauce to stew, and some of it is made into butter. In making butter, which is done every few days, women first accumulate a sufficient supply of sour milk. Two types of containers are used in making butter: one a gourd suspended from a wooden tripod (Fig. 64), and the other a large pottery jug (Fig. 65). In making butter in a gourd, a girl or woman shakes the suspended gourd back and forth on the tripod, stopping the process every few minutes to let air escape by means of a small hole which otherwise is blocked with a piece of wood, some grass, or a cloth, until finally the milk turns to butter. When butter is made in the large pottery jug, the jug, filled with milk, is placed on mats on the ground. The milk is first stirred with a large pronged stick, which the woman rotates between her hands. Then she puts a skin cover over the pot and rocks it back and forth until butter is formed. The latter method of making butter is an ancient one, for it is illustrated on Mesopotamian bas-reliefs dating from the third millennium B.C. and is still practiced there today.[89] Every third or fourth time a butter gourd or jug is used, it is washed out and smoked with the wood of oleaster or of *avalo.*

Fresh butter commonly serves as a base for medicine or is applied directly to the head as a cure for headaches. It is also mixed with

[89] Contenau, 1954: 58–59.

flowers and other aromatic substances and used as a pomade. If it is to be eaten, it is usually boiled and spiced. In this form it can be safely stored in pottery containers, bottles, or gourds for a month or two and sometimes even for an entire year, though it turns black after long storage. The common way of eating butter is as an ingredient in stew.[90]

The people of Northwest Ethiopia do not make true cheese, though they prepare various milk solids. When, for example, the buttermaking process is complete and the butter has been removed from the butter-maker, the buttermilk which remains is boiled in a pot over a slow fire for perhaps an hour. During the boiling, the buttermilk separates into two parts: a solid which is called *aive*, and a liquid which is called either *telela* or *telela agwot*. The solid is either eaten alone or, when there is a shortage of the ordinary stew ingredients, it is added to stew directly or mixed with the liquid, *telela*, and spices. In addition, *aive* is occasionally added to milk, and the mixture heated and stirred until a new solid forms on the bottom of the pot (cottage cheese?) which, with the remaining whey, is called *azor*. Around Gondar, people call this *azorish* or *azorish ikaffinye* from an Amharic verb *azora* meaning "to turn around." Because it is easy to prepare, *azor* is often served by women to their friends when they visit.

Milk is not usually found in the marketplaces of Ethiopia, since it is either consumed entirely at home or sold or bartered to neighbors. It is common, however, to find spiced cooking butter and butter pomade in the market, sold by women who display it in pats which are placed on leaves or wrapped in them.

Beekeeping

As people travel through the countryside of Northwest Ethiopia, they commonly watch for the nests of wild honeybees (*Apis unicolor*) and stingless bees (*Trigona* and *Melipona*) which abound there, as in much of the savanna area of Africa. When a nest is discovered along the trail, travellers often stop to get the honey. To accomplish this, a small smoky fire is first built as close to the nest as possible, and then a man, using an ax, chops at the tree trunk or branch to make an opening through which he can remove the comb. If, because of the ferocity of the bees, he abandons the project before reaching the comb, a more intrepid companion takes over and completes the job.

In addition to the simple honey gathering described above, many people in the Northwest practice a rudimentary beekeeping, building

---

[90] Though William Harris (1844, III: 49) reported that the pagan Galla made offerings of butter to the deity, I did not hear of this use in the Northwest.

hives and placing them in trees in the countryside for swarming bees to enter (Fig. 66). Ethiopian beekeepers sometimes make a special effort to make their hives attractive to bees, rather than trusting to chance alone that the bees will find and enter them. One method is to smoke the hive over a fire of green oleaster leaves so that it will have a pleasant odor. Another is reported by Henry Salt for Wojjerat in Tigre Province, where the natives, having found a wild hive, placed near it a wooden box smeared with honey to attract the bees.[91] After a swarm has taken possession, the hive may simply be left in the tree to provide a known place from which to gather honey, or it may be carried home and placed in a convenient location nearby. It is not the practice of the Gumis and Kumfel to bring the hive home; instead, they lash it to the branch of a tree with bark or rope and cover it with grass. As a result of this practice, the approach to a Gumis or Kumfel village is announced to the traveller long before he sees the village itself. Some Gumis and Kumfel explain their failure to bring the hives home by saying that their bees give an unusually painful sting, whereas others say that bees will provide more honey if the hive is left in the country. One Gumis man even claimed that if a hive were removed from its tree the bees would abandon it. Nevertheless, the Amhara and other peoples of the Northwest sometimes bring home a hive that bees have entered, commonly placing it either in the wall of a house (Sketch 3), as in the Hadhramaut,[92] or nearby about three feet off the ground on a forked pole.

Some people, instead of attracting bees to the hive or waiting for a chance swarm of bees to enter it, actively seek out and capture swarming wild bees to bring home. When the bee hunter finds a wild swarm, he sprinkles the bees with water, catches the queen, and puts her into a small temporary cage. When the bees have dried their wings somewhat and followed the queen into the cage, the beekeeper simply wraps the cage in a robe, carries the bees home, and then transfers them to a permanent hive.

In the practices described above, which are common throughout Africa, we may have the steps by which man progressed toward the complicated practices of modern beekeeping: first the simple gathering of honey from wild hives, then the placing or hives in the countryside for wild swarms to enter, and finally the bringing of the hives home for convenience.

In Northwest Ethiopia, as almost everywhere in Africa,[93] the hunting of honey and the putting out of hives to attract the swarms of bees is the work of men. This suggests that in the progression of man to

[91] Salt, 1814: 489.   [92] Ingrams, 1936: 52.   [93] Bodenheimer, 1951: 166.

agriculture from hunting-gathering, in which stage the collection of wild hives was probably the work of male hunters, men simply continued their ancient responsibilities.

SKETCH 3.—Beehive in the wall of a house.

TYPES OF HIVES AND THEIR CONSTRUCTION.—The common types of beehives in Northwest Ethiopia are cylindrical wickerwork hives (Sketch 3) and cylindrical clay hives (Fig. 67), though other types of hives, and plank barrels, have also been reported [94] in Ethiopia.

The cylindrical wickerwork hive, always made by men, is the most widespread type in the region. It is an elongated cylinder made of a framework of rather heavy wooden ribs interwoven with lighter, more pliable ones. Near Gondar, the wood used for the beehive framework is *satabirt* (*Commelina* sp.), *girowa* (*Vernonia* sp.), or *zigita* (*Carissa edulis?*), while the lighter strips for interweaving are made from the most supple branches of *satabirt* or from a vine called *azo areg* in Amharic. Wickerwork hives are usually smeared with a mixture of mud, chaff, and, where available, cow dung. To protect the hive from rain it is sometimes covered with grass which is tied in place with three or four ropes; such covered hives last for as long as ten years.

[94] Seyffert, 1930: Karte II; Bodenheimer, 1951: 168.

The cylindrical clay beehive, which is sun-dried rather than fired, is common among the Agow of Sahalla and the neighboring highland Amhara. This type of hive is also found among the K'amant, but there it seems to be losing popularity in favor of the wickerwork hive, because, it is said, the clay beehive is made by women, and men who use it are therefore regarded as lazy. Cylindrical clay beehives among the Agow of Sahalla are made in two sizes, both about a foot in diameter; the longer one is about 150 centimeters long, and the shorter one about 50 centimeters long. The long hive is used for a young active swarm so that it will have ample space to store its honey. When the swarm is old and the bees produce less honey, the beekeeper commonly saws the hive in two with a knife. One half is left for the bees who occupied the large hive, and the other half is used for a new swarm. Cylindrical clay beehives usually have a round hole about two inches in diameter at the center of the cover at one end of the cylinder, through which bees enter the hive. Sometimes, however, the hole is filled in, and a crack is made along the edge of the cover to enable the bees to enter. Clay beehives are usually kept outside of the house, raised a few inches off the ground on rocks, and then covered with grass weighted with stones or covered with bark or wood.

To house the queen bee, a separate section is sometimes built and placed within the hive. It is usually made from a piece of bamboo four or five inches long which is split into several pieces and woven together loosely with a grass or sedge or soft bark.

SEASONS AND METHODS OF HONEY-TAKING.—By tradition, men in the Gondar area clean the hives they have at home on the first day of the Ethiopian new year in early September. The hives are prepared at this time so that they will be ready for the approaching season when the bees will be active gathering nectar from the flowers that grow in profusion just after the rains. The hives are cleaned at night by men, who first burn incense in a small fragment of pottery near the entrance to each hive "to celebrate the new year." Then, while one man holds a lantern, another places smoldering cow dung near the entrance to drive the bees back. He then removes about two-thirds of the wax and old black honey, leaving the hive in good condition to receive its new supply. Five or six weeks after the new year's cleaning, the men collect honey from the hive for the first time, usually about half of the honey then available. After several more weeks, the beekeeper takes honey again, though, after that, most people take no more honey until the following new year.

The Gumis and Kumfel, who keep their hives in trees in the countryside, collect the honey once or at most twice a year, usually in Sep-

tember or October and again in March. Two or more men or boys go
out at night, when the bees are less active, to the tree where the hive
is located. One man, carrying a rope, climbs the tree. When he reaches
the hive, he lowers the rope to his companion who ties to it a gourd
filled with smoldering wood. The climber places the smoking gourd in
front of the hive, which drives the bees away, and then digs out most
of the honey with his hands or with a knife. The smoldering wood is
then thrown from the gourd and the honey is put into it and lowered
to the ground. It is interesting to note that neither the Gumis, Kumfel,
nor any of the other peoples of Begemder protect themselves against
the stings of the bees, and that their heads, necks, arms, legs, and feet
are always uncovered.

TYPES OF HONEY.—The original quality and taste of honey depend on the plants from whose flowers the nectar was gathered, though
they are often altered by smoke when the bees are driven from the
hive, or when the honey is separated from its comb over a fire, or
when impurities such as soil, dirt, and wood are introduced.[95] In most
parts of Northwest Ethiopia, four types of honey (Amh.: *mar*) are
distinguished: white (Amh.: *nech' mar*), red (Amh.: *k'aī mar*), black
(Amh.: *t'ik'ur mar*), and bitter, reddish-yellow honey, *din*. Fresh honey
taken from a hive during the fall season of flowering is usually light
colored. If, however, honey is left in the hive until the end of the dry
season (April), it is said to become dark in color. I have been told
that red honey is found wherever the bees gather nectar from the
flowers of the acacia (Amh.: *girrar*), though Carl Seyffert said that
acacia honey is white or at least very clear.[96] The bitter, reddish-
yellow *din* is said to be produced by bees who are not very active.

White honey is the preferred type and commands the highest price
in the market, whereas *din* is least preferred and is cheapest. Not only
does *din* have a bad taste, but it is said to be bad for the stomach.
When it is used for making mead, it is said to make the mead bitter.
Thus, people often mix other types of honey with *din* to make it
more palatable.

STORAGE AND USES OF HONEY.—Around Gondar, honey is stored in
pots or gourds. Gourds normally have tightly fitting lids to keep out
ants and bees. Pots, however, must be specially fitted with covers made
of leaves plastered over with dung, mud, and chaff. Honey is usually
stored for only a short time, but it is said to keep for long periods
without spoiling. In highland Begemder and Semyen, honey is most
valued for its use in making several beverages: 1) mead, 2) *birz*, a

[95] Seyffert, 1930: 71-73.
[96] Seyffert, 1930: 72.

mixture of honey and water, 3) *telba chilka,* made of one part of honey, five parts of water, and one part of crushed flaxseed, 4) *avīsh chilka,* made like *telba chilka,* but with fenugreek instead of flaxseed, 5) *marinautit,* made by boiling one part of honey with five parts of fresh milk, and 6) *marinakevi,* made by mixing and boiling honey, butter, and turmeric. Honey is not usually eaten on bread, but it is often eaten directly in the comb and is considered a delicacy. The Gumis of Bodella and the Kumfel of Yīkaho eat most of their honey in two forms: in the comb or simply with the comb crushed. The Gumis sometimes make honey water and mead, but the Kumfel claim they do not make mead, perhaps because honey is valuable and is an excellent trade item for them. Thus, the Amhara and other highland peoples, who have more advanced beekeeping practices than the lowlanders, also have more varied ways of using honey.

HONEY AS A TRADE ITEM.—Though many of the people of the highland sell honey in the market or to traders, the people of the lowland, because of the deficiency of other trade goods and the abundance of honey, probably market a great deal more honey than do the highlanders. Indeed, at the Kumfel village of Yīkaho in the lowland, honey is the principal trade item. It is said that generations ago the Kumfel even paid taxes in honey, though today they sell their honey to traders from K'wara and Alefa in the highland, and pay their taxes in currency.

The Agow of Sahalla, who also have an abundance of honey, often market it in the dry season when prices are high. They walk as much as seven days to Makalle in Tigre Province, or to Sokota or Samre to market their pots of honey. The Agow say that honey is such a valuable trade item that only rich people can afford to make mead from it for themselves.

Though the Italians in their drive for self-sufficiency urged the exportation of honey to Italy, little was done in that direction, and even today only small amounts of honey are exported from Ethiopia (valued at about $34,000 U.S. in the year ending September 10, 1950 [97]). Beeswax, though it was third among the exports of Ethiopia in the 1930's, is now only a minor export, accounting for less than 1 per cent of exports by value in 1956 ($348,000 U.S.).[98]

[97] Ethiopian Government, Ministry of Commerce and Industry, 1951: 54.
[98] Statistical Office of the United Nations, 1957: 196.

Chapter VIII

Fishing, hunting,

AND GATHERING ACTIVITIES

In Northwest Ethiopia, though the products of herding and farming form the basis of sustenance, people do not overlook fishing, hunting, and gathering to supplement their food supply and to obtain other useful products.

FISHING.—Though it might seem that all of the peoples of the Middle East and East Africa, where shortages of animal protein are common, should be eager to obtain fish for food, some of them, including certain Ethiopian groups, reject it because of a deep-rooted cultural prejudice. Noble Somali, for example, not only reject fish, but despise fish eaters.[1] Likewise, the Galla living near the Blue Nile a century ago, abhorred the eating of fish,[2] and even today only Galla too poor to afford meat or bread consume fish.[3] The true Kaffa of southern Ethiopia do not fish, though the Manjo, a submerged group of hunters living in Kaffa country, do.[4] In Northwest Ethiopia, most peoples catch fish and eat them without prejudice, though there is one group, the Agow of Sahalla, who make no use of fish even though they live near the Tekezzay River, in a region where many fish are available. The Agow say, however, that they have no prejudice against eating fish, and that they would do so if shown how to catch them and to eat them without risk of swallowing bones. Apart from the case of the Agow, the only suggestion that any other group in the Northwest ever avoided fish is the statement of James Bruce, who reported in the late eighteenth century that the K'amant did not eat them.[5]

Except for the Wayt'o fishermen of Lake T'ana and some Amhara specialists who spend part of the year at it, fishing is an occasional activity undertaken by farmers when they have spare time. If the farmer-fishermen have a surplus of fish, they generally give or barter

[1] I. M. Lewis, 1955: 75.   [2] Plowden, 1868: 306.
[3] Huntingford, 1955: 28.   [4] Huntingford, 1955: 110.
[5] Bruce, 1790, IV: 275.

them to neighbors and friends. Neither they nor the professional fishermen generally sell fish in the marketplace though they sometimes peddle them in the streets of larger settlements such as Gondar and Azezo.

Though the net, trap, snare, spear, bow and arrow, and hook and line are used sometimes in fishing, perhaps the most common way of catching fish in Northwest Ethiopia is by the use of fish-stupefying plants. Because of the need for relatively still water to make the stupefacients effective, most fishing is done during the dry season, when streams are flowing slowly or are ponded. The gathering of the stupefying plants, all of which are wild, is generally in the hands of the men. The common stupefacients include the seeds of the tree *Milletia ferruginea* (Amh.: *birbirra*), the leaves of the shrub *Maesa lanceolata* (Amh.: *killabo*), the bark of *aura* (*Lantana trifoliata?*), and the fruit of the *Solanum marginatum* (Amh.: *imboy*). Other plants sometimes used, but which I cannot identify, are, by their Amharic names, *tibirbir, k'utina,* and *shorīta.* To ensure the effectiveness of his fish-stupefying plants the fisherman avoids sexual intercourse the night before gathering them. After gathering, he commonly lets certain of the agents dry in the sun for about two days, and then crushes them in a mortar or between two stones, and mixes them with the other stupefying agents. Finally, he bundles the mixture into a cloth, and takes it to a spot in the stream above a quiet pool. Before starting his fishing, however, he usually pours libations or casts offerings into the water for good luck. *Arak'i,* the distilled liquor, is considered most effective for this purpose, though flat bread, milk, or other food is often substituted for it. After making his offering, the fisherman takes his bundle of stupefacients, and presses and rubs it in the water, releasing the active agents. From one to several hours later, when the dazed fish rise to the surface of the water, the fisherman picks them up by hand or with a net. They are eaten after cleaning and cooking, but without treatment beyond that.

Among the nets found in Northwest Ethiopia are the gill net, the cast net, and the scoop net. The gill net is used by Wayt'o fishermen in Lake T'ana, who commonly go a short distance from shore in their balsas, spread the net parallel to the shore in shallow water, and then beat the water between the net and the shore with a long pole, which frightens the fish into the net. The cast net, which is found in many places, is circular, about eight feet in diameter, and weighted around its edge with chains or lead. In using the cast net, which does not generally bring an abundant reward, the fisherman stands on the shore or in shallow water, casting the net in such a way that it traps any fish beneath it, and then retrieves the net by means of a rope which is tied to the center of the net. Cast nets such as those of Northwest Ethiopia have a wide distribution in the coastal regions of Africa, though they are also found along the great rivers of the continent. The distribution of cast nets in Africa suggests, according to some writers, that the cast net was originally foreign to Negro Africa,[6] and that it was introduced from the Mediterranean area, from India, or from Indonesia, where it is common. Though I have not seen plunge baskets in Northwest Ethiopia, scoop nets are used around Gondar to pick up fish caught on the line or dazed by stupefacients.

Though today the hook and line, usually baited with bread or meat, are used by many highland people, as well as by the Gumis, the hooks I found were of foreign origin. This, and the fact that fishing with the hook does not seem to have been common in the past in Ethiopia [7] and that one traveller [8] reported having seen no hooks at all in the country, suggests that the hook is a recent introduction to the area.

Among the other fishing techniques found in the Northwest are the use of the spear among the Wayt'o and Gumis, the use of the bow and arrow among the Gumis, and the trapping of fish in fast-flowing streams by damming them with rocks and placing, in an opening in the dam, a basketry trap, its open end facing upstream for unwary fish to enter. One other technique, observed in Semyen, is the use of a braided horsehair loop suspended from a long stick to jerk the unwary fish from the water.

Among the fish of Lake T'ana and streams nearby are the catfish (*Clarias* sp.), called in Amharic *ambasa*, the largest of which weigh about twenty-eight pounds, the carp-like *nachasa* (*Barbus* sp.), which may reach a weight of ten pounds, the perch-like *karoso* (*Tilapia nilotica*), which reaches two to three pounds, and the *beyehso* (*Varicorhinus beso*), about two pounds. The Amhara speak of a fish "as large as a man," called *sorz*, which is found in Lake T'ana; some writers suspect that this may be the Nile perch (*Lates niloticus*), which reaches a size of one hundred pounds at Khartoum in the Sudan. No foreigners have ever seen the *sorz*, however, and it remains doubtful that the Nile perch actually does exist in Lake T'ana. Other unidentified fish mentioned by the people of Gondar are *ye bahir assa* ("the lake fish"), *assamadenges,* and *warekeda.*

Usually, fresh fish are cooked and added to stew, though they are sometimes fried or roasted. Fish are not usually dried, smoked, salted,

[6] Leth and Lindblom, 1933: 45.   [7] Lagercrantz, 1934: 21.
[8] Hayes, 1905: 97.

or pickled. In Marīam Deber village near Gondar, however, when large batches of forty or fifty fish are caught, they are sometimes sun-dried, crushed in a mortar, mixed with cayenne pepper and salt, and stored in pots. When this mixture is used, it is added with butter to boiling water to make a sort of porridge.

HUNTING.—There has been a serious depletion of game in northern Ethiopia since firearms became common in the country.[9] To illustrate the former abundance of game in the region, there are a number of observations by travellers. A century ago, for example, one writer said that the favorite occupation of the lowland Negroes was hunting and that they ate the flesh of elephants, rhinoceroses, and other animals.[10] Another writer said that young men of Tigre tried to distinguish themselves by killing first an elephant, then a Negro or a Galla.[11] Sir Samuel Baker, moreover, described an abundance of large game, including elephants and rhinoceroses, in the lowland border regions of Ethiopia and the Sudan. Today, on the other hand, large game animals along the Sudan border are few in number. We saw none on our trip into the border country and people there say that only a few large game animals and lions remain and that they seldom approach human settlements.

In Lake T'ana, there has been an equally serious destruction of animal life. In the late eighteenth century, for example, the lake contained large numbers of hippopotami.[12] At the beginning of the last century they constituted a veritable plague for the farmers of the area and rendered navigation dangerous.[13] In the mid-nineteenth century, Walter Plowden had to wait along the shore all night because a herd of hundreds of hippopotami blocked the passage of his balsas.[14] Even in the early years of this century, Lake T'ana is said to have been a paradise for hunters, who left the remains of hippopotami strewn on the shores of the lake.[15] By 1928, however, R. E. Cheesman warned of the threatened extinction of the hippopotami in the lake, for their numbers already had been seriously depleted. The destruction had gone so far by 1937 that the Missione di Studio al Lago Tana in three months on Lake T'ana saw only two hippopotami.[16] The killing of the hippopotami of Lake T'ana thus seems to have taken place largely within this century, and has apparently been associated with the acquisition of firearms by the Wayt'o hunters.[17] The Italians, in an effort to save the remaining hippopotami, passed a law protect-

[9] Maydon, 1925: 112; R. E. Cheesman, 1936: 327. [10] Salt, 1814: 380.
[11] Pearce, 1831, I: 217–18. [12] Bruce, 1790, III: 402.
[13] Grottanelli, 1939: 190. [14] Plowden, 1868: 193–94.
[15] Grottanelli, 1939: 190; Rava, 1913: 84. [16] Grottanelli, 1939: 190.
[17] Grottanelli, 1939: 189–90.

ing them. Today, however, there are few, if any, left in the lake, though the hippopotami still found in the Blue Nile could presumably repopulate the lake if given the opportunity. Of the people living near Lake T'ana, none seem to care that there are no hippopotami left, except the Wayt'o for whom the animals were a major source of meat and a focus of ceremonial life. Their incautious destruction of the hippopotamus resource has placed the Wayt'o in a precarious economic position, for they own no land for cultivation and few, if any, cattle for plowing. Despite these disadvantages, it seems that the only way they can survive is by making a painful transition to agriculture.

The highland sections of the Northwest have few large game animals. In highland Semyen, the Walia ibex (*Capra walia*), which may have been numerous in ancient times, survives today only in small numbers in the roughest and most remote sections. The lesser game animals, including various creatures of the antelope type, are still pursued by man, though the restrictions imposed upon hunting rifles gives them a chance for survival.

The Amhara traditionally have hunted either mounted or on foot with spear, gun, club, and dog.[18] I have heard of spring loop traps being used for catching birds, of snares for capturing various animals, and larger traps for leopards and lions. In the Northwest, as already pointed out, the sling is used to frighten birds from the fields of grain, but is not used seriously for hunting, although it serves as a weapon among some other peoples of Ethiopia.[19] The Amhara deny ever having used arrow poisons, though the Wayt'o,[20] certain groups of Agow,[21] and the lowland Negroes[22] have been reported as using them. The poisons in question were made either by boiling the "roots of an evergreen tree"[23] or from the juice of a currant-like fruit.[24] Though the euphorbia plant occurs in many places, and though its juice is used as an arrow poison among the Lugbara of the Congo-Uganda border,[25] I have not heard of this use in the Northwest.

GATHERING.—Gathered wild plant materials are used in an impressive variety of ways in Northwest Ethiopia: for food, in the preparation of beer and liquor, for fuel, fiber, and construction, as detergents for washing, as charms, medicine, spices, stimulants, incense and perfumes, cosmetics, dyes, skin softeners and tanning materials, fish intoxicants, rat poisons, and, where used, arrow poisons. Even though

[18] Harris, 1844, III: 83.   [19] Lagercrantz, 1950: 217.
[20] Plowden, 1868: 72; Beckingham and Huntingford, 1954: 58.
[21] Beckingham and Huntingford, 1954: 57–58.
[22] Wylde, 1901: 453; Foster, 1949: 128.   [23] Wylde, 1901: 453.
[24] Foster, 1949: 128.   [25] Baxter and Butt, 1953: 121.

imported commercial preparations are replacing many gathered plant materials in Addis Ababa and in the larger towns of Ethiopia, the rural areas of the Northwest are still surprisingly free of commercial substitutes.

Wild roots, berries, and nuts are usually gathered for food only by children, especially by shepherd boys in the country. Poor people sometimes collect wild foods for sale in the marketplace, though the effort generally is not considered worth the return. Other wild products are usually collected as needed by the person who uses them. Thus, the housewife collects her basket grasses, perfume plants, cosmetics, and spices, the fisherman gathers his stupefacients, the smith his wood for charcoal, and the tanner his tannin. There are certain well-known and widely used wild plants, but others, especially medicinals, are known only to a few people who keep their knowledge secret.

Gathered plant materials serve such a diversity of uses and supplement agricultural produce so nicely that it is sometimes difficult to tell where cultivation ends and gathering begins. Often, when a field or garden is cleared, useful wild plants are left growing. Sometimes wild plants, especially detergents and basket grasses, are transplanted or their seeds planted near the house so that they will be available when needed.

Northern Ethiopian grain farmers, unlike grain farmers of Western societies, are perhaps as acutely aware of their environment and make as extensive use of it as do many rainforest peoples. Despite this, botanists seem to know far more about the gathering activities of rainforest peoples than of farmers such as those of Ethiopia. A study of the place of gathered plant materials in the Ethiopian economy should, therefore, be extremely rewarding.

Chapter IX

Food, Cooking, and Nutrition

CULTURAL PREJUDICE AS A LIMITATION ON THE USE OF AVAILABLE FOOD RESOURCES.—In Northwest Ethiopia, only part of the food resources available are used because of the limitations imposed by group food prejudices. In some ways, however, a much more complete use is made of such resources than would be made by Europeans in a similar environment. Thus, besides the foods included in the daily diet, there are roots, berries, and other wild products which are not ordinarily eaten by adults but are important food supplements for children. Every adult, moreover, knows these wild products from the days of his youth and in times of scarcity and famine he also eats them.

The strongest of the food prejudices of the Northwest Ethiopians are centered about animal products. Thus, the Amhara and most other peoples of the region are revolted at the thought of eating lizards and snakes, hyenas, certain wild fowl, hippopotami, wild and domestic pigs, dogs and cats, horses, mules, donkeys, and camels. Contempt for chickens and eggs, which is common among the Galla, Danakil, and Somali, is not found, as has been observed previously, among the Amhara or any other of the peoples of Begemder and Semyen. I observed no prejudice against eating fish, though such a prejudice was reported in the eighteenth century among the K'amant and is still found among the Galla and many peoples of Ethiopia and East Africa. Though the flesh of mature cattle is relished, veal was, in the past, considered disgusting in some parts of Tigre and in other sections of Ethiopia.[1] The milk of donkeys, mares, and camels is also rejected as food by most groups.

In his admirable study, *Insects as Human Food,* F. S. Bodenheimer [2] has shown that insects are quite nutritious and are eaten by many peoples of the world. That other Western writers have largely overlooked the importance of insects as food may be due to their own cultural prejudice against insects and to their belief that only starving men would eat them. That this belief is false is attested to by abundant

[1] Bruce, 1790, III: 293; Parkyns, 1868: 207–8.   [2] Bodenheimer, 1951.

references to the relish with which locusts, termites, caterpillars, worms, spiders, and even lice are eaten in parts of Negro Africa and elsewhere. In the region in and around Ethiopia, though other insects are generally ignored, many peoples eat locusts. For example, they are eaten by the people of Sennar [3] as well as elsewhere in the Sudan,[4] by Yemen Arabs,[5] by Ruwala bedouin,[6] by the Danakil,[7] and by the Moslems of Tigre.[8] Ethiopian Christians, on the contrary, are not permitted to eat locusts and everywhere in the Northwest they deny ever eating them. Indeed, in the past when Christians ate locusts in times of famine and confessed to the act, their priests imposed "on them a terrible penance," and did not even regard them as Christians until they had been re-baptized.[9] To support their rejection of locusts as food, which may be simply another negative reaction to Islamic ways, Ethiopian Christians have even denied that John the Baptist ate locusts; they say rather that he ate the fruit of a tree.[10]

The Amhara, besides rejecting the animal products mentioned above, refuse to eat the meat of any animals, wild or domestic, that are not slaughtered by Ethiopian Christians. Similarly, the K'amant, Falasha, and Jabartis refuse to eat the meat of animals killed by any-one of a religion other than their own. Such attitudes are common throughout the Middle East, where in some places Moslems extend them to include fish and even locusts. In Northwest Ethiopia, the lone Negro group, the Gumis, are the only ones who have no prohibitions against eating the flesh of animals killed by members of other re-ligious groups, a situation which again clearly indicates the Gumis' affinities with Negro Africa where such prohibitions are not general.

People who violate the majority prejudices against animal foods are shunned by those who observe them. Thus the Wayt'o, who, so far as I can determine, depart from the accepted food patterns only in eating hippopotamus flesh and the meat of certain forbidden wild fowl, are despised by the Amhara, and most Amhara refuse to eat food prepared by the Wayt'o. Some Amhara feel so strongly about this that they will not even enter Wayt'o homes. I have even been told by an Amhara that should he give a vessel of water to a Wayt'o, the con-tainer would never be used again, but would be thrown away. The Amhara also look down on the Negroes of the Sudan border for their reputed violations of the accepted foodways, which the Negroes deny and try to hide from others lest they suffer still greater loss of status.

[3] Parkyns, 1868: 147.
[5] Bodenheimer, 1951: 162.
[7] Bodenheimer, 1951: 162.
[9] Gobat, 1834: 295.

[4] Bodenheimer, 1951: 162–63.
[6] Forde, 1949: 319.
[8] Gobat, 1834: 295.
[10] Parkyns, 1868: 147.

Besides the foods mentioned previously that are rejected outright, there are other foods which are sometimes eaten, but are not highly valued. Such foods, which can best be termed "second-class foods," include roots and tubers, leafy vegetables and fruits, and the milk of goats and sheep. Thus, among the Amhara the only common root crop used for food is the white potato, though sweet potatoes do quite well in the area and yams, coco-yams, and other root crops probably would do well, too. Though leafy vegetables are now grown wherever there is a market for them among local Western inhabitants, the Amhara do not consider them worth cultivating for their own use. Similar attitudes about leafy vegetables are held in Addis Ababa [11] and among the Galla,[12] as well as in some other parts of Africa. Though many kinds of fruit trees such as lemon, orange, and grapefruit do well in parts of Ethiopia, the people of the Northwest show little interest in them. Lemons, for example, are found both cultivated and wild in the area, but are nowhere important in trade or in the diet. Where cows' milk is not abundant the milk of goats and even of sheep may be used, but otherwise it is generally used only by poor people, by shepherds, or for medicine.

THE IMPORTANT FOODS AND THEIR PREPARATION.—The basic foodstuffs everywhere in Northwest Ethiopia are grains and legumes. Important supplements are barley-malt beer, cows' milk and butter, eggs, spices, and vegetable oil. Honey, coffee, chicken flesh, and other meat are expensive and, though people relish them, they cannot afford them every day.

There are many ways of utilizing grains and legumes for food, ranging from those requiring little preparation to those needing involved processing. Some of the simplest ways of using grains and legumes are eating raw horse beans, chick peas, green peas, and lentils; roasting unripe grain on the stalk over a fire, producing a product known as *ishat t'ibs;* roasting heads of mature grain in the coals of a fire; parching grain, peas, or beans on a pan over a fire to make *k'olo;* and popping sorghum and maize which is called *ababa k'olo,* meaning "flower parched grain." Some of the more complex forms of prepared grain and legumes are whole grain porridge *(nifro)* of which there are several types, porridge made from flour *(genfo),* flat, unfermented bread *(kītta),* pancake-like, fermented flat bread *(injera),* raised bread *(dabo),* and hard bread balls *(dabo k'olo)* which are carried as food by travellers. *Injera* is the most common food of the Semitic- and Cushitic-speaking peoples of the Northwest. It is usually broken into pieces and

[11] Messing, 1955: 430.   [12] Huntingford, 1955: 28.

used to dip up bits of the stew, *wot'*, which is generally eaten with it. The Negro Gumis, on the other hand, do not make either flat bread or raised bread. Instead, the principal dish of the Gumis is a meal porridge made of sorghum, maize, or finger millet.

Various types of grain are used in making *injera*. *T'eff* is preferred, though barley is probably the most common *injera* grain in the highland, and sorghum in the lowland. If the grain harvest is small, green peas, horse beans, or haricot beans are also commonly used. To make *injera*, flour and water are mixed together and stored in a pottery jar for three or four days to ferment. Since the jar is never washed, the bits of old dough left in it apparently enable ready fermentation. After the flour and water have fermented, more water is stirred into the mixture to make a batter similar in consistency to pancake batter. This batter is poured onto a large, greased flat pottery or scrap metal skillet and cooked over an open fire until done. *Injera* is so important in the Amhara diet that a woman usually prepares fresh *injera* for her family two or even three times a week, storing it until it is needed.

Stew, which is known as *wot'*, is prepared in a variety of forms, too, differing according to ingredients. Meat stew, *k'eh wot'*, is preferred, but ordinary people cannot afford meat stew often and they must settle for stews made of grain and legumes for their everyday food. Stew is made tasty by adding to it the hot sauce *dilih* which is made of water and many spices, such as cayenne pepper, black mustard, ginger, garlic, fenugreek, basil, coriander, turmeric, Amharic cabbage seed, the herb *t'enadam* (*Ruta* sp.), and *Nigella sativa* and *Afromomum corarima*. To make the hot sauce, spices are ground fine on a special grinding stone, salt is added, and the whole cooked in water to mix the ingredients thoroughly. The resulting sauce is too highly seasoned to be palatable to most Europeans. Ethiopians themselves, though accustomed since childhood to heavily spiced foods, confess that certain especially hot sauces cause them to break out in perspiration. In addition to the *dilih,* which is the sauce in common use, there is another sauce called *awazi,* usually made without mustard and often carried in a powdered form by travellers. Sauce is stored in gourds or pots until needed. It is usually added to the stew directly. When Ethiopians are travelling and stew is not available, they sometimes spread their bread (*injera, kitta,* or *dabo*) with a mixture of *awazi* and water, or they simply dip the bread into the mixture.

There are some suggestions that the raised bread *dabo* may be a fairly recent introduction to Northwest Ethiopia. The Negro Gumis do not use it, and a century ago in Ethiopia its use was restricted to the upper classes.[13] Even today in the Northwest, most Amhara housewives make raised bread only for holidays and other special occasions, or for carrying on trips. Wheat is the grain commonly used in making raised bread, though I have heard of barley, sorghum, maize, and even t'eff used with it. To make raised bread, a portion of t'eff injera dough which has stood for a few days is mixed with water, spices, and flour. This mixture is allowed to rise. Then the dough is kneaded and baked over a fire in a covered pottery dish until done. As a substitute for dough yeast, the housewife may skim the froth from beer and use it in making bread, demonstrating the close ties that bread making and brewing still have in Ethiopia. Mansfield Parkyns observed a century ago that a little honey wine was also sometimes used as leavening in making bread.[14]

EATING HABITS.—In highland Begemder and Semyen people usually eat three meals a day: breakfast at seven or eight in the morning, lunch at noon, and supper in the evening after dark. In the late afternoon they sometimes eat a snack with beer or coffee and, whenever visitors arrive, food is offered to them, too. Breakfast is a small meal, consisting of bread or parched grain, grain porridge, and coffee if it is available. It is said that country people often have no breakfast at all. At noon, people usually have a substantial meal of stew and flat bread, wot' and injera, with milk or beer. In the evening they eat wot' and injera again. At mealtimes, husband and wife eat first together and, after they have finished, the children and servants eat what is left.

Ethiopia is a land in which all major religious groups have a tradition of feast and fast. Christians, Moslems, and Jews alike have not only weekly fast days but long fast periods each year during which they avoid eating animal products of any sort. Usually the long fast periods are followed by great feasts such as the Easter feast of the Christians. The need for avoiding animal products on fast days has encouraged the development of a whole series of special foods made of grain, legumes, spices and vegetable oils, and probably stimulated the breeding and dispersal of oil plants such as nug, safflower, and sesame, as well as protein-rich legumes of various sorts.

ALCOHOLIC DRINKS: Beer.—Beer, called in Amharic t'alla, is the common household drink of the people of the Northwest, and its preparation is the work of the housewife. People do not like water very well, and when they have no beer they often pour water into a beer pot and slosh it around to get some of the beer flavor into the water. Every family makes beer about once a month for its own use, though

[13] Harris, 1844, III: 175.   [14] Parkyns, 1868: 201.

an additional supply is made for holidays or other celebrations. I have never seen beer sold in the marketplaces although there is a small-scale, local sale of beer to beerhouses, which will be discussed later.

In making beer, four ingredients are commonly used: water, *gesho* (*Rhamnus prinoides*), malt, and the flour of an unsprouted grain. The following procedure is followed by Amhara women. The leaves of *gesho* are dried, then crushed in a small mortar and pestle, and soaked in a jug of water for three days. The *gesho*, like hops, gives the beer a bitter taste.[15] Meanwhile, to provide the malt, grains of barley are put in another jug of water and soaked for twenty-four hours. The water is then poured from the barley and the barley is placed between two layers of leaves and stored in the rafters of the house until the sprouts of barley have reached a length of about one and one-half inches.[16] The sprouted barley is crushed slightly in a mortar until the grains are broken open. After this, the barley is placed on a metal plate or on a skin in the sun for a full day (Fig. 68). Finally, the sprouted grains are ground on a grindstone into flour. Then, flour made from other unsprouted cereal grains is made into a paste which is allowed to stand for about three days and is then cooked on a circular metal plate over an open fire (Fig. 69). The resulting cake is broken up and mixed with the ground, sprouted barley. This mixture is added to the pot of *gesho* and water and allowed to ferment for four days. After fermentation, a great deal more water is generally added to the mixture, which sometimes is then allowed to stand for several more days.

When the beer is considered ready for drinking, it is poured from the pot in which it was made into a freshly smoked pot. The grain remaining in the first pot is then mixed with water, and this mixture and additional ingredients are poured into a second smoked jar and allowed to stand for a day or so. The resulting second beer is regarded as an inferior drink and is consumed largely by children and servants. The alcoholic content of Ethiopian beer is usually low and one must drink it in quantity to feel its effect. It is a grey liquid with bits of grain floating in it, and has a pleasant sour taste. Beer is usually served in small gourds or in imported glasses.

[15] Nastrucci (1940: 412–13) mentions the use of small quantities of the leaves of oleaster, of *girowa* (*Vernonia*), and of *missana* (*Croton macrostachys*) in beer occasionally. I have heard of Amhara women using *girowa* leaves to wash out their beer pots and of Kumfel women using them as a substitute for *gesho*, but I have not heard of the use of the leaves of oleaster or of *missana* in beer in Northwest Ethiopia.

[16] Though I asked everywhere, I was unable to find grain fermentation started by chewing or holding grain in the mouth as practiced by some primitive peoples of Southeast Asia. Ethiopians laugh at the idea that such a procedure should be followed.

Though barley is universally used as the malt grain in highland Begemder and Semyen, among the Gumis both sorghum and maize serve as malt grains. Because the Gumis beer lacks barley malt and usually contains no *gesho*, the highlanders consider it an inferior product. Sometimes the Gumis and their neighbors the Kumfel purchase *gesho* brought from the highland for use in their beer. Moreover, the Kumfel also substitute the leaves of the wild plant *girowa* (*Vernonia* sp.?), which they gather, dry, crush into powder, and use exactly like *gesho*. *Girowa* leaves are commonly used in the highland, too, but in a green state for washing out the beer jugs; when there is a shortage of *gesho*, however, even highland women add *girowa* to beer as an alternate. In addition, I have heard that some Amhara in Debre Tabor on occasion use the leaves of tobacco and *ch'at* (*Catha edulis*) for *gesho* in making beer.

Wine.—Wine making, which has been discussed in the section on grapes, under cultivated plants, has been carried on at least since Portuguese times, when wine was used both in Christian communion services and at home by nobles and kings as an intoxicant. Today, however, the church has what amounts to a monopoly on the making of wine and it is made for home use rarely, if at all.

Mead—Mead (Amh.: *t'edj*) is believed to be a more ancient beverage in Ethiopia than wine. Indeed, the name for wine in Amharic, *weyn t'edj*, means "grape mead." Ethiopian mead is a clear amber liquid, the best of which has a delicious flavor which makes it a favorite drink of the people. Because honey is expensive, however, few people can afford mead often and it is consumed regularly only by wealthy men.

The making of mead, like the making of beer, is the work of women. The woman first puts honey into a pot with water and *gesho*, the proportions of honey and water depending on the strength of mead desired. She then covers the pot and lets it stand, usually from three to ten days, depending on the temperature. Then she opens the pot, removes the *gesho* leaves, and, if the wax was not removed from the honey before the process began, she filters the liquid which is then ready for consumption. In the past, one writer, Charles Jacques Poncet, spoke of the Ethiopian use of barley malt in making mead,[17] though other writers are silent on the question, and I found no one in the Northwest using malt in making mead today.

Arak'i.—*Arak'i*, the only native distilled liquor of Northwest Ethiopia, is made throughout the highland, but not among the Kumfel, Gumis, or Agow of Sahalla, all lowland groups. This suggests that the

---

[17] Foster, 1949: 120.

distillation of liquor, a more complicated process than the simple
fermentation of beer and mead, may be a relatively recent introduction to Ethiopia, one which has diffused among the advanced peoples
of the highland, but not to the relatively backward lowlanders. This
suggestion is supported by the similarity of the Amharic word *arak'i*
to words used in the Middle East and Central Asia for various distilled liquors (*arrak, arak'a, aker*), which may indicate an introduction
from that area, perhaps by pre-Moslem Arab traders.

The usual Ethiopian *arak'i* is a clear liquid which looks and tastes
rather like the *anice* of the Italians. It is strong, has a slightly smoky
taste, and should be drunk only in small quantities. Important Amhara
officials, when travelling across country, often carry *arak'i* in leather-
covered Italian canteens. They serve the drink in small horn cups
which are a little smaller than European whiskey glasses. When serving *arak'i*, the official first presents the cup to his guest or to the most
important person present, who drinks and then passes the cup back
to the host to be refilled and offered to someone else.

The best *arak'i* is made of finger millet, though other grains, such
as wheat, barley, maize, rye, or sorghum, are sometimes substituted for
it. It is common also to make *arak'i* of combinations of grains, most
frequently wheat and finger millet, wheat and barley, and wheat and
maize. Wealthy people sometimes also use honey as an ingredient,
though ordinary people cannot afford to do this.

To make *arak'i*, the woman whose work this is follows the same
procedure as in making beer, but for the final dilution she adds only
half the amount of water ordinarily added. The thick brew is then put
into a large pot, whose top is then sealed with a mud, straw, and cow-
dung mixture. A bamboo tube is inserted into a hole in the side of
the pot near the top, and the air space around it is sealed with mud.
The woman then places the pot over a fire and boils the liquid, the
steam escaping down the bamboo tube and condensing in a special
copper or brass kettle set in water, which is changed frequently.[18]
When the *arak'i* has cooled, it is poured into imported glass wine
bottles, which are covered with paper or corked with corn cobs.

In a few towns of the Northwest, *arak'i* is made commercially,
usually by aged Christian widows who have no other source of income.
The town of Debre Tabor has a number of such women producing
an *arak'i* which is considered to be the best made in the Northwest,

---

[18] These special copper or brass kettles are not made in Ethiopia, but are imported from abroad. Some of these kettles, presumably of English manufacture, find
their way into Ethiopia from the Sudan; others of French manufacture enter the
country by way of Harar; and still others, probably of Italian manufacture, come
by way of Asmara.

if not in all of Ethiopia. Debre Tabor *arak'i* is shipped to Gondar and elsewhere in the province and some of it even reaches Addis Ababa. Since *arak'i* is shipped only in small quantities, it is carried by poor merchants, many of whom have only one donkey. When they arrive at Gondar, they deliver it to friends who live there, and the friends, in turn, sell it to the drinking houses. Debre Tabor *arak'i* is not sold in the Gondar market because it is too expensive; instead, most Gondar people buy local *arak'i* which is sold both in the marketplace and directly by the old widows who make it.

A great deal of liquor is consumed in the beerhouses and mead-houses which are found in the larger towns of the Northwest and which are popular gathering places for men. Many of the women who work in these houses are prostitutes, and men can obtain sexual satisfaction there as well as food and sometimes lodging. Besides this, they have a good time talking to their friends and listening to the songs of the professional musicians who gather there. Ethiopian Moslems as well as Christians frequent these houses, though Arab Moslems do not usually go into them.

State of Nutrition and Health

There are suggestions, in the typically distended stomachs of young children and in the small average stature and generally low resistance to disease of the people of the Northwest, that the normal diet does not provide all of the nutritional elements necessary for a vigorous, healthy life. A 1958 general nutritional survey of Ethiopia, involving dietary, biochemical, and clinical studies, seems to confirm this. The survey revealed a daily caloric deficit of as much as 400 calories per person, which contributes to the leanness so characteristic of Ethiopians. There was also an insufficiency of protein, which was manifested especially in the characteristic growth retardation of children and in the occurrence of the disease kwashiorkor. Endemic goiter, which is widespread in Africa, was found in several areas. Though analysis of foodstuffs failed to provide convincing evidence of an iodine deficiency to account for the goiter, it was noted that the salt used by the people was low in iodine and not a significant source of it. Mild rickets were present in as many as 30 per cent of preschool children, which apparently indicates a moderate deficiency of vitamin D, which could be remedied by encouraging greater exposure to the sun. Clinical data revealed a significant incidence of lesions which were attributed to a lack of vitamin A. In the Northwest, cayenne pepper, eggs, and milk provide the major share of vitamin A to the diet. The failure of the people of the Northwest to eat yams denies them an excellent source of this vitamin, and one which is utilized by the root cultivators of the southern highland. In four of the regions sampled, intakes of ascorbic acid were low and apparently this is associated with the failure of people to consume much citrus fruit, though cayenne pepper again was an important supplier of vitamin C. In view of the deficiencies mentioned above, it is noteworthy that Ethiopian intakes of thiamine, riboflavin, niacin, and calcium were adequate, and that the intake of iron was at fantastically high levels, the latter apparently resulting from the use of *t'eff* which is so unusual in its iron content. Though studies reveal widespread infestation of Ethiopians with intestinal and other parasites, the plentiful supply of iron in the diet has meant that the parasites have not depleted the body supply of iron. In fact, anemia was less common in the survey group than would have been expected in an American survey population. Other favorable aspects of the Ethiopian state of health were a low prevalence of dental caries, a strikingly low level of cholesterol in the blood, a low average blood pressure, and an infrequency of hypertension.[19]

The deficiencies and strengths of the Ethiopian diet are clearly related to the attitudes toward food, which in some cases deny people excellent and necessary nutrients. Though the subject has not been adequately investigated, it is likely that Ethiopian dietary deficiencies become more acute during the prolonged religious fasts, when people are required to abstain from animal products. It is then, when their resistance is low, that people are most likely to succumb to the frightening local array of respiratory, venereal, intestinal, skin, and other diseases.

[19] Interdepartmental Committee on Nutrition for National Defense, 1959: 1–2, 58, 73, 77–86. For other dietary information, see Showalter, 1950, and Simmons *et al.*, 1951: 64–72.

Chapter X

CRAFTS AND INDUSTRIES

Ethiopians, despite their proximity to the Mediterranean and Middle Eastern centers of civilization, have little skill in artistic expression; not only is their silverwork and other metalwork less accomplished than that of Egypt and Arabia, but they have no fine wood carving such as is found in West and Central Africa. This may result in part from the constant warfare and the uncertainty of life that has characterized the region in most of the past, for men of action on the frontiers of civilization have seldom been notable for artistic productivity. It is true, of course, that Christian Ethiopians are proud of their churches, and their colorful paintings, umbrellas, and silver crosses, but these things are often crude and shabby and do not elicit much enthusiasm among foreign travellers.

Despite the general deficiency of Ethiopian craftwork, the Amharic and Tigrinya-speaking peoples have a limited craft tradition that is superior to those of the Negro and Cushitic-speaking groups of the country. They not only produce a higher grade of silverwork, mostly jewelry of various kinds and silver crosses, but they are the only groups with elaborate church paintings, which appear to be of Byzantine inspiration. Much of the best work has been done in the centers of political authority, where nobles and kings have encouraged church painting through their endowments, and have supported court artisans, both native and foreign, so as to enable them to create articles of quality befitting the station of their masters.

Unlike most peoples of rainforest Africa, who honor and respect craftsmen, Ethiopians, like Arabians, generally ignore or look down on many types of craftsmen, some of whom belong to despised classes or to ethnic minorities. In the Northwest, for example, iron smithing and pottery work are generally done by the Jews, or Falasha; weaving is largely in the hands of Ethiopian Moslems and Jews; the making of balsas is the work of the Wayt'o; and leatherwork is done by a lowly Amhara class of tanners. Contrary to the general pattern, saddle makers, horn craftsmen, and silverworkers are respected in Northwest Ethiopia.

174

LEATHERWORKING

Most farmers in Northwest Ethiopia process some cattle hides and sheep and goat skins for their own use. In addition, there are professional tanners who earn their livelihood by making leather, and in whose hands exclusively lie the tanning activities. These tanners are known as *fak'ī*, Amharic for "scrapers," or *arabenya*, which connotes "a person skilled in making imported, prestigeful goods," [1] or *develansa*. Though tanners regard themselves as Amhara, they comprise a lowly class with whom other Amhara do not commonly intermarry. They also generally live in separate hamlets in the Amhara country, and are especially numerous in Dembya and around Lake T'ana. Tanner classes, to my knowledge, are not found among the Agow or K'amant of the Northwest, though they are found among other Cushitic groups of Ethiopia.

Tanners use the hides and skins of their own animals, as well as buying them locally, often arranging for their purchase or processing at times of feasting, when animals are slaughtered. The tanners perform all the tasks connected with leatherworking, including the gathering of wild materials used in the leathermaking and tanning processes and the selling of finished products. The wives of the tanners, although they do not generally participate in leather production, work with finished leather, sewing it to woven grass baskets and trays to reinforce and decorate them for women of other groups, who look on this work as beneath their dignity. Tanners and their wives commonly sell their goods and services in nearby hamlets or in the nearest market; they regularly come, for example, to the Gondar weekly market where the men sit in one group with pieces of leather and finished leather bags for sale, and the women gather in another group nearby, sewing leather on baskets (Fig. 70).

TECHNIQUES OF SKIN PROCESSING: CATTLE HIDES.—When a man wants to prepare a cattle hide to sell, he simply pegs it to the ground and lets it dry for two days or so before taking it to market. Sometimes he treats the hide by scattering ashes on the flesh side, assertedly to eliminate the odor, but perhaps also to make it heavier, since hides are sold by weight. If he intends to use the hide for making thongs, whips, or other items which do not require tanned skins, he will process the hide himself, making it into chamoised leather. If, however, he has need of a tanned hide, he will have a professional tanner do the work for him.

In making chamoised leather, the man first soaks the hide in a big

[1] Messing, 1957: 204.

pot, known in Amharic as *madiga,* in a solution of cattle urine and
the crushed astringent fruit of the bush *imboy (Solanum marginatum).*
About a week later, when the hair has loosened, he scrapes it from the
hide with a knife, and lets the hide drain for a few hours. He then
soaks the hide again, for eight to fourteen days, in a mixture either
of milk and crushed castor beans, milk and Amharic cabbage seed, or
water, *nug,* and flaxseed. Finally, the hide is removed from the pot and
placed on skins on the ground to drain. For an hour or two every day
for several days, men work over the skin by trampling on it with their
feet or kneading it with their hands (Fig. 71). Each day after the skin
has been worked on, it is covered with leaves or with another skin to
keep it from drying out. Finally, the hide is soft enough to use, and, if
it has not been cut before soaking, it is now cut into the desired shapes,
and marrow, fat, or butter is rubbed on the leather as a preservative.
The process just described results in a chamoised leather which is
preserved by the decomposition products of the oil and fat; this
leather is, however, a product distinct from tanned leather, which is
made only by members of the tanner class.

The tanners begin their work by carrying out a process similar to
that just described, after which they proceed with their tanning
activities. The important local source of tannin is the bark of the
tree *bibisha (Cassia goratensis?),* though the bark of *k'eret (Osyris
abyssinica)* and the kernels of the fruit of *inkwoi (Ximenia* sp.) are also
used in some places. The bark and kernels are crushed in a mortar,
mixed with water, and rubbed on the skin while it is pegged to the
ground. After the skin dries for three or four days, it is reddish-brown
in color and ready for use. Today, tanners also buy tannin, called
k'elem or "color," which is imported from the Sudan, and which produces a skin brighter in color than one treated with local tannins.

PREPARATION OF SHEEP AND GOAT SKINS.—Though generally sheep
and goat skins receive less processing than cattle hides, differences in
the extent of the processing occur from place to place and also according to the use for which the skin is intended. The Gumis, for example,
as a rule merely peg their sheep and goat skins, hair side down, allow
them to dry for about one-half hour, then sprinkle salt and water on
them, and finally rub the skins with a smooth stone for one-half hour
or so. After further drying, the skins are ready for use. Among the
Amhara, the preparation of a sheep or goat skin may be either simple
or quite involved.

When the Amhara wish to make a skin into an apron or sitting pad,
they generally peg the skin to the ground, dry it for a day, smear it
with butter, work it a little, and use it. In preparing a goat skin bag,

by contrast, the processing is more complex. First, the farmer carefully slits the skin at the rear and peels it forward, leaving holes only at the legs, neck, and tail. Then he sews closed with cattle tendons all the openings except one, fills the skin with a mixture of urine and *imboy*, ties the opening shut, and allows the skin to stand for two or three days. Then he drains off the liquid and blows air into the skin through one of the legs. He beats the inflated skin with a stick for three to six hours, places it in the sun for a while, and then blows it up and beats it again. The skin bag is stretched under this treatment until it reaches the desired size. Then the farmer lets the air from the skin and soaks it in a pot in a mixture of crushed flaxseed, *nug*, and water. After it has soaked for two weeks, he hangs it up to drain and then kneads it until it is soft enough to use. From village to village in the Amhara country, the process of making the goatskin bag varies, but everywhere people soften the skin and then stretch it by blowing it up and beating it. In some places, they fill the skin with beans in the final process, and use it at home as a seat for several days before they finally use it for carrying grain to market or for other purposes. Besides the uses mentioned above, sheep and goat skins are used by scribes in making the parchment for church paintings and religious writings. In making parchment, the scribe stretches the processed skin taut between poles, then carefully scrapes it with a knife or a sharp adze, and rubs it with a stone and finally with a piece of pottery until it is smooth enough for use.

SADDLE MAKING

Though saddles are sometimes imported to the Northwest from Addis Ababa or elsewhere, usually they are made by local craftsmen known as *anat'i*, who do not comprise a separate class, though some of them are members of minority groups. Saddles are usually sold in the house of the saddle maker rather than in the marketplace.

SILVERWORKING

The traditional center of silverworking in Ethiopia is Axum, the political and religious heart of the ancient north Ethiopian state. Its pre-eminence in silverworking was probably encouraged by the presence there of foreign silversmiths who were brought in to work for the king and lords of the country. Following the decline of the Axumite Empire, the city maintained its position in silverworking because of its prestige as a center of Christianity, though in recent years the new capital, Addis Ababa, has become a major rival.

It appears likely that silverworking skills were introduced to Northwest Ethiopia in fairly recent times from Axum, for neither the Agow-speaking peoples nor the Negroes of the region know these skills, and even today the majority of silverworkers have learned, or claim to have learned, their trade in Axum. Moreover, most of the silver-workers of the Northwest are Amhara Christians, respected people who intermarry freely with other Amhara, though in other parts of Ethiopia silverworkers are commonly Moslems and members of craft classes. A silverworker commonly trains one of his sons in his job, but other sons usually follow other occupations. Though the number of silversmiths in the region is small, there are individual silversmiths in many villages, and in Gondar itself there are several who occupy small shops on back streets near the marketplace (Fig. 72).

The principal source of silver in the Northwest is the Maria Theresa dollar, which is melted down to make bracelets, ankle chains, earrings, charm necklaces, rings, and crosses of various forms, by the *cire perdue* process. The finished article is commonly boiled in a solution of lemon juice, water, and salt for an hour or so and then soaked in a cold solution of water and the crushed fruit of the shrub *indod*, be-fore receiving a final scrubbing with a metal brush. In making such things as bracelets, the smith pours molten silver into a *v*-bottomed metal form to produce a wire which can be bent readily into the desired shape. In addition to working silver, silversmiths commonly also work copper, though not usually other metals.

IRONWORKING

ANTIQUITY OF IRON AND IRONWORKING IN ETHIOPIA.—It has been suggested that iron may first have been introduced to northern Ethi-opia by Egyptian mercenaries in the third century B.C.[2] Though there is no historical or archeological confirmation of this suggestion, it is apparent that iron remained in short supply in much of the region for a long time after that. In the first century A.D., for example, iron was still traded to Ethiopia by Greek traders,[3] and in the sixth century A.D. the Axumites traded iron, of what origin it is not stated, to peoples to the south.[4] Moreover, when the Portuguese arrived in Ethiopia, iron bars circulated as money, a situation similar to that which existed in parts of Negro Africa until modern times, and which probably in-dicates a continued shortage of iron. Though we know no more about the time of introduction of ironworking techniques than of iron, I am inclined, in view of the present-day shortage of ironworkers among the Negroes of the Sudan border and among lowland Agow, toward

[2] Wainwright, 1945: 18.   [3] Schoff, 1912: 24.   [4] Cosmas, 1898: 52–53.

the position that ironworking was introduced to Ethiopia in fairly recent times.

SOURCES OF IRON.—It is clear from the historical record that in the past there were numerous small iron mines and a small-scale regional trade of iron ore in Ethiopia. James Bruce, for example, reported in the late eighteenth century that the mountains of Begemder were full of iron mines.[5] Nathaniel Pearce, who was in northern Ethiopia in the second decade of the nineteenth century, said that ironstone was plentiful in all parts of the country, but especially in Godjam, Wojjerat, Salora, and Bora.[6] The ironstone was treated by heating it in a fire until it was thoroughly hot, and then pounding it with large oval stones, the operation being repeated until it was free of all earth and suitable for use.[7] In the Gondar area even a generation ago, the ironworkers obtained some iron ore by trade from Armadchīo, and some from Shoa and Godjam provinces, where it was mined. Today blacksmiths no longer obtain their iron from domestic deposits, but instead use scrap iron, which they buy in the local marketplaces. The shift to the use of scrap iron apparently has taken place since Italian times, when it first became abundant, and parallels the virtual disappearance of the indigenous iron-smelting industry throughout Africa under the impact of European trade.[8]

SOCIAL POSITION AND OCCURRENCE OF BLACKSMITHS.—Northwest Ethiopia straddles the border between Negro Africa, where most peoples regard blacksmiths as members of an honored profession, and the Middle East, where blacksmiths commonly form separate lowly groups, whether classes, castes, or tribes.[9] Because of this, some groups of the Northwest, including all Semitic and most Cushitic groups, look down on smiths, and others, including the Gumis and Kumfel, respect them. The Agow of Sahalla belong to the Middle East in this regard, for they purchase their iron goods from members of an inferior Agow class of blacksmiths, called *t'ebīb,* who live in Lasta. Among the K'amant living in Ch'ilga, one of the centers of the K'amant people, ironwork is done by the Falasha, or Jews, who sell their goods either to people who come to their homes or in the marketplace, or travel here and there as itinerants. Similarly, among the Amhara and Jabartis, ironwork is generally done by the Falasha, one family of whom live in almost every village. Though I heard of an occasional Amhara blacksmith in the northern and western parts of highland Begemder and

---

[5] Bruce, 1790, III: 253–54.　　[6] Pearce, 1831, II: 202–3.
[7] Pearce, 1831, II: 203.　　[8] Tax, Eiseley, Rouse, and Voegelin, 1953: 18.
[9] Forschungsinstitut für Kulturmorphologie, Heft 2: 8.

Semyen, Amhara blacksmiths appear to be common only in the Debre Tabor area. There, they are called t'eyb, and, though they claim to have learned their skill from the Falasha, they do not intermarry with them. Like the Falasha, the t'eyb live in hamlets by themselves, the men making iron goods and the women pottery. There is also a group living in Amhara country at Ibinat (Ebbenat), east of Lake T'ana, who are called gafat, and who work iron, as well as making leather goods and pottery. Though these people speak only Amharic, they are said to be related to the Agow and may be ancient migrants from the Gafat district of Godjam.

Among the Gumis and Kumfel peoples of the western lowland, the blacksmiths do not belong either to a low class like the t'eyb or to an ethnic minority like the Falasha. Instead, they are respected men who practice their craft without stigma; indeed, in one village, the people laughed heartily at the very idea that men might be looked down upon because they were blacksmiths. Despite their high social position, there are few blacksmiths among the Gumis and Kumfel, and generally people buy a large share of their iron goods either from traders coming from the Sudan or from the Ethiopian highland. There are also few indigenous blacksmiths among the Baria and Cunama of western Eritrea, and among other tribes of the Sudan border. The shortage of blacksmiths among these peoples may mean either that ironworking techniques have come to them only in fairly recent times or that they have always been able to obtain their iron goods from others and have felt no need to increase their own production of them.

In most of Ethiopia, blacksmiths are feared as well as scorned. This fear is coupled with the belief that smiths possess supernatural powers, such as the ability to give the evil eye, to cause sickness, and to change themselves into the form of hyenas or other animals, and to attack and eat people. Because of this, blacksmiths have often been persecuted in the past, and once King Zara Yaik'ob (1434–68) went so far as to kill large numbers of them as sorcerers.[10] The fear of blacksmiths finds expression today in terms which are commonly applied to them, such as t'ebib, literally "one who has secret knowledge," and buda, "a sorcerer" or "evil spirit." It may be that the belief in the supernatural powers ascribed to blacksmiths originally sprang from the mystery which early man associated with the processes of metalworking. In Ethiopia even in modern times the ability of the smiths to change the shape of metal is believed to result from magical forces which can be offset by the use of certain charms. William Harris observed a century ago in Ethiopia, for example, the belief that the presence of any

10 Beckingham and Huntingford, 1954: 55.

Christian emblem or portion of scripture is sufficient to neutralize the ability of the god of metalworking to transform metal.[11]

TECHNIQUES OF IRONWORKING.—Today, the blacksmiths of the Northwest soften their scrap iron in a charcoal fire, then cut and hammer it into the desired shape. Though, in the last century, Galla smiths smelted iron in furnaces made of beaten clay,[12] I saw no furnaces of any kind in Begemder and Semyen. The charcoal used for softening iron is produced locally, sometimes by the smith himself and sometimes by other villagers, who either sell it to the smith or give it to him when they want some work done. Smiths are permitted to gather wood almost everywhere in the village, for their activities, in making and sharpening agricultural and other implements, are considered essential. Many types of wood are used for charcoal; near Gondar, charcoal made of oleaster and juniper wood is used to make a hot fire quickly, but charcoal made from *imbus* wood is considered to be better because it burns slowly.

The smith usually starts his work in the cool of early morning, and sometimes works for the entire day. He builds his charcoal fire in a circular pit about one foot deep and one or two feet in circumference (Fig. 73). The pipe-ends of two bellows are placed down one end of an iron pipe which extends underneath the charcoal fire. An apprentice operates the bellows, one in each hand, moving them rhythmically up and down. The iron to be worked is buried in the hot coals of the fire and the bellows are operated for five minutes or so until the iron is red-hot. Then the smith picks up the iron with long pincers and places it on an anvil [13] while he either pounds it himself or holds it while someone else pounds it with a heavy hammer. Often, two men or boys pound the iron in turn or with alternating blows. When the iron cools, it is replaced in the fire and reheated. To bend the end of a hoe or plow point, the smith stretches the iron between two rocks and pounds down on it. To make holes in an implement, he places a small iron plate with a hole in it on the anvil, places the red-hot implement over it, and then pounds it with a hammer and chisel until a hole is formed above the hole in the plate.

Ironwork done for fellow villagers is usually paid for in grain when

---

[11] Harris, 1844, II: 295.   [12] Huntingford, 1955: 71.

[13] Before Italian times, anvils were made of hard rock found in stream bottoms. In the past Kaffa and Galla smiths used flat slabs of basalt as anvils (Huntingford, 1955: 71, 131). Moreover, Galla smiths used pieces of flat basaltic stone for hammers (Huntingford, 1955: 71) and Kaffa smiths had hammers of wood for fine work (Huntingford, 1955: 131). Today the Somali smiths use an anvil "as often made of stone as of metal" (I. M. Lewis, 1955: 133). Near Gondar I have seen only steel anvils, apparently salvaged from the Italians.

there is no money available, the ironworker accepting whatever grain the farmer has in abundance. Sometimes payment is put off for three to six months until the harvest is in and grain can be spared.

Ironworking among the Falasha is not necessarily a hereditary trade. A blacksmith may learn his trade from his father or from a neighbor or relative. Among the Falasha, one son may become an ironworker and another a weaver, usually on the parents' decision. Smithing is not usually a man's only activity, for he combines his ironwork with farming and animal husbandry; he does not, however, commonly work silver.

Horn Craftsmanship

In the Amhara country of Ethiopia, there are respected Amhara horn craftsmen (*wanch'a antach*), who make cups of cattle horn, and who do not comprise a separate class. The center of horn craftsmanship is reputed to be Godjam Province, though a few horn craftsmen have moved to Begemder and Semyen, and others visit some of the southern towns of Begemder, such as Dengel Ber, as itinerants. Their cups, known in Amharic as *wanch'a*, are made in both small sizes for *arak'i* and larger sizes for mead and beer, and may be purchased from merchants in the large markets of Begemder and Semyen.

Boat Construction

Ethiopian Disinclination toward Navigation.—Most Ethiopians have traditionally been disinclined toward navigation.[14] This disinclination is found not only among plateau groups such as the Amhara, but to some extent even among coastal peoples such as the Danakil and Somali,[15] and has led foreign seafarers to dominate through all of history in carrying the produce of the region abroad. It is quite understandable that peoples of the plateau area show little interest in navigation, for most of the region is unsuited to boating; rivers, for example, in the rainy season are commonly wild torrents and in the dry season are shallow bodies of water that in many cases are ponded. An additional deterrent to inland navigation by the plateau Ethiopians may be their fear of disease in the low-lying river valleys where navigation is most feasible. Among the Kaffa of the south, the deficiency of boating skills is so complete that the people take no voyages on their rivers and streams, and their language contains hardly any words that pertain to navigation or to the sea.[16]

[14] A similar distrust of the sea in inland South Arabia hindered the military expansion of Islam in its early days (Hornell, 1946: 229–30).

[15] Paulitschke, 1893: 239.

[16] Forschungsinstitut für Kulturmorphologie, Heft 3: 16.

OCCURRENCE AND CONSTRUCTION OF VESSELS.—As might be expected, the people of the Northwest in the past had little skill in boat construction and were satisfied with crude craft or none at all. James Bruce described, for example, one inept crossing of the Blue Nile by the King of Abyssinia and his army, in which, though the river ran fast and deep and though many died in the passage, no skin floats were used, nor were rafts built except for a few women in the party.[17] Nathaniel Pearce reported a similar case of a caravan from Gondar which attempted in early July to cross the Tekezzay River, which was swollen with rain. The caravan lost five slaves, several donkeys, and a merchant before half of the party turned back to spend the season in Semyen. Nevertheless, Pearce added, messengers and people without loads crossed the river throughout the rainy season on rafts,[18] which apparently were very crudely constructed and quite dangerous craft.[19]

The situation in Northwest Ethiopia has changed very little in modern times, for there are still no native-built boats. Instead, rude temporary floats and rafts are made, where necessary, to navigate streams. In Sahalla, for example, the Agow sometimes make simple floats, called *gwena*, to cross the Tekezzay River. Such floats are made of several logs, each a few inches in diameter, lashed together with bark. The person wishing to cross the stream ties his goods on the float, and, holding onto it, he pushes and kicks his way across the river. David Buxton pictures some equally crude rafts on Lake Haik in Wollo Province in northeastern Ethiopia, made of bamboo and used by fishermen to balance on while spearing fish.[20] Inflated goatskins have been reported as used on one of the tributaries of the Tekezzay River at the northern tip of Begemder and Semyen,[21] and there have been scattered reports of rafts supported by inflated skins in use in several other parts of the country, including the Omo River in southern Ethiopia.[22] Another peculiar type of raft found in Ethiopia is the *jandi*, which was reported in use on the Blue Nile. This raft is made by taking a tanned oxhide with holes punched all round the edges, piling dry grass on it, and tying the whole together with hide ropes that pass through the holes. Goods are transported inside the *jandi*, whereas people squat on the top or let their legs dangle in the water; in either case, swimmers pull and push the *jandi* across the stream.[23] James Hornell believes that the *jandi* may possibly be a survival of military pontoons used by Greeks in the time of Xenophon and

[17] Bruce, 1790, III: 448–52.　　[18] Pearce, 1831, I: 254–55.
[19] Pearce, 1831, I: 239.　　[20] D. Buxton, 1950: Plate 50.
[21] Parkyns, 1868: 432.　　[22] Wylde, 1901: 442; Hornell, 1946: 32.
[23] Rey, 1927: 114–15.

Alexander the Great,[24] which it very much resembles. I heard of no coracles, earthen jars, or gourds used as floats or rafts in Northwest Ethiopia. Gourd rafts have, however, been reported in use in the Sudan on the River Rahad, a tributary of the Blue Nile,[25] and if the testimony of Francisco Alvarez is to be trusted, gourds, together with reeds and wood, were used in making rafts in the sixteenth century on Lake Haik in Ethiopia.[26]

Craft more complicated than rude rafts and floats have been reported in use in Northwest Ethiopia only along Lake T'ana. There, simple reed balsas, called in Amharic *tankwa* (Fig. 21), are made by the despised Wayt'o fishermen. The *tankwa* vary in size, but the largest are said to be capable of taking fifty mule loads, or a total weight of about two and three-quarters tons.[27] Some of these *tankwa* are sold by the Wayt'o to Amhara and Jabarti merchants who use them for lake trade, especially for carrying coffee from Zegie Peninsula at the south end of Lake T'ana to lakeshore market towns such as Delgī, where it is shipped by mule to the Sudan and elsewhere. The Wayt'o use *tankwa* for fishing with gill nets and hook and line near the shore, and on calm days they venture far out into the lake, crossing large expanses of open water.

Tankwa are made of papyrus, which grows here and there along the lakeshore, particularly at the south end of the lake. In that region, one village, Dengel Ber, present capital of Alefa *wereda*, is even named for the abundant growth of papyrus along the lakeshore nearby (*dengel*: papyrus, *ber*: gate; thus "papyrus gate"). Since the Wayt'o own no land, even along the lakeshore, they must get permission from Amhara landowners to collect papyrus, which is usually given to the Wayt'o in exchange for fish they supply to the landowners. To make the *tankwa,* the Wayt'o man ties together stalks of papyrus with rope made from the bark of the wild fig tree. A wooden stick runs the entire length on the bottom inside the *tankwa* to give the craft strength and rigidity. On the inside of the craft, mat-like bundles of reeds, *kofe,* overlap one another to form a rough deck. The boatman sits on another mat of reeds with his legs bent and a knee resting on each side of the unstable craft to help balance it. Since no attempt is made to waterproof the craft, the boatman usually becomes quite wet. He propels the *tankwa* with a stout pole ten to twelve feet long which is excellent for punting in the shallow waters near the lakeshore. The same pole, without any blade or other expansion at the end, is used to paddle in deep water, a practice similar to that followed by the

[24] Hornell, 1946: 21–22.   [25] Hornell, 1946: 37.
[26] Alvarez, 1881: 150.   [27] R. E. Cheesman, 1936: 121.

Tasmanian aborigines [28] in propelling their balsas at sea. Though the paddle would be far more satisfactory for use in deep water, it is not found on Lake T'ana, though it is reported in use on Lake Zwai. The *tankwa* generally becomes useless and is discarded when the material becomes saturated and rotten after a few weeks.

James Hornell has suggested that the *tankwa* of Lake T'ana is the "lineal descendant of the papyrus canoes used by the nobles of Ancient Egypt when fowling in the marshes, and by the fishermen of the eleventh dynasty when netting on the Nile." The *tankwa* and the ancient Egyptian craft have surprising similarities: "the use of papyrus as the material of construction, the pointed and curved ends, and, in particular, the filling up of the hollow between the sides to form a raised deck." [29] Today, reed rafts are no longer built in Lower Egypt, and in Upper Egypt they are seen only rarely as temporary craft for crossing canals or the Nile itself.[30] Balsas are still found today, however, among the Nilotic peoples of the Sudan, and in many places farther up the Nile, though in both regions dugout canoes are the most common means of water transport. Besides the Upper Nile, the Lake Chad area is the only other place in Africa where there is a variety of types of reed floats and reed balsas, though they occur sporadically elsewhere in Africa where marshy conditions make rafts the only practicable craft for navigating the shallow water.[31] In Ethiopia, balsas are found also on Lake Abaya in the Rift Valley.

Dugout canoes, which are in general use along the upper Nile and in rainforest Africa, are not found on the lakes and rivers of Northwest Ethiopia, though they have been reported in the Gumis country.[32] Plank boats, which were known to the Axumites from the Red Sea trade, and which spread up the Nile from Egypt into the Sudan and also occur in Negro Africa on Lakes Tanganyika, Victoria, and Edward, are not used either on the lakes or rivers of Ethiopia. Dhow-like plank boats, however, are used along the coastal margins of the region by the Somali, Danakil, and other peoples. In the Lake T'ana region, although on several occasions foreigners have built and used boats, the Ethiopians have remained aloof and disinterested. There is a record from the seventeenth century that an Egyptian *Abuna* made a boat on Lake T'ana, but that it was badly calked and sank on its first voyage.[33] One of the early Portuguese, too, made a little boat, calked it with "incense," and made several voyages on Lake T'ana.[34]

---

[28] Sollas, 1924: 117.　　　　[29] Hornell, 1946: 53.
[30] Hornell, 1946: 51.　　　　[31] Hornell, 1946: 54–55.
[32] Cerulli, 1956: 19.　　　　[33] Beckingham and Huntingford, 1954: 37.
[34] Beckingham and Huntingford, 1954: 37.

The Wayt'o, however, have chosen to ignore these and other examples, and continue to use their *tankwa,* which are readily built from the reeds that are available along the shore of the lake.

WEAVING OF COTTON AND WOOL

ANTIQUITY OF CLOTH IN ETHIOPIA.—It is known that cotton was cultivated and cloth made in ancient Meroe in the Sudan, and that cloth was imported to Ethiopia as early as the first century A.D.,[35] but it is not known when the practice of weaving cloth was first introduced to the land. There are, however, suggestions that cotton cloth replaced skin clothing only gradually. Thus, Duarte Barbosa, writing in the early sixteenth century about Red Sea trade, observed that the clothes of Abyssinians were made of hides, and that they had a law which permitted only certain families and ranks to wear cloth clothing; in the seventeenth century, on the other hand, both Jerome Lobo and Charles Jacques Poncet asserted that cloth clothing was used by common people and upper-class people.[36] Father Francisco Alvarez,[37] writing of Tigre in the early sixteenth century, mentioned that some women wore sheepskins, whereas others wore cloth clothing. Manoel de Almeida observed in the early seventeenth century that whereas Ethiopian men generally wore cotton clothing, cloth was less generally used by women. Poor women, he said, possessed only dressed oxskins or skins with the hair still on, but tanned and soft.[38] He noted further that in Dembya and Godjam, which at the time were strongholds of Agow-speaking peoples, many women who were not very poor wore skins.[39] James Bruce, in the late eighteenth century, commented that the clothing of the Agow of Godjam was all of hides.[40] Today, in southern Ethiopia among the Galla and Sidamo [41] and among the Konso,[42] women still wear skins, though men wear cotton clothes. The above observations, together with the fact that lengths of cloth have been used as a medium of exchange in Ethiopia, suggest that the use of cloth has spread across the country in fairly recent times. At first, it was used by people of wealth and high status, then by men generally, and finally by women; first it was used by Semiticized peoples, and later by unassimilated tribes such as the Agow. Today in the Northwest, cloth clothing is in general use, though there are suggestions, in the skin capes worn by boy deacons and other young boys, and in the leather aprons worn by some farmers in Semyen when working in the field, that animal skins served as garments not very

---

[35] Schoff, 1912: 24.   [36] Barbosa, 1866: 19.   [37] Alvarez, 1881: 92.
[38] Beckingham and Huntingford, 1954: 60.
[39] Beckingham and Huntingford, 1954: 60.
[40] Bruce, 1790, III: 739.   [41] Smeds, 1955: 14–15.   [42] Nowack, 1954: 41.

long ago. The practice of weaving, however, is still not of equal importance among all of the ethnic groups of the Northwest. There are, for example, no native weavers among the Agow of Sahalla, only a few among the Agow-speaking K'amant and they have learned their craft from the Falasha, and in the Gumis villages I visited, I encountered only one native weaver.

The position of men as innovators in the introduction of new styles of dress seems to be characteristic not only of Ethiopia, but of other parts of Africa, too. On the Central Plateau of Nigeria, for example, men of the pagan tribes have generally adopted cotton clothing, whereas many women still go naked except for a leafy branch worn front and back, fastened to a thong belt. Even when pagan women start wearing cloth skirts, they often continue to wear their leafy branches as undergarments.

WEAVING OF COTTON.—Weavers in Begemder and Semyen are always men. They do not comprise a separate class, though they are usually looked down upon because their work is considered to be beneath the dignity of strong men and warriors. Some of the weavers are Amhara and some Falasha, but most of them are Jabartis.

Some weavers are itinerants who travel to distant villages to set up their looms and weave, and now and then one encounters one of these weavers travelling by foot on rough back trails with his loom on his shoulder, on his way to a new location. Generally, however, the weaver remains at home, performing his work in a hut adjoining his house. If there are two or three weavers in a village, they commonly set up their huts nearby so that they can converse and pass the long hours of work more pleasantly. Within his grass-roofed hut, the weaver sits with his feet and legs in a pit in the dirt floor, facing his suspended, one-bar loom, and throwing his shuttles back and forth across the fabric, whose fibers are separated by simple, wooden shed-sticks. The fabric is wound onto the beam of the loom as it is finished.

If a person wants to have a weaver make the cloth for a *shamma,* the characteristic shawl worn by the Amhara, he must provide the weaver with thread. To do this, he buys raw cotton in the market, and some woman in his household then removes the seed by hand, spins the thread, and winds it into a form suitable for the weaver to use. Since in the Northwest cloth is not dyed, clothing is characteristically white (Fig. 75). If a colored pattern is desired in the fabric, imported colored thread is purchased and given to the weaver along with the white thread.

WOOL AND WOOL WEAVING.—In most parts of the Northwest, the wool of sheep is never cut. Where it is cut, it is generally used at home rather than sold. One exception occurs in Semyen, where some farmers shear their sheep and sell the wool in small quantities for use as pillow stuffing, some of which is traded as far as Gondar. Nevertheless, the idea of raising sheep commercially for the sale of wool does not exist there, nor are there any special breeds of sheep raised for their wool. Indeed, I heard from one European that he had introduced several wool sheep to Shoa from abroad and, when he offered to give them to an Amhara friend, the friend refused them, saying that everyone would laugh at him if he owned such strange-looking sheep.

I have never seen a weaver of wool at work in Northwest Ethiopia, though such men are found in the cold, high mountain areas of the region: on Guna Mountain east of Debre Tabor, and in the Beyeda district near Mt. Ras Dedjen. Even in these places, a village has only a few wool weavers, because their products cannot compete successfully with imported woolen goods traded from Addis Ababa. In Semyen, I was told that formerly there were many weavers who made rugs for the Empress Taitu, who died in 1918. Henry Salt,[43] too, early in the last century mentioned Semyen as a center of carpetmaking. Today, however, the Semyen weavers have turned to other activities and, though some still do a little weaving, they now make only rude black and brown blankets of undyed thread. Shepherd boys in the highland of Semyen, nevertheless, still commonly wear woolen skull caps (Fig. 57) which they weave while watching their animals in the field. Sometimes such caps may be found for sale in the market. Wool weaving in the Guna area has not suffered as complete a decline as in Semyen, and weavers there make ponchos, blankets, saddle blankets, rugs, and hats, some of quite good workmanship.

In both Semyen and Guna, the wool weavers are Amhara Christian men and do not comprise a special class. In Guna, these men are said to weave cotton, too.

POTTERY MAKING

Generally among the Amhara, Jabartis, Agow, and K'amant of the Northwest, all housewives make their own sun-dried containers of mud and dung, but they have neither knowledge of nor inclination toward making fired pottery, an activity which is considered undignified. Instead, among these groups, pots are commonly made by women of the Falasha ethnic minority, though near Debre Tabor there are Amhara potters of the low-class group known as *t'eyb,* and at Ibinat there are potters of the *gafat* group. The only instance I found of ordinary Amhara women making pots without losing status was at the

43 Salt, 1814: 426.

village of Wehinī (where the kings of Abyssinia imprisoned rival claimants to the throne; thus, the name *wehinī*, which in Amharic means "prison"), the last settlement on the road to Metemma before one reaches the country of the Gumis. It may be that the people of Wehinī have been influenced in this by the Gumis who, together with the Kumfel of the western lowland, regard pottery making as a respected occupation, and have neither a special potter class nor an ethnic minority such as the Falasha to do this work.

Generally potters work at home and sell their goods there or in a nearby market. There are, however, a few itinerant potters, such as certain poor Falasha of Mīnata (Mīlata?) village in Semyen who regularly, in groups of four or five, travel to the Agow village of Silaszī in Sahalla to practice their craft. In Silaszī, the Falasha potters live in a house which is set aside for them, staying for several months and sometimes even for as long as a year, until the local demand for pots is met; it is common, if there are no Falasha in residence at the moment, for the Agow to travel to Mīnata to buy pots.

Pots are made by the coil method, are decorated with incised designs, and are baked in an oxidizing fire out-of-doors (Fig. 74). Though such pots have a characteristic red color, they are sometimes blackened by being smoked over burning dung. Since the firing and blackening leave the pots porous, they must be waterproofed before use. This is generally done by the woman who purchases the pot; she applies oily substances such as milk, butter, and cottonseed to the inside of the pot after it has been heated. An alternate method of waterproofing in Ethiopia, reported by Simon Messing,[44] is resin-coating, the resin coming from plant materials. It is curious that the potters of the Northwest have adopted neither the kiln nor the potter's wheel, though both have been in use in nearby areas of the Middle East since ancient times, and that they have not taken over the use of slip, paint, glaze, or additions to the surface of the pots, other than those mentioned above.

BASKETRY

Basketmaking is the work of women, and every young girl learns this craft, for, when she marries, one of her responsibilities is to keep her household supplied with baskets. Baskets are not generally made for sale, although sometimes a Falasha woman who is entirely occupied with pottery making will trade her pots for baskets.

Generally, baskets are made, by coiling methods, of the fiber of wild plants, which are sometimes transplanted near the house for con-

[44] Messing, 1957a: 134.

venience. Among the common fiber plants are the grasses or sedges *sindodo* (*Pennisetum schimperi*), which is ordinarily used to form the coils, and *gramta* (*Cyperus fischerianus*) and *akirma* (*Chloris* spp.), which as a rule are split and used for wrapping coils and fastening them together. If a woman does not have enough material for making a basket, she may buy undyed grasses and sedges in the marketplace. In addition, it is common for women to purchase all of their colored *gramta* and *akirma*, for the dying of basket fibers is done only by Jabarti women. The common fiber dyes are purple, fuchsia, and blue-green, and they are imported from abroad. Among the other materials sometimes used in basketmaking are the root of the euphorbia, the root of the thorn acacia, and the inside of the leaf of the plant *biska*. It is usual to dry the fiber plants in the sun, and to store them in the rafters of the house until they are needed.

In making a basket, the woman first splits the stalks, if necessary, and soaks them strip by strip in water to make them flexible enough to work. Then she constructs the basket using her hands and one tool, a metal punch made by Falasha ironworkers. The punch is used to make the holes through the last coil completed so that a strip of fiber can be threaded through and wrapped around the top coil to secure it in place. Some women say that they think out the colors and designs of their baskets before they start work on them. Others say that they work in the design as they make the basket. Most of them agree, however, that for a basket they want to be especially good, they must plan the size, shape, designs, and colors in advance.

In Northwest Ethiopia, except among the Gumis, people have numerous baskets in a variety of colors and in many forms. There are, for example, small circular baskets with tight-fitting peaked covers which are used for storing small miscellaneous items. Larger circular baskets are used for storing cotton and thread and sometimes for temporarily storing small amounts of grain. Sometimes a woman will have a large circular basket covered with leather, and provided with one leather thong for fastening the lid down and another to serve as a carrying strap. Such baskets are often used by travellers for carrying food or clothing, and locally for carrying food from the house to the field at the times of sowing and harvest. Most houses also have a large basket, about fifty centimeters in diameter and flared at the top, which is used as a general carryall. Such baskets are used to carry grain from place to place in the house, to hold freshly ground flour, to hold freshly cut meat, and sometimes to carry or to store mud. Occasionally, woven grass containers are also made to protect horn cups and glass drinking bottles at home and when travelling.

Another common basketry item is the serving tray used for the flat bread *injera*. The *injera* basket has a circular base wider at the bottom (about thirty centimeters) than at the top (about seventeen centimeters), and is usually about thirty centimeters high. A flat circular tray (fifty centimeters in diameter) is attached to the top of the base. At mealtime, this basket, piled with *injera,* is set on the floor in the living section of the house along with a pot of hot stew. The diners squat around the tray, breaking off pieces of flat bread, dipping them into the stew and eating them. Such serving trays are usually provided with woven covers, presumably to keep the flat bread warm. Though almost all Ethiopian basketry is skillfully executed and attractive, basketmakers lavish most care on their serving trays, which frequently have beautiful patterns worked into them, generally by weaving together grasses of different colors, and less commonly by variation in the weaving.

Housewives usually also have flat basketry trays to toss grain up and down to allow the wind to blow away the last bit of chaff. These trays are sometimes bound with leather around their edges to strengthen them. Another common household item is a circular sieve made of a coiled frame and a screen of stiff, straight pieces of grass placed very close together and tied in such a way that small spaces occur at regular intervals. The sieves are used to remove dirt and coarse pieces in sifting flour.

Another common basketry item found in the highland is a milk container made of coiled grass. Such containers are gourd-shaped, are about twenty-five centimeters high, and have a diameter of about ten centimeters. Before the basketry milk containers are used, they are smoked. It is said that these containers leak a little at first, but that the deposit of fat from the milk soon prevents leakage.

Though coiled baskets, such as those mentioned above, are found among most peoples of the Northwest, they do not occur among the Gumis. Instead, the Gumis have twined baskets, which are made from bamboo strips by men. Twined baskets are also found, in addition to coiled baskets, in a few places in the highland, near Gondar where men make large, shallow storage baskets of stiff material such as the branches of the shrub *lenquata* (*Grewia ferruginea*), and in the Fart'a area of Gaïnt, from which they are shipped to the Debre Tabor market for sale.

Chapter XI

Markets and Trading

Trade in the Past

TRADE IN AXUM.—Axum's importance in trade was based on its geographical position between the interior Cushitic and Negro tribes and the maritime traders of the classical world. Already in the third century B.C.,[1] with the spread of the influence of the Ptolemies south along the Red Sea, Axum was drawn into extensive foreign trade. One trading post was established by the Ptolemies on the Red Sea coast at Adulis, near present-day Massawa, and another, nearer the source of supply, in the plateau at Cohaitu (Coloe), not far from the present town of Adi Caieh. Though Axum apparently also maintained overland commercial ties with the Sudanese kingdoms of Napata and Meroe and, through them, with Egypt, these ties must have been far less important than those with the maritime traders.

Most of Axum's imports were finished goods: cotton and linen cloth, cloaks, mantles, and robes, glass, brass, copper, iron and steel, axes, adzes, and swords, copper drinking cups, coins, a little wine, olive oil, and, for the king, gold and silver plate.[2] These goods came not only from Arabia and Egypt, but also from as far away as Syria, Italy, Ceylon, and India. Its export goods, on the contrary, were raw materials: ivory, rhinoceros horn, tortoise shell, gold, and slaves, which seem to have come not from Axum itself, but from south and west of the Axumite dominions. Though much of the goods from the tribes to the south and west must have been passed from one trader to another before finally reaching Axum, there were also armed trading expeditions, organized by the lords of Axum, which penetrated country far to the south. Cosmas, writing in the sixth century, described such a trading expedition, organized by the King of Axum with the coöperation of the governor of the Agow, which reached an area to the south known as Sasu, a land of frankincense and gold. The traders, who numbered more than five hundred, brought with

---

[1] Longrigg, 1945: 12.   [2] Schoff, 1912: 24.

them oxen, salt, and iron for trade. When they arrived at their destination, they built large compounds fenced with thorns, and then exchanged their goods by "silent trade," without coming into direct contact with the natives, who brought gold to the edge of the compound.[3] The traders remained in the country only for several days until their trade goods were gone, though the entire expedition took a total of six months.

The trade of Axum was seriously disorganized by the Persians' seventh-century conquest of the ports along the African coast. The rise of Islamic power later in the seventh century and the expansion of the Beja nomads (see Map 3) forced most of the foreign traders to flee the coastal towns, made more tenuous Axum's economic and cultural ties with the civilized world, and contributed to its decline as a great power.

TRADE IN ABYSSINIA.—In pre-modern times, Abyssinia continued to occupy a trade position similar to that of Axum: primarily as an intermediary exchanging the raw materials of the interior peoples for the manufactured goods of the maritime traders. A sixteenth-century account of the Red Sea trade indicates that there were several ports serving the area that today comprises Ethiopia: Mogadisho and Afuni on the Indian Ocean, and Met, Berbera, Zeila, Dalaqua (Dahlak Islands?), and Massawa on the Red Sea coast.[4] Most of the trade of northern Ethiopia, including that of the Kingdom of Abyssinia, apparently passed through Massawa. There, where the plateau is closest to the seacoast, traders had to cross only a narrow coastal plain, thus limiting the unpleasantness of high temperatures, the danger of malaria, and the likelihood of armed raids by the warlike pastoralists who preyed on caravans passing through their semidesert homeland. Among the raw materials shipped out were gold, rhinoceros horn, ivory, civet, coffee, honey and wax, spices, hides and skins, and mules. Trade contacts of Abyssinia with the Sudan were perhaps more extensive than in Axumite days, for there developed in highland Abyssinia a demand for cotton as cotton clothing became generally accepted. Indeed, at the close of the seventeenth century, the King of Sennar even maintained a customs officer in the highland at Ch'ilga to collect duty on cotton imported from the neighboring lowland regions, a duty which was divided evenly between the King of Sennar and the King of Abyssinia.[5]

The Red Sea ports serving Abyssinia were usually under the political control of Moslems, who discriminated against Christian merchants from the highland. Sometimes the Christians were simply made to feel unwelcome or were taxed more heavily than Moslems. At other times,

[3] Rawlinson, 1910, I: 363.   [4] Barbosa, 1866: 16–18.   [5] Foster, 1949: 113.

they were robbed and killed or sold into slavery. This inequitable treatment of Christian merchants provided Abyssinian Moslems an opportunity to dominate the trade to the coast, which they soon did. This gave them a great advantage in the domestic trade as well, for they were more familiar with foreign trade goods and could obtain them directly from the coastal traders, and so in time, they came to dominate the domestic trade. Considerable numbers of them settled in the market towns in the Christian parts of the country, either selling directly to the public or acting as personal agents for wealthy Christians. Though most of the Moslem merchants were natives or Jabartis, there were also Moslems from Arabia, Morocco, Tunisia, Libya, Egypt, Turkey, Ormuz, and India.

Despite their importance in the domestic economy, Moslem merchants were despised and treated with contempt by important Abyssinian Christians, both for their religion and for their occupation, which was regarded as undignified. Because of this double stigma, they paid dearly for the privilege of trading in the country. Sometimes, for example, they had to pay tribute or make gifts to local lords and to the king, and sometimes the lord or king took gold or other goods from them by force or threat of force. Usually, too, Moslems were made to occupy separate quarters in market towns, a situation that they may have liked, for their quarters were usually in inconspicuous locations on low ground.

Trading was a hazardous occupation in Abyssinia, and wealthy merchants travelled with large numbers of armed men who were as much accustomed to hard fighting as were soldiers. In crossing the lowland from the Red Sea ports, the danger was from ambush by Galla, Danakil, and other pastoral groups who did not hesitate to slaughter everyone in the caravan. Along the Sudan border in Wolk'aīt, bands of Negroes of up to one thousand men often ambushed caravans, sometimes surprising and slaughtering an entire group.[6] To the south, the valley of the Blue Nile was particularly dangerous, for hundreds of fierce Galla horsemen often lay in wait there for merchant caravans and frequently cut off and destroyed them almost to a man.[7] Even in the highland, there was considerable danger, for political conditions were usually uncertain and merchant caravans were a great temptation for the many Abyssinian rebels and bandits.

In addition to the burdens and risks of trade in Abyssinia just mentioned, there were onerous tariffs and tolls both on imports and on domestic trade. Since the Christians did not control the ports along

[6] Plowden, 1868: 130–31.   [7] Plowden, 1868: 129.

the Red Sea coast or the lowland toward the Sudan, they established customs posts in the highland along the principal trade routes, where the merchants paid their tariffs. Such posts were usually found in mountain passes that caravans could not readily avoid. The revenue from a customs post might go to the king, to the local lord, or to the customs collectors themselves. Almeida [8] reported that in the seventeenth century the king reserved for himself the tariffs collected at the customs post at Lamalmon, but allowed subsidiary nobles to control other posts in the country. In James Bruce's time, tax collectors paid their superiors for the right to collect duties,[9] and then established posts where they wished. Bruce [10] in 1769 encountered five such customs posts between Massawa and Adowa. In Walter Plowden's time, a *nagadi ras* ("chief of merchants") was appointed for each of six towns in Ethiopia. The *nagadi ras* paid money to the great chiefs, and then collected taxes not only at his principal post but at additional minor posts that he established.[11] Apparently there were no fixed rates of duty at these posts. The Reverend Samuel Gobat, for example, was asked fifty dollars for sixty copies of the Bible, but after protest was permitted to pass without charge.[12] If merchants refused to pay the sum requested by the tariff collectors, however, they might be delayed for months [13] or even robbed of everything they owned.

Sometimes the impediment of tariffs and local customs posts so restricted trade that the king was forced to limit them. King Īyasu the First (1682–1706), for example, established legal tariffs and customs posts and vowed that those who violated them would be severely punished.[14] Nevertheless, at most times duties were so unreasonable that they must have seriously hindered trade. The plight of the merchant in Ethiopia was vividly described by Walter Plowden in the nineteenth century, when he said that after the merchant had paid his tolls and warded off all human enemies, he still had to overcome the difficulties of raging floods, steep mountains, bad roads, and wild animals that destroyed his mules.[15] It is not surprising that Ethiopia has remained backward and poor when one examines the hindrances to what elsewhere is considered normal trade. It is a tribute to generations of resourceful, patient, and long-suffering merchants that trade has been carried on as well as it has been. Though interior customs posts continued until the Italian occupation, fortunately they no longer exist today.

[8] Beckingham and Huntingford, 1954: 87. [9] Bruce, 1790, III: 105.
[10] Bruce, 1790, III: 105. [11] Plowden, 1868: 130.
[12] Gobat, 1834: 99. [13] Bruce, 1790, III: 105.
[14] Beckingham and Huntingford, 1954: 87. [15] Plowden, 1868: 131.

PRESENT-DAY MARKETS IN THE NORTHWEST

IMPORTANCE AND DISTRIBUTION OF MARKETS.—A system of markets, widely scattered across the Northwest, is the foundation of trade today, the means by which most locally produced goods are exchanged, the means of distributing to consumers goods from distant places, and the means of assembling surplus local products for shipment to places where they are in demand. Most villagers are far from any settlement where there is a shop, so that without markets they would be able to exchange goods only with their neighbors or perhaps with peddlers or with travelling merchants who pass by. Without markets, merchants could not accumulate quantities of goods for shipment except at great expense, for they would have to approach many villagers in order to gather together even a small amount of grain or produce. Today, even with help from local officials, grain is often difficult to purchase from individuals in the back country; the traveller must make use, instead, of local markets or he must carry sufficient food and supplies with him for his journey, for rural folk in Ethiopia are not accustomed to dealing outside of the market system.

The greatest number of markets is found in the middle highland, across which trade routes run, which has the greatest variety of agricultural products, and which enjoys a position intermediate between the lowland and cold highland, each of which has a different assemblage of cultivated plants. Markets appear to be absent in the country of the Gumis, Kumfel, and Sahalla Agow, a situation which has never been explained, but which may be partly due to the inability of the lowland to attract much trade from the highland because of the fear highlanders have of venturing into the lowland. Another factor that may have contributed to the failure to establish lowland markets is that lowland regions have been frequented by bandits who prey on merchants and travellers, thus discouraging trade. A third possibility is that the market system is a relatively recent innovation in the Northwest and that, because the highland is the most advanced part of the country and the principal avenue of cultural introduction, the markets would tend to have been established there.

CHARACTERISTICS OF THE MARKET.—Most markets in Northwest Ethiopia are held regularly once a week, on any day except Sunday.[16] Saturday is by far the most common market day, though Monday, Tuesday, and Thursday are also popular. Several important towns,

---

[16] R. E. Cheesman (1936: 55) reports that a large market is held on Sunday outside of Addis Ababa, but that such disregard for the Sabbath is exceptional.

such as Gondar, Azezo, Debre Tabor, and Nifas Moch'a, have daily markets as well, but in every case the daily market is much smaller than the weekly market, and attracts mostly local people. Because it requires so much less space, the daily market may be held in a different location, often nearer the center of town than the weekly market. The daily town markets and the small back-country weekly markets on the average have perhaps two hundred people attending, whereas the most popular of the Gondar markets attract as many as seven thousand people (Fig. 75). Though marketplaces are usually situated in or near villages or towns, in some cases a market is in a spot of no apparent importance, though at an earlier date there might have been a settlement nearby or an important trail junction which has since lost its significance. Markets, however, do not necessarily remain fixed in one spot over a long period of time. They may, for example, be moved by government order, as was the case with the K'olediba market after the Dembya epidemic of 1953–54, or they may be abandoned and later reopened at a nearby place; in such cases, either the name of a market may be changed or the former name may move with it.

Markets are held in the open, and vendors generally have neither tables nor chairs, but sit on the ground (Figs. 77 and 79), or on the simple raised stone steps or the earth mounds which are found in most marketplaces. Women, it is true, often hold umbrellas for protection from the sun, but men have only hats or shawls with which to shield themselves. The only shelters found are built by occasional Arab merchants to protect their wares. The markets of the Northwest are roughly divided into sections in which different types of goods are sold. This division is often hardly apparent in small markets, but very obvious in the large ones such as the Gondar weekly market. Thus, in the latter market there is a section in which men sell iron goods and scrap iron, another section for cloth, clothing, and thread, and a few rows of leatherworkers selling skin bags, tanned skins, and other goods. Some distance away sit the wives of the leatherworkers covering baskets brought to them by customers. To one side mules, horses, donkeys, sheep, goats, and cattle stand dumbly while buyers and sellers discuss their merits. Wood, sold by women, is stacked neatly in bundles to one side, while the huge center section of the market is occupied by vendors, mostly women, selling food and spices in great variety. In small groups nearby are the Arab merchants with their imported odds and ends of trinkets, spices, coffee, razor blades, turmeric, and so forth, and men selling silver crosses and other jewelry.

The Gondar market and most other markets of Begemder and Semyen have no baskets or pots for sale, though basket grasses are a common item.

The process of selling goods in the market is often a friendly affair, with neighbors and family grouped around their respective produce, patiently awaiting purchasers. There is none of the loud competition for customers found in other parts of the world. Rather, the buyer wanders unhindered about the market pricing and selecting his purchases. Sometimes a small group forms around a buyer, usually a foreigner or stranger, as he discusses the price and merits of the merchandise. Spectators and other vendors may join in, too, for everyone enjoys the repartee of negotiating a sale to such a person. Once the purchase has been made, commonly at more than double the normal price, the group of spectators melts away as fast as it was formed.

TRADE OF AN IMPORTANT REGIONAL MARKET: DEBRE TABOR.—To illustrate the nature of goods exchanged and the extent of the trade contacts of a large regional market, let us consider the weekly market of Debre Tabor which dominates the trade of the southeastern part of the province and attracts, at its largest, two or three thousand people. The list of goods I found in this market on a Saturday in November, 1953 (Table 5) is not complete, but it shows clearly the

TABLE 5

Types of Goods Found in Highland Markets

	Debre Tabor Weekly Saturday Nov. 2, 1953	Debre Tabor Daily Oct. 28, 1953
Cereals and Oilseeds		
sorghum	x	
maize	x	x
barley	x	x
wheat	x	x
finger millet	x	x
t'eff	x	x
nug	x	x
flaxseed	x	x
Pulses		
green peas	x	x
horse beans		x
chick peas	x	x
lentils	x	x

	Debre Tabor Weekly Saturday Nov. 2, 1953	Debre Tabor Daily Oct. 28, 1953
Vegetables (potatoes)	x	x
Spices, Stimulants, and Aromatics		
aromatic flowers		x
fenugreek	x	x
t'enadam	x	
cayenne pepper	x	
salt	x	
shallots	x	x
garlic	x	x
basil	x	
ginger	x	
sprouted barley	x	
gesho	x	x
cumin	x	
coffee	x	x
leaf mustard seed	x	
black mustard seed	x	
incense	x	
coriander	x	
turmeric	x	
Animals and Animal Products		
eggs	x	x
butter	x	x
chickens	x	x
sheep and goats	x	
donkeys, horses, and mules	x	
milk		x
Household Goods		
pottery	x	
basket grasses	x	
straw mats	x	
indod, a detergent	x	
soap	x	
firewood		x
Cotton Goods		
cotton	x	
cotton thread	x	
cotton cloth	x	
clothes	x	

	Debre Tabor Weekly Saturday Nov. 2, 1953	Debre Tabor Daily Oct. 28, 1953
Woolen Goods		
woolen thread	x	
wool saddle blankets	x	
Leather Goods	x	
Metal Work		
local iron goods	x	
razor blades	x	
needles	x	
silverwork	x	

nature of the agricultural produce of the region in its great variety of cereals and pulses, oilseeds, spices, stimulants, and aromatics, and its deficiency of green vegetables, fruits, and root crops. It shows, too, an overwhelming emphasis on domestic products, with only a scattering of imported goods such as razor blades, needles, thread, cloth, soap, and spices. Most of the domestic goods originated in villages within three days journey of Debre Tabor (see Map 7). Others, however, came from greater distances: cotton from Belessa (four days) and Wolk'aīt (eleven days), spices from Dembya (four days), silverwork from Dessie (nine to ten days), salt from the Danakil Depression (about two weeks), and coffee from southern Ethiopia (about one month).

Though most of the goods in the market were sold by villagers or local traders, there were also long-distance traders working either for themselves or for wealthy merchants. Such traders operate mainly in the dry season from mid-November to June, carrying goods by mule and donkey caravan principally to and from Gondar, Dessie, and Godjam. In Debre Tabor, many camp in a large grassy field not far from the center of the town near the town spring. Their animals graze in the field nearby by day, and are tied and guarded from hyenas at night, for hyenas are especially numerous and bold at Debre Tabor. Such traders carry a variety of goods to Debre Tabor, their nature at any one time being determined largely by local supply and demand. Among the goods they carry out are hides and skins, grain, oilseeds, butter, and honey, some of which is used domestically and some of which finds its way into the world market.

Debre Tabor could be reached by motor road in Italian times from Dessie and Gondar. Today, however, the old Italian roads have fallen into disrepair; the bridges were either destroyed by the Italians in their retreat before the British liberators or were permitted subsequently to fall into ruin. There are now more than twenty fords be-

PLACES OF ORIGIN OF NATIVE PRODUCTS
IN THE WEEKLY MARKET, DEBRE TABOR,
NOVEMBER 2, 1953

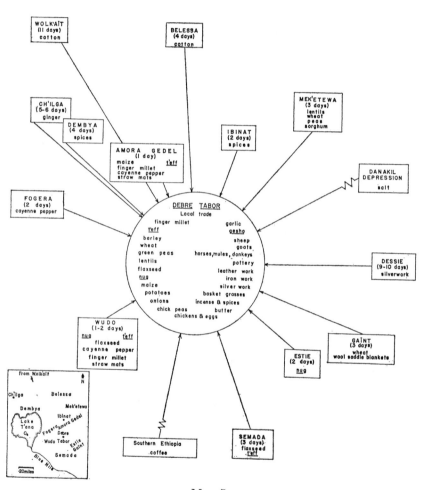

MAP 7

tween Gondar and Debre Tabor across streams which once were bridged. In many places where bridges have been destroyed, there is no apparent indication that a detour and ford are necessary and a driver unfamiliar with the road may approach the empty, yawning span before he realizes that he has made a mistake and backs up to look for the ford which is somewhere nearby. Such fords are shallow in the dry season, only a foot or so in depth, and the bottoms are rocky and solid. The approaches, however, may be steep or strewn with boulders and roots so that one must be careful. Unfortunately, the Imperial Highway Authority has no funds available to maintain the Debre Tabor road, let alone to rebuild it. If it were not for makeshift repairs done by mission people and others who use it, the road would be completely impassable. As it is, the road is impassable eastward from Nifas Moch'a to Dessie, and westward to Gondar it is passable only in the dry season starting about September. Very few commercial vehicles make the trip from Gondar to Debre Tabor, however; in November, when we returned to Gondar from Debre Tabor, for example, we met the first truck going in. It was hauling supplies for the Seventh-Day Adventist Mission at a cost of about four dollars U.S. per quintal. In past years, the road proved to be so rough that truckers were discouraged from making the trip, for one breakdown in the back country could cost the owner dearly. Thus, the Debre Tabor market, despite its importance, remains largely what it always has been: a regional market center to and from which goods are carried largely by humans, donkeys, horses, and mules.

TRADE IN THE BACK COUNTRY.—Most country people away from such large regional markets as Debre Tabor continue to trade, as they have in the past, in small markets which may be as far as a week from their homes, exchanging surplus produce for the few necessities or luxuries that they cannot obtain in their own villages. To illustrate the nature of commerce in the back country, let us consider the case of Silaszī, an isolated Agow settlement at about 5,500 feet elevation in Sahalla, not far from the Tekezzay River. Since the people of Silaszī have no market in their village, they must travel long distances to exchange their goods. As can be seen on the accompanying map (Map 8), the markets they depend on are in the highland. The nearest market town, Islamgie, is a two-day walk away and the farthest market they normally visit, Makalle, is a seven-day walk. Because of the effort involved, a Silaszī family usually goes to market only about once a month, though in the rainy season when the streams become rushing torrents, many villagers do not go to market for the entire season. People going to market usually carry goods of such small value that the trip seems scarcely worth the effort (Fig. 76). It should be noted, however, that in Silaszī, as in many other parts of the world, it is not the exchange of goods alone that is important, but the pleasures of com-

MAP 8

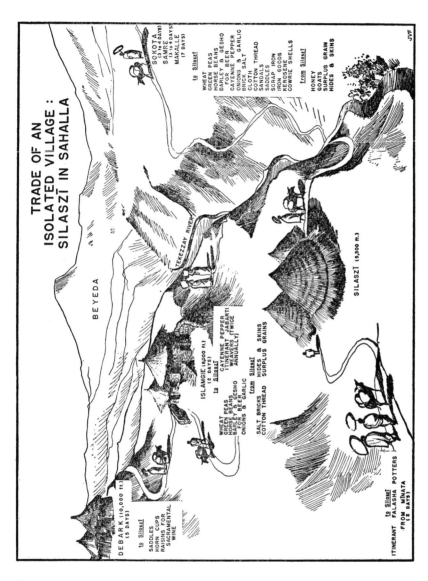

TRADE OF AN
ISOLATED VILLAGE :
SILASZĪ IN SAHALLA

BEYEDA

TEKEZZĀY RIVER

SILASZĪ (5,500 ft.)

DEBARK (10,000 ft.)
(5 DAYS)

to Silaszĭ

SADDLES
HORN CUPS
RAISINS FOR
SACRAMENTAL
WINE

ISLAMGIE (8000 ft.)
(2 DAYS)

to Silaszĭ

WHEAT PEAS
HORSE BEANS
BARLEY & GESHO
FOR BEER
ONIONS & GARLIC

from Silaszĭ

HIDES & SKINS
SURPLUS GRAINS

CAYENNE PEPPER
ITINERANT 'JABARTI
WEAVERS (TWICE
ANNUALLY)

SALT BRICKS
COTTON THREAD

to Silaszĭ
ITINERANT FALASHA POTTERS
FROM MĬNATA
(2 DAYS)

SOKOTA
(3 to 4 DAYS)
SAMRE
(3 to 4 DAYS)
MAKALLE
(7 DAYS)

to Silaszĭ

WHEAT
GREEN PEAS
HORSE BEANS
BARLEY & GESHO
FOR BEER
CAYENNE PEPPER
ONIONS & GARLIC
BRICK SALT
CLOTH
COTTON THREAD
SANDALS
SADDLES
SCRAP IRON
IRON GOODS
KEROSENE
COWRIE SHELLS

from Silaszĭ

HONEY
GOATS
SURPLUS GRAIN
HIDES & SKINS

JVF

panionship along the way, the visiting with relatives and friends, the exchange of gossip, and the gathering of news about the outside world. The *joie de vivre* of Ethiopian travellers is an emotion that contrasts sharply with the goal-oriented, sometimes frantically hurried travel of foreign visitors to the country.

Since the region around Silaszī is poor, dry scrub country, it provides little surplus produce other than honey and goats and occasionally hides and skins (see Map 8). The people trade most of their honey and goats in the markets of Samre, Sokota, and Makalle to the east, where they get higher prices than in the markets to the west. From the former markets, they get salt and cotton thread, imported and locally made cloth, scrap iron and iron goods, kerosene, men's sandals locally made from old tires, and cowrie shells, as well as agricultural produce. The people of Silaszī, in turn, exchange the salt and cotton thread in the Islamgie market to the west and sometimes in other small markets in Beyeda and Belessa for dyed and undyed basket grasses, imported Italian sickles, coffee from southern Ethiopia, barley, *gesho* for beermaking, cayenne pepper, onions, garlic and other spices, peas, horse beans, and wheat which is important in the ceremonies of the Christian church at Silaszī. Horn cups from Godjam, saddles, and the raisins imported from Yemen for making sacramental wine are traded either directly from Debark or by way of Islamgie.

Itinerant Falasha women potters come to Silaszī from Minata, a Falasha settlement about two days to the southwest, to make pots for the Agow women who never make pots themselves. Such potters usually come in groups of four or five accompanied by a man. They live in a special house reserved for them, staying for several months and even for as long as a year. While they are in Silaszī, people from the country nearby go to them to order pots. If there are no Falasha potters living at Silaszī, women go to Minata to buy pots. Similarly, itinerant Moslem weavers visit Silaszī to weave *shammas* for the local people, remaining perhaps several weeks until their work is finished. Besides buying iron goods from blacksmiths in the market, the Agow of Sahalla are served by Agow ironworkers from Sokota who visit Silaszī once a year, usually in February or March, and, using scrap iron supplied by the villagers, make hoes, plowshares, and other implements. Such ironworkers build shelters outside of the village and camp there for from two weeks to a month before moving on.

Such is the simple pattern of trade in Silaszī. The village produces little that is reflected in the economic statistics compiled by the Ministry of Commerce and Industry in Addis Ababa. Perhaps a few skins and a little beeswax eventually reach the world market, but nothing

more. Just as Silaszī gives little to the world, so it takes little, remaining
steadfast to the ancient Ethiopian pattern of near self-sufficiency.

TRADE ROUTES AND PRACTICES

TRADITIONAL TRADE ROUTES.—The mountainous character of the
country, the many factors complicating the local flow of trade to and
fro, and the shifting of trade routes according to political conditions
in the country, have led to an extremely complex system of trade
routes which has not been unravelled in all its intricacy even today.
Traditionally, the trade routes of Gondar, the main center of commerce in the region, have been to the west to the Sudan by way of
Metemma, to the south along either side of Lake T'ana to Godjam
Province and southern Ethiopia, to the east to Debre Tabor and
Dessie and thence to the coast or to Shoa Province, to the northwest to
Om Ager and the Sudan, and to the northeast across the Tekezzay
River to Tigre Province and Eritrea. These trade routes, which are
still used by caravans today, are rough trails, but are quite satisfactory
for the men and pack animals that use them.

Apparently the regional governors and village chiefs bear the re-
sponsibility for maintaining trails, but they generally work on them
only when ordered to do so by higher authorities, who, unfortunately,
live far away in the political capitals and never see the trails in the
back country. It is a characteristic of Ethiopia that when His Majesty
plans to make a trip, people along the route he is to take are put to
work improving the route, so that for the short time he travels over
it, it is in far better condition than beforehand and afterwards when
it is permitted to lapse into its previous condition of neglect. The
custom of improving roads before the expected visit of a higher
authority extends down at least to the level of Governor-General of a
province. Such improvements, unfortunately, remain isolated and
temporary expedients rather than permanent, well-thought-out plans.
Merchants, of course, must sometimes improve a trail to make it passable, but this is an effort they make only when absolutely necessary.

TRADE ALONG THE SUDAN BORDER.—In the past, the caravan route
from Gondar to Sennar and Khartoum was an important one, and the
border town of Metemma was a way station of considerable significance
with a great market where Ethiopian and Sudanese merchants mingled to exchange highland coffee for Sudanese cotton. In Metemma a
century ago, for example, Sir Samuel Baker observed thousands of
bales of cotton and rows of sheds occupied by coffee merchants, and a
confusion of transport camels, mules, and donkeys.[17] The accessi-

[17] Baker, 1867: 503.

bility of the place is shown by the fact that the Sheikh of Metemma
and the people living there were "tukroories," migrants from Darfur
and West Africa who were loyal to the King of Abyssinia but who
were also forced to pay tribute to the Egyptians who then controlled
the northern Sudan.

Since the last century, Metemma has lost its position as a great
emporium. Its decline was brought about principally by two develop-
ments: 1) the establishment of railways in the Sudan which opened
new and more profitable markets for Sudanese cotton and also enabled
the Sudanese to obtain coffee from abroad at low prices, and 2) the
construction of motor and rail routes from highland Ethiopia to the
Red Sea, which directed more Ethiopian trade in that direction. Today, while a few goods are still imported and exported at Metemma
(coffee from the highland; British cloth; Japanese and Indian cotton
thread; tea, soap, kerosene, and copper arak'i pots from various foreign
sources), the trade is a thin trickle compared to that of former times.
Metemma has not only lost its position as a great international trading
center, but it has declined as a regional trading center to the point
where it has few shops and no market. This decline has been encouraged by the abandonment by the Sudan Government of their
border post nearby at Gallabat and their establishment of a new
administrative center back from the border, and by the maintenance
of high tariffs by the Ethiopians. The high tariffs have led to high
prices for imported goods in Metemma, which, in turn, stimulated
organized smuggling and encouraged the frontier people to cross the
ill-defined border into the Sudan to trade.

Though Metemma has lost its position as a trade center, the border
country itself continues to be an important source of cotton for the
highland as well as supplying some sorghum, goatskins, and honey. At
the village of Bodella south of Metemma, we saw more merchants
than we had ever seen before in one place, all trying to purchase
cotton from the villagers who were harvesting it at a leisurely pace.
Most of the merchants were highlanders from Gondar, Alefa, Serak'o,
and K'wara. Such merchants camp in Gumis villages sometimes for
weeks until they can obtain enough cotton by barter or by purchase to
load their animals for the trip back to the highland. The price for
cotton in the Sudan is about four times greater than that paid by the
highland traders, but few Sudanese traders attempt to buy the Ethiopian cotton because it is sold in such small quantities that it is not
worth handling. Besides selling cotton directly to traders, border people sometimes go to the highland to sell or barter their cotton. Some
of the Kumfel people, moreover, act as intermediaries in the move-

ment of cotton to the highland, journeying into distant regions occupied by Gumis and carrying cotton home, later to exchange it for other goods with highland traders who come to their country. Far to the north of Metemma along the border, there is probably even more important highland-lowland trade in cotton at Om Ager in Eritrea.

THE ARAB TRADER AND SHOPKEEPER.—Arab merchants from Yemen play an important part in the trade of the Northwest, for they are the principal shopkeepers in Gondar and in the larger towns, and suppliers of other merchants. Arab shops in the towns are usually located near the marketplace. In Gondar, for example, the daily marketplace is partly enclosed by such shops. Because Gondar is a large trade center, Arab shops are also found in the Italian-built *piazza* and in the European section of the town. Arab shops contain a remarkable collection of goods, rivalling the general store of the United States in variety of merchandise. In Gondar, for example, one such shop might contain American and Ethiopian cigarettes, razor blades of British or Czechoslovakian make, fly flicks made locally, kerosene of Persian Gulf origin, lanterns from Britain and Germany, tennis shoes from Japan and Poland, leather shoes, cotton thread, and cloth from India, Britain, and the United States, ready-made clothes tailored locally, needles made in Britain, soap, resin, salt, spices, and candy, imported umbrellas, leather goods and saddles, cooking pans from abroad, imported mattresses and blankets, dates, peanuts, cowrie shells, and countless other items. A few shops in Gondar also carry European canned goods and candy for the foreign population and wealthy Ethiopians; tinned butter from Kenya costs two dollars U.S. per half pound; other imported goods include Nestlé's chocolate from Switzerland, tea from India and England, tinned biscuits from England, tinned fruit from South Africa, Australia, Britain, and Italy, wine from Eritrea, and liquor from various countries.

Arab traders are found, however, not only in towns and cities but also in many small market villages. As an example of the activities of such traders, let us consider the case of a trader I met in Mecane Birhan in Semyen (Fig. 80), who was one of three merchants living in the village. He had been in Eritrea and Ethiopia for twenty years, first living in Asmara, then in Gondar, and finally in Mecane Birhan. Unlike Arab merchants in the larger towns, he had no shop, but made the rounds of three nearby markets, Derasgie, Islamgie, and Inch'etkab, on a mule with resin, spices, salt, soap, and other goods packed in skin bags. He was a picturesque sight riding to market perched on his mule puffing thoughtfully on his pipe. When he was short of supplies, he sent a list of the goods he needed to a merchant friend in Debark, on the motor road two days away, and they were packed out to him by mule or donkey. Village traders such as this man are more isolated from civilization than any other foreigners in Ethiopia, and they participate more fully in Ethiopian life than any others. This trader, for example, had taken two Ethiopian wives though he still had another wife in Yemen. Ordinarily, too, such village traders are pleasant and cheerful, quite unlike the Arab merchants in the towns who usually are loud and aggressive and often treat ordinary Ethiopian customers with brusqueness and thinly veiled contempt.

The Yemen Arab shopkeepers have a clear advantage over the Ethiopian Moslems, who generally have narrower contacts and less organizational skill. Nevertheless, most of the small trade of the Northwest is in the hands of the Ethiopian Moslems, for they are far more numerous than the Yemen Arabs.

MODERN COMMERCE: MOTOR AND AIR TRANSPORT.—After their military conquest of Ethiopia, the Italians built many motor roads, which made possible a vast expansion of modern commercial activities. In the Northwest, they constructed a graded road from Gorgora north to Tigre and Eritrea, with branch roads or tracks connecting with Dessie by way of Debre Tabor, with Metemma, with Om Ager by way of Wolk'aït, and with Godjam around Lake T'ana. Today, most sections of the branch roads and tracks are completely impassable, though others, such as those to Debre Tabor and Nifas Moch'a, to Ch'ilga, and to Tikil Dingaï, are passable in the dry season by jeep or truck. The main graded road north, on the other hand, is maintained by the Ethiopian Government, is passable throughout the year, and has tended to focus trade along a north-south line running through the province, for it is far cheaper to transport goods by truck to distant markets than it is to pack them by donkey and mule caravan. The transport of cotton from the Sudan border to Gondar is perhaps one example of the high cost of animal transport, for a small bale of cotton purchased in Bodella village is sold for twice as much in Gondar, one hundred fifty miles away. This situation makes trade difficult for local producers, for it means that foreign goods reaching Massawa by boat can be transported inland by truck to Gondar to compete favorably with those Ethiopian goods produced close at hand but transported by donkey.

Along the graded motor road running north from Gondar to Asmara in Eritrea pass huge Italian-built trucks loaded high with the bags of cereals, pulses, and oilseeds, and hides and skins which comprise the principal exports of the region. The trucks arriving in Gondar from Asmara carry oil and gas, tires and auto parts, textiles, soap, shoes and other foreign manufactured goods, building materials, sugar, salt, tea, wines and spirits, as well as canned goods and imported food for the small foreign population. The number of trucks arriving and departing from Gondar is small. At the maximum, for example, there are a half-dozen arrivals in a day, and at a minimum there are no arrivals for two or three days. Addis Ababa can be reached by motor road only by first driving north to Adowa and Adigrat and then south again, a long, expensive journey which limits trucking between Addis Ababa and the Northwest to a minimum.

Trucks are owned by trading firms or by private truckers, and are driven by Italians and Eritreans. It is a tribute to the resourcefulness of the drivers and their helpers that the vehicles continue to operate, for the road is rough and the vehicles take tremendous punishment. It is a common sight to see a vehicle alongside the road with the driver and his helper peering under the hood, dismantling the engine, or fixing a flat tire. They must sleep in their vehicles in villages along the way, eating food that they take with them or that they can buy in rough native cafés where the proprietress knows how to prepare Italian *pasta* for them. The rocky road is very hard on the tires of the heavily laden trucks, which are repaired again and again. Often drivers simply bolt rubber or metal patches onto a tire. Such patches commonly make a clicking sound as they strike the road when the vehicle labors majestically along. Even when tires are finally beyond repair, they are not discarded, but are sold to shoemakers in the large towns who resole shoes or make sandals of them.

Ethiopian Airlines planes from Asmara and Addis Ababa land about twice a week at the airport south of Gondar, but shipments by plane are too expensive for most merchandise and air shipments contribute at best an insignificant volume to local commerce.

Chapter XII

THE EFFECT OF MAN'S ACTIVITIES ON VEGETATION AND SOIL

THE MODIFICATION OF THE VEGETATION COVER.—According to local tradition and to the statements of many foreign observers, the isolated trees (Fig. 66) and clusters of trees that are found in the wetter parts of northern and central highland Ethiopia are the relics of a forest which once covered much of the plateau and which was destroyed by man. In the initial phases of the destruction of the ancient forest cover, it was apparently the clearing of land for agriculture and grazing that destroyed most woody vegetation, aided by the deliberate and accidental use of fire, to which there are numerous references in the literature.[1] Even today, these destructive activities of man continue, for more woody vegetation is destroyed with every new field brought under cultivation and with every fire set by a herdsman to encourage the growth of succulent grasses for his domestic animals. Indeed, the destruction has gone so far that sizable forests occur on the plateau today only in southern Ethiopia, where the plow is a fairly recent introduction and where in many places a system of "plantation" agriculture is followed which does not require such extensive clearing as the field agriculture of the north.

In later times, with the northern and central plateau largely under cultivation, it was the cutting of wood for fuel, and to a lesser degree for building materials and artifacts, that constituted the most severe drain on the remaining trees and shrubs, for like most peoples of Africa and the Near East, the Ethiopians use firewood and not coal, gas, or oil for fuel. To satisfy the demand for firewood, steady streams of women went into the countryside each day to chop down trees and shrubs and struggled home or to market bowed under enormous loads of brush and branches (Figs. 81 and 82). The drain on the wood re-

[1] Bruce, 1790, III: 125; Gobat, 1834: 70; Plowden, 1868: 232; Parkyns, 1868: 165; Dove, 1890: 28–29; R. E. Cheesman, 1936: 259–60; Fuertes and Osgood, 1936: 182; Grabham and Black, 1925: 116.

source was especially severe near large settlements. Already in the seventeenth century, according to Almeida, the camp of the emperor had to be moved every few years when the neighboring hills and valleys had been stripped bare of firewood.[2] Almeida reported further that Ethiopians were amazed to hear that elsewhere in the world big cities could remain for many years on the same site without suffering from a shortage of firewood. James Bruce,[3] in a similar vein, spoke of the greater shortage of trees along the routes most commonly followed by armies. Because many people live on the plateau, the destruction of woody vegetation there was more complete than in the sparsely settled lowland regions, which today contain the principal reserves of wood in northern and central Ethiopia and to which wood gatherers are turning increasingly to obtain their supplies of firewood.

The shortage of wood has become so acute in some highland regions that people must depend largely on dried cattle dung for fuel. It is common in such regions for women, accompanied by little girls, to go into fields where cattle have been grazing and collect the dung in baskets, and carry it home for burning (Fig. 83). This, of course, makes impossible the utilization of the dung for fertilizer and cuts off from the soil an important natural supply of nutrients. In one place, at Derasgie in Semyen, women also collected the droppings of our horses and mules for burning, though this is exceptional.[4]

Because people have been so active in destroying vegetation, it seems, at first glance, surprising that there are any woods left in the high parts of the plateau of Begemder and Semyen. Still, such woods do exist here and there. In Semyen, for example, there are juniper woodlands on the plateau several miles east of Debark, as well as near the village of Gasha Jagri. The people of Gasha Jagri say that they take no legal measures to preserve their juniper woods, that villagers may cut down trees if they need the wood. One traveller, on the other hand, mentions camping by a grove of trees in Semyen which his Ethiopian companions avoided in gathering firewood because it was an ancient burial ground.[5] It may be that the woods of juniper I saw in Semyen were protected not by law but by respect for the dead or by superstition. Elsewhere in the region, the K'amant worship in groves of trees, which are saved from destruction for that reason, and the Gumis, who are said [6] to venerate trees, may do likewise. The pagan Galla of central and southern Ethiopia not only maintain special

[2] Beckingham and Huntingford, 1954: 82.   [3] Bruce, 1790, III: 560.

[4] Bruce, in travelling across the high plateau of Semyen in the late eighteenth century, reported similarly that people used dried cakes of cow and mule dung for burning (Bruce, 1790, III: 192).

[5] Maydon, 1925: 89.   [6] Cerulli, 1956: 32.

sacred trees, but they occasionally plant a sycamore fig (*Ficus syca-morus*) or a coffee shrub over the grave of a priest, and then hold it sacred. Though the "cedar" (*Juniperus procera?*) is said to be the most common sacred tree among the Galla, they are not particular as to the species of tree they worship under.[7] Besides the Galla, many other Ethiopian groups venerate sacred trees, including the Sidamo, Danakil, and Somali,[8] as well as the Kaffa,[9] and the Tigre tribes.[10] To the Sidamo, their sacred trees represent the sacred forest of Uraga, where man originated.[11] Against this background, the presence of groves of trees within the compound of every Christian church, a char-acteristic of highland Ethiopia (Fig. 84), seems more understandable. We are probably dealing here with a remnant of the ancient religious habit of the country. Without its persistence, the Ethiopian country-side would be a far less attractive place, for churches, surrounded by groves of trees, crown many hills on the plateau and add beauty to what otherwise would be a drabber landscape. Preserved within the church compounds are trees unrivalled in size by any of the same species growing in the countryside. Perhaps the most conspicuous trees within the church compounds are the junipers, which often tower high above the church itself. Other trees commonly found around churches are the oleaster, wild fig, and *wanza* (*Cordia abyssinica*).[12] In the region of Sahalla, which is too low in elevation for junipers, stately candelabra euphorbia plants commonly take the place of trees in church compounds.

The only considerable attempt at reforestation in Ethiopia is around Addis Ababa where there was such a shortage of firewood at the end of the nineteenth century that Emperor Menelik established extensive plantations of eucalyptus and ordered that anyone who cut down a tree must plant another in its place.[13] Many farmers on the Shoa Pla-teau around Addis Ababa have followed Menelik's example and planted eucalyptus trees around their farmsteads, thus creating an attractive landscape of circular houses with thatched, conical roofs and clusters of tall, slender eucalyptus amid the fields of grain. In Northwest Ethiopia, there has been extensive planting of eucalyptus around many of the towns, much of it apparently at the time of the Italian occupation. These trees have grown and multiplied with such vigor that today many towns such as Gondar, Azezo, and Debre Tabor look as if they were built in woods (Figs. 5, 75, 82). In villages back

[7] Rochet d'Héricourt, 1841: 166.
[8] Trimingham, 1952: 260; Cerulli, 1956: 129–30.
[9] Huntingford, 1955: 133.   [10] Frazer, 1938: 496.   [11] Cerulli, 1956: 130.
[12] Dove, 1890: 21.   [13] Logan, 1946: 27.

from the motor road, however, eucalyptus trees are not usually grown at all.

THE EROSION OF SOIL.—A few writers have asserted that soil erosion in Ethiopia appears to be far less severe than in many other parts of Africa. On the other hand, the Blue Nile alone has been estimated to carry fifty million tons of Ethiopian silt into the Sudan each year, a situation which attests to the large-scale erosion in the country. The traveller can find additional indications of large-scale erosion in the landscape. Steep trails commonly become rutted and develop into gullies. Gullies also can often be seen in plowed fields, cutting back and destroying good farmland. Though its effects are less readily discernible, sheet erosion must take place on an equally large scale.

In Northwest Ethiopia, there are certain agricultural practices which undoubtedly inhibit erosion. One of these is the custom of leaving boulders and tree stumps in cleared fields. Another is the practice of plowing along the contour. Others are the practice of strip cultivation, the cutting of diagonal drains down many hillsides, and the establishment of stone walls and rudimentary terraces on exceptionally steep slopes. It does not appear, however, that Ethiopian farmers follow these practices in an attempt to retard erosion, though inadvertently that is their effect. Farmers leave boulders and tree stumps in their plowed fields, for example, because they simply do not consider it worth the effort to remove them, but would rather plow around them. Contour plowing is probably done because it is easier on steep slopes to walk and to control plow and oxen by going along the contour than by going up and down. The practice of strip cultivation may be followed, at least in part, because of systems of fallowing and land ownership, rather than specifically for preventing erosion. The systems of diagonal drains, where I have seen them, seem to be built to assure the drainage of soils that are likely to become waterlogged. Terracing of steep slopes, and the building of rough stone walls, though neither practice is followed universally, seem to indicate a desire to retard erosion, but might just as well indicate a desire to develop level plots of ground that can be worked with greater ease. Where I have seen gullies developing in trails and in plowed fields, farmers have made no effort to block them. The indifference of most Ethiopians to the loss of arable land through soil erosion and to the destruction of woods and forests provides little basis for optimism about the future economic development of the land.

CONCLUSIONS

It is implicit in this work that the concern of the peoples of North-west Ethiopia with maintaining ritual purity, and their use of certain domestic plants and animals as group and status symbols, have been critical factors in inhibiting the acceptance of new plants and animals and in contributing to the development of the cultural landscape. Thus, both Semitic and Cushitic groups, whether Moslem, Christian, or pagan, have rejected the domestic pig as an impure animal, though in some other parts of sub-Saharan Africa the domestic pig has been widely diffused and has become an important element in the economies of many groups. With respect to certain other plants and animals, religion has led to sharp differences within Northwest Ethiopia in use and rejection, with non-Moslem groups commonly refusing particular plant and animal foods because they are identified with Islam. The Christians, for example, regard the eating of camel flesh as a Moslem habit, and reject it for that reason. Similarly, the use of tobacco, the use of the indigenous stimulant *Catha edulis,* and at an earlier date the use of coffee, were regarded as Moslem habits, and other religious groups refused such products and did not cultivate them. Indeed, in the past strong sanctions, such as excommunication or, in the case of tobacco, mutilation, were sometimes applied by the Amhara against those of their group who used such forbidden items. Not only have the Amhara rejected the use of certain foods and stimulants as Moslem habits, and inhibited the diffusion of the plants and animals involved, but they have tended, perhaps by extension of the custom of looking at things in this way, to regard the roots, tubers, and vegetatively reproduced crops, such as the banana-like ensete (*Ensete edulis*) which is grown by many of the Cushitic groups to the south, as beneath their dignity. Instead, they have preferred the cereals and pulses, including their favorite t'eff (*Eragrostis teff*), which dominate the agriculture of the North. The attitudes of the Amhara, according to the thesis of W. Stiehler, may have led to a large-scale recession of ensete planting in northern Ethiopia in favor of cereals and pulses.

Though there is only incomplete historical evidence that such a recession of ensete actually did take place, the sociopsychological basis for it is present. In any event, the prejudice of the Amhara against ensete has prevented its becoming important as a food crop in those sections of the northern plateau of Ethiopia which are suited to its cultivation. As a result of this and of the use of the plow in the north, there are striking differences between the southern plateau areas of ensete cultivation, with their closely spaced plantations and their considerable forest cover, and the northern plateau areas of cereal cultivation, which have an open landscape with trees surviving only in places difficult of access or in places, such as church compounds and cemeteries, where they are protected by custom or superstition.

Not only have Amhara attitudes led to north-south differences in the Ethiopian Plateau itself, but they have contributed to highland-lowland contrasts. Amhara concern with cattle, horses, and mules as status symbols, and their preference for the cereal *t'eff* and for barley-malt beer flavored with the leaves of the shrub *gesho* (*Rhamnus prinoides*), encouraged them to avoid settling in the hot, arid lowland borders of the plateau, which are unsuited to their favorite plants and animals as well as being excessively hot and disease-ridden. As a result, the Amhara have extended their effective control into the lowland borders of the Northwest only when the highland itself has been free of internal strife and they have wished to control trade routes and to secure the approaches to the plateau. This has meant that the plateau today is the most advanced part of the region culturally and agriculturally, and that the lowland is a neglected frontier occupied largely by impoverished Cushites and Negroes. This probably also accounts for the ease with which Britain, France, Italy, and Egypt seized the lowland borders of Ethiopia, and the severe defeats the armies of the latter two countries suffered when in the last century they tried to extend the area of their control over the center of Amhara power in the highland.

Northwest Ethiopia well illustrates the general need for geographers to assess the role of cultural attitudes in affecting the use of the environment.

GLOSSARY, REFERENCES CITED, AND INDEX

GLOSSARY OF SCIENTIFIC NAMES

OF PLANTS MENTIONED FREQUENTLY

IN THE TEXT

Plants have been identified by name, usually from Italian sources, especially Chiovenda, 1912.

acacia, *Acacia* sp.
akirma, Chloris sp.
Amharic cabbage or leaf mustard, *Brassica juncea?*
avalo, wood, not identified
azo areg, unidentified vine
bananas, *Musa sapientum*
barley, *Hordeum* sp.
basil, *Ocymum basilicum*
berberei, Capsicum frutescens
black mustard, *Brassica nigra*
broad beans (horse beans), *Vicia faba*
castor beans, *Ricinus communis*
cayenne pepper, *Capsicum frutescens*
ch'at, Catha edulis
chick peas, *Cicer arietinum*
citron, *Citrus medica*
coco-yam, *Colocasia antiquorum*
coffee, *Coffea arabica*
cone wheat, *Triticum turgidum*
coriander, *Coriandrum sativum*
cotton, *Gossypium* spp.
cumin, *Cuminum cyminum*
dengel, Cyperus sp.
emmer wheat, *Triticum dicoccum*
enset, Ensete edule
eucalyptus, *Eucalyptus globulus*

euphorbia, *Euphorbia* sp.
fenugreek, *Trigonella foenum graecum*
feyt'o, Lepidium sativum?
fig, *Ficus* sp.
finger millet, *Eleusine coracana*
flax, *Linum usitatissimum*
Galla potato, *Coleus edulis*
garlic, *Allium sativum*
gesho, Rhamnus prinoides
gibto, Bipinus termis
girowa, Vernonia sp.
gourd, *Lagenaria vulgaris*
gramta, Cyperus fischerianus Schimper
grape vine, *Vitis vinifera*
green peas, *Pisum abyssinicum*
guaya, Lathyrus sativus
haricot beans, *Phaseolus vulgaris*
horse beans (broad beans), *Vicia faba*
imboy, Solanum marginatum
imbus, unidentified wood
indod, Phytolacca sp.
juniper, *Juniperus procera*
leaf mustard or Amharic cabbage, *Brassica juncea?*
lemon, *Citrus limonum*
lentils, *Lens abyssinica*

lupine, *Bipinus termis*
macaroni wheat, *Triticum durum*
maize, *Zea mays*
missana, Croton macrostachys
nug, Guizotia abyssinica
oats, *Avena* sp.
oleaster, *Olea chrysophylla*
onion or shallot, *Allium ascaloni-cum*
pearl millet, *Pennisetum typhoi-deum*
potato, *Solanum tuberosum*
prickly-pear cactus, *Opuntia* sp.
rye, *Secale cereale*
safflower, *Carthamus tinctorius*
sesame, *Sesamum indicum*
shallot, *Allium ascalonicum*

sorghum, *Sorghum vulgare*
squash, *Cucurbita maxima* and *Cucurbita pepo*
suf, Carthamus tinctorius
sweet potato, *Ipomoea batatas*
sycamore fig, *Ficus sycomorus*
t'eff, Eragrostis teff
t'enadam, Ruta sp.
tobacco, *Nicotiana tabacum* and *Nicotiana rustica*
turmeric, *Curcuma longa*
wanza, Cordia abyssinica
warka, Ficus vasta
wheat, *Triticum* sp.
yam, *Dioscorea bulbifera* and *Dioscorea abyssinica*
zigita, Carissa edulis?

REFERENCES CITED

Abd Allah ibn Ahmad, called Ibn al-Baitar. *Heil- und Nahrungsmittel*. Translated by Joseph v. Sontheimer. Stuttgart: Hallberger, 1840–42. 2 vols.

Addis Ababa, University College. Ethnological Society. *Bulletin* No. 2 (December, 1953). 38 pp.

Aïyer, A. K. Yegna Narayan. *Field Crops of India*. Bangalore: The Government Press, 1947. 653 pp.

Allen, W. E. D. *Guerrilla War in Abyssinia*. Harmondsworth, England: Penguin Books, 1943. 126 pp.

Alone, J. P. H. M., and D. E. Stokes. *The Alone-Stokes Short Manual of the Amharic Language*. London: Macmillan and Co., Ltd., 1946. 206 pp.

Alvarez, Francisco. *Narrative of the Portuguese Embassy to Abyssinia during the Years 1520–1527*. Translated and edited by Lord Stanley of Alderley. Hakluyt Society Works, Vol. 64. London: The Hakluyt Society, 1881. 412 pp.

Ames, Oakes. *Economic Annuals and Human Cultures*. Cambridge, Mass.: Botanical Museum of Harvard University, 1939. 153 pp.

Azaïs, R. P., and R. Chambard. *Cinq Années de Recherches Archéologiques en Éthiopie, Province du Harar et Éthiopie Méridionale*. Paris: Librairie Orientaliste Paul Geuthner, 1931. 348 pp.

Baker, Sir Samuel W. *The Nile Tributaries of Abyssinia*. London: Macmillan and Co., 1867. 596 pp.

Barbosa, Duarte. *A Description of the Coasts of East Africa and Malabar in the Beginning of the Sixteenth Century*. Translated by Henry E. J. Stanley. Hakluyt Society Works, Vol. 35. London: The Hakluyt Society, 1866. 336 pp.

Baumann, Hermann, Richard Thurnwald, and Diedrich Westermann. *Völkerkunde von Africa*. Essen: Essener Verlagsanstalt, 1940. 665 pp.

Baxter, P. T. W., and Audrey Butt. *The Azande, and Related Peoples of the Anglo-Egyptian Sudan and Belgian Congo*. Ethnographic Survey of Africa, East Central Africa, Part 9. London: International African Institute, 1953. 152 pp.

Beckingham, C. F., and G. W. B. Huntingford. *Some Records of Ethiopia, 1593–1646*. Hakluyt Society Works, Series II, Vol. 107. London: The Hakluyt Society, 1954. 267 pp.

Bent, J. Theodore. *The Sacred City of the Ethiopians*. London: Longmans, Green and Company, 1893. 309 pp.

Bisschop, J. H. R., "Parent Stock and Derived Types of African Cattle, With Particular Reference to the Importance of Conformational Characteristics in the Study of Their Origin," *South African Journal of Science,* XXXIII (1937), 852–70.

Blanford, W. T. *Observations on the Geology and Zoology of Abyssinia.* London: Macmillan and Co., 1870. 487 pp.

Bodenheimer, F. S. *Insects as Human Food.* The Hague: W. Junk, 1951. 352 pp.

Boettger, Caesar Rudolf. *Die Haustiere Afrikas.* Jena: Veb Gustav Fischer Verlag, 1958. 314 pp.

Bollettino della R. Società Geografica Italiana, "Un articolo russo sul limite di estensione verticale delle piante coltivate in Abissinia," Serie VII, Vol. II (1937), pp. 305–11.

Brehm, Alfred. *Die Säugetiere.* Revised by Max Hilzheimer and Ludwig Heck. Vol. 13. Leipzig and Vienna: Bibliographisches Institut, 1920. 714 pp.

Briggs, L. Cabot. *The Living Races of the Sahara Desert.* Papers of the Peabody Museum of Archaeology and Ethnology, Harvard University. Vol. XXVIII, No. 2. Cambridge, Mass.: Peabody Museum, 1958. 217 pp.

British Ministry of Information. *The Abyssinian Campaigns.* London: His Majesty's Stationery Office, 1942. 143 pp.

Brooke, Clarke. "Settlements of the Eastern Galla, Hararge Province, Ethiopia." Unpublished Ph.D. dissertation, University of Nebraska, 1956. 315 pp.

Brooke, Clarke. "The Rural Village in the Ethiopian Highlands," *The Geographical Review,* XLIX (1959), 58–75.

Bruce, James. *Travels to Discover the Source of the Nile, in the Years 1768, 1769, 1770, 1771, 1772, and 1773.* London: G. G. J. and J. Robinson, 1790. 5 vols.

Budge, Sir E. A. Wallis. *A History of Ethiopia.* London: Methuen and Co., 1928. 2 vols.

Burkill, I. H. *A Dictionary of the Economic Products of the Malay Peninsula.* London: Crown Agents for the Colonies, 1935. 2 vols.

Buxton, David. *Travels in Ethiopia.* New York: Medill McBride Co., 1950. 200 pp.

Buxton, P. A. *Trypanosomiasis in Eastern Africa, 1947.* London: His Majesty's Stationery Office, 1948. 44 pp.

Candolle, Alphonse de. *Origin of Cultivated Plants.* New York: D. Appleton and Company, 1885. 468 pp.

Candussio, Renzo. "Il miglioramento del 'neuk' (*Guizotia abyssinica* Cass). Prime indagini ed osservazioni e direttive del lavoro di selezione," *L'agricoltura coloniale,* 35 (1941), 347–54.

Castaldi, Angelo. "Gli Habab," *Le vie d'Italia,* 42 (1936), 209–19.

Castro, Lincoln de. *Nella terra dei Negus.* Milan: Fratelli Treves, 1915. 2 vols.

Cerulli, Enrico. "Folk-Literature of the Galla of Southern Abyssinia," pp. 10–228 in *Varia Africana III.* Harvard African Studies, Vol. III. Cambridge,

Mass.: The African Department of the Peabody Museum of Harvard University, 1922. 374 pp.

Cerulli, Ernesta. *Peoples of South-West Ethiopia and Its Borderland.* Ethnographic Survey of Africa, North-Eastern Africa, Part 3. London: International African Institute, 1956. 148 pp.

Cheesman, E. E. "Classification of the Bananas," *Kew Bulletin,* 1947, pp. 97–117; 1948, pp. 11–28.

Cheesman, Robert E. *Lake Tana and the Blue Nile.* London: Macmillan and Co., 1936. 400 pp.

Childe, V. Gordon. "The Diffusion of Wheeled Vehicles," *Ethnographisch-Archäologische Forschungen,* 2 (1954), 1–17.

Chiovenda, Emilio. "Le piante alimentari nelle nostre colonie," *Atti* della Società Italiana per il Progresso delle Scienze, 17 (1928), 543–58.

Chiovenda, Emilio. *Osservazioni botaniche, agrarie ed industriali fatte nell' Abissinia Settentrionale nell'anno 1909.* Monografie e rapporti coloniali, No. 24. Rome: Ministero delle colonie, Direzione centrale degli affari coloniali, Ufficio di studi coloniali, 1912. 132 pp.

Ciferri, Raffaele, and Enrico Bartolozzi. "La produzione cerealicoltura dell' Africa Orientale Italiana nel 1938," *L'agricoltura coloniale,* XXXIV (1940), 441–50, 502–15.

Ciferri, Raffaele, and Guido Renzo Giglioli. "La cerealicoltura in A.O.I. I. I frumenti duri," *L'Italia agricola,* 76 (1939), 247–57. 1939a.

Ciferri, Raffaele, and Guido Renzo Giglioli. "La cerealicoltura in Africa Orientale. II. I frumenti piramidali, turgidi, polacchi e dicocchi," *L'Italia agricola,* 76 (1939), 379–87. 1939b.

Ciferri, Raffaele, and Guido Renzo Giglioli. "La cerealicoltura in Africa Orientale. III. I frumenti volgari e compatti," *L'Italia agricola,* 76 (1939), 765–74. 1939c.

Ciferri, Raffaele, and Guido Renzo Giglioli. "La cerealicoltura in Africa Orientale. IV. Caratteristiche dei gruppi minori di frumenti etiopici e loro 'formulazione,' " *L'Italia agricola,* 76 (1939), 837–44. 1939d.

Ciferri, Raffaele, and Guido Renzo Giglioli. "I frumenti dell'Africa Orientale studiati su materiali originali." Vol. I of *I cereali dell'Africa Italiana.* Florence: Regio Istituto Agronomico per l'Africa Italiana, 1939. 1939e.

Ciferri, Raffaele, and Isaia Baldrati. "Il 'Teff' (*Eragrostis Teff*). Cereale da panificazione dell'Africa Orientale Italiana montana." Vol. II of *I cereali dell'Africa Italiana.* Florence: Regio Istituto Agronomico per l'Africa Italiana, 1939.

Ciferri, Raffaele, and Isaia Baldrati. "La cerealicoltura in Africa Orientale. VI. Il 'Teff' (*Eragrostis Teff*)," *L'Italia agricola,* 77 (1940), 170–76.

Cipriani, L. *Ricerche antropologiche sulle genti.* Vol. V, Missione di Studio al Lago Tana. Rome: Reale Accademia d'Italia, 1940. 468 pp.

Cohen, Marcel S. R. *Nouvelles études d'éthiopien méridional.* Paris: Edouard Champion, 1939. 472 pp.

Conklin, Harold C. "An Ethnoecological Approach to Shifting Agriculture,"

Transactions of the New York Academy of Sciences, Ser. II, Vol. 17 (1954), pp. 133–42.

Contenau, Georges. *Everyday Life in Babylon and Assyria.* New York: St. Martin's Press, 1954. 324 pp.

Copertini, Spartaco. "Il 'pane' di fecola di banano abissino," *L'agricoltura coloniale,* 32 (1938), 444–46.

Corfield, F. D. "The Koma," *Sudan Notes and Records,* XXI (1938), 123–65.

Cosmas Indicopleustes. *The Christian Topography.* Translated and edited by J. W. McCrindle. Hakluyt Society Works, Vol. 98. London: The Hakluyt Society, 1897. 398 pp.

Crowfoot, J. W. "Further Notes on Pottery," *Sudan Notes and Records,* VIII (1925), 125–36.

Dainelli, Giotto. "Case abissine dell'Eritrea," *Le vie d'Italia,* XLII (1936), 82–93.

Dainelli, Giotto. *Geologia dell'Africa Orientale.* Rome: Reale Accademia d'Italia, 1943. 4 vols.

Dalziel, J. M. *The Useful Plants of West Tropical Africa.* London: The Crown Agents for the Colonies, 1937. 612 pp.

Dove, Karl. "Kulturzonen von Nord-Abessinien," *Petermanns Geographischen Mitteilungen,* Ergänzungsheft No. 97 (1890), pp. 1–34.

Engler, Adolf. *Die Pflanzenwelt Ost-Afrikas und der Nachbargebiete.* Theil B. Berlin: Geographische Verlagshandlung Dietrich Reimer, 1895. 535 pp.

Ethiopian Government. Ministry of Commerce and Industry. *Economic Handbook of Ethiopia.* Addis Ababa: Ministry of Commerce and Industry, 1951. 212 pp.

Forde, C. Daryll. *Habitat, Economy and Society.* London: Methuen and Co., Ltd., 1949. 500 pp.

Forschungsinstitut für Kulturmorphologie. *Atlas Africanus.* Hefte 1–8. Munich: C. H. Beck'sche Verlagsbuchhandlung Oskar Beck, 1921–31.

Foster, William, ed. *The Red Sea and Adjacent Countries at the Close of the Seventeenth Century.* Hakluyt Society Works, Series II, Vol. 100. London: The Hakluyt Society, 1949. Part III, pp. 93–165, "A Narrative by Charles Jacques Poncet on his Journey from Cairo into Abyssinia and back, 1698–1701."

Frazer, Sir James George. *The Native Races of Africa and Madagascar.* London: Percy Lund Humphries and Co., Ltd., 1938. 578 pp.

Fuertes, Louis Agassiz, and Wilfred Hudson Osgood. *Artist and Naturalist in Ethiopia.* New York: Doubleday, Doran and Co., Inc., 1936. 249 pp.

Gobat, Samuel. *Journal of a Three Years' Residence in Abyssinia.* London: Hatchard and Son; and Seeley and Sons, 1834. 371 pp.

Grabham, George W., and R. P. Black. *Report of Mission to Lake Tana, 1920–1921.* Cairo: Government Press, 1925. 207 pp.

Grottanelli, Vinigi L. *Ricerche geografiche ed economiche sulle popolazioni.* Vol. II, Missione di Studio al Lago Tana. Rome: Reale Accademia d'Italia, 1939. 298 pp.

Grottanelli, Vinigi L., and Claudia Massari. *I Baria, i Cunama e i Beni Amer.* Vol. VI, Missione di Studio al Lago Tana. Rome: Reale Accademia d'Italia, 1943. 416 pp.

Gulliver, Pamela, and P. H. Gulliver. *The Central Nilo-Hamites.* Ethnographic Survey of Africa, East Central Africa, Part 7. London: International African Institute, 1953. 106 pp.

Haggenmacher, G. A. "G. A. Haggenmacher's Reise im Somali-Lande 1874," *Petermanns Geographischen Mitteilungen,* Ergänzungsheft No. 47 (1876), pp. 1–45.

Hahn, Eduard. *Die Haustiere und ihre Beziehungen zur Wirtschaft des Menschen.* Leipzig: Duncker and Humblot, 1896. 581 pp.

Halim, Ahmed Abdel. "Native Medicine and Ways of Treatment in the Northern Sudan," *Sudan Notes and Records,* XXII (1939), 27–48.

Harris, William C. *The Highlands of Aethiopia.* London: Longman, Brown, Green, and Longmans, 1844. 3 vols.

Harrison, Paul W. *The Arab at Home.* New York: Thomas Y. Crowell Co., 1924. 345 pp.

Hartmann, R. *Abyssinien und die übrigen Gebiete der Ostküste Afrikas.* Leipzig: G. Freytag, 1883. 304 pp.

Haudricourt, A. "L'Histoire du Tef," *Revue de botanique appliquée et d'agriculture tropicale,* 21 (1941), 128–30.

Hayes, Arthur J. *The Source of the Blue Nile.* London: Smith, Elder and Co., 1905. 315 pp.

Hövermann, Jürgen. "Über glaziale und 'periglaziale' Erscheinungen in Erithrea und Nordabessinien," *Abhandlungen der Akademie für Raumforschung und Landesplanung,* 28 (1954), 87–111.

Holm, Henrietta M. *The Agricultural Economy of Ethiopia.* Foreign Agricultural Service, United States Department of Agriculture, FAS M–13. Washington: U.S. Government Printing Office, 1956. 44 pp.

Hornell, James. *Water Transport, Origins and Early Evolution.* Cambridge, England: University Press, 1946. 307 pp.

Hotten, John C. *Abyssinia and Its People.* London: John C. Hotten, 1868. 384 pp.

Huntingford, G. W. B. *The Galla of Ethiopia. The Kingdoms of Kafa and Janjero.* Ethnographic Survey of Africa, North-Eastern Africa, Part II. London: International African Institute, 1955. 156 pp.

Ingrams, W. H. *A Report on the Social, Economic and Political Condition of the Hadhramaut.* Colonial Office Report, No. 123. London: His Majesty's Stationery Office, 1936. 177 pp.

Interdepartmental Committee on Nutrition for National Defense. *Ethiopia:*

Nutrition Survey. Washington: Interdepartmental Committee on Nutrition for National Defense, 1959. 140 pp.

Isenberg, Karl W., and J. L. Krapf. *Journals of the Rev. Messrs. Isenberg and Krapf.* London: Seeley, Burnside, and Seeley, 1843. 529 pp.

Istituto Agricolo Coloniale Italiano. *Relazione di una missione di agricoltori in A.O.I.* Relazioni e monografie agrario-coloniali, No. 43. Florence: Istituto Agricolo Coloniale Italiano, 1937. 46 pp.

Jensen, Lloyd B. *Man's Foods.* Champaign, Illinois: The Garrard Press, 1953. 278 pp.

Kew, Royal Gardens. "I. Teff (*Eragrostis abyssinica*)," *Bulletin of Miscellaneous Information,* 1887, pp. 2–6.

Kirk, R. "Some Vegetable Poisons of the Sudan," *Sudan Notes and Records,* XXVII (1946), 127–52.

Lagercrantz, Sture. *Contribution to the Ethnography of Africa.* Studia Ethnographica Upsaliensia, Vol. I. Upsala: 1950. 430 pp.

Lagercrantz, Sture. *Fish-Hooks in Africa and Their Distribution.* Smärre Meddelanden, No. 12. Stockholm: Statens etnografiska museum, 1934. 39 pp.

Laurent-Täckholm, Vivi. "The Plant of Naqada," *Annales du Service des Antiquités de l'Égypte,* 51 (1951), 299–312.

Laurent-Täckholm, Vivi, and Mohammed Drar. *Flora of Egypt,* Vol. III. Bulletin of the Faculty of Science No. 30. Cairo: Cairo University Press, 1954. 644 pp.

Leslau, Wolf. "The Black Jews of Ethiopia," *Commentary,* 7 (1949), 216–24.

Leslau, Wolf. "The Meaning of 'Arab' in Ethiopia," *The Muslim World,* 39 (1949), 307–8. 1949b.

Leslau, Wolf. *Ethiopic Documents: Gurage.* Viking Fund Publications in Anthropology, No. 14. New York: The Viking Fund, Inc., 1950. 176 pp.

Leslau, Wolf. *Falasha Anthology.* Yale Judaica Series, Volume VI. New Haven: Yale University Press, 1951. 222 pp.

Leth, T., and K. G. Lindblom. *Two Kinds of Fishing Implements: 1. The Plunge-Basket (Stülpkorb), in Africa and Elsewhere. 2. The Circular Cast-Net in Africa.* Smärre Meddelanden, No. 11. Stockholm: Statens etnografiska museum, 1933. 48 pp.

Lewis, D. J. "The Tsetse Fly Problem in the Anglo-Egyptian Sudan," *Sudan Notes and Records,* XXX (1949), 179–211.

Lewis, I. M. *Peoples of the Horn of Africa. Somali, Afar and Saho.* Ethnographic Survey of Africa, North-Eastern Africa, Part I. London: International African Institute, 1955. 200 pp.

Lindblom, K. G. *The Use of Oxen as Pack and Riding Animals in Africa.* Smärre Meddelanden, No. 10. Stockholm: Statens etnografiska museum, 1931. 77 pp.

Lobo, Jerome. *A Voyage to Abyssinia.* Translated from the French edition of M. LeGrand by Samuel Johnson. London: Elliot and Kay, 1789. 186 pp.

Logan, W. E. M. *An Introduction to the Forests of Central and Southern Ethiopia*. Institute Paper No. 24. Oxford: Imperial Forestry Institute, 1946. 58 pp.

Longrigg, Stephen H. *A Short History of Eritrea*. London: Oxford University Press, 1945. 188 pp.

Maydon, H. C. *Simen, Its Heights and Abysses*. London: H. F. and G. Witherby, 1925. 244 pp.

Messing, Simon David. "Changing Ethiopia," *The Middle East Journal*, 9 (1955), 413–32.

Messing, Simon David. "The Highland-Plateau Amhara of Ethiopia." Unpublished Ph.D. dissertation, University of Pennsylvania, 1957. 770 pp.

Messing, Simon David. "Further Comments on Resin-Coated Pottery: Ethiopia," *American Anthropologist*, 59 (1957), 134. 1957a.

Mikesell, Marvin K. "Notes on the Dispersal of the Dromedary," *Southwestern Journal of Anthropology*, 11 (1955), 231–45.

Murdock, George Peter. *Africa: Its Peoples and Their Culture History*. New York: McGraw-Hill Book Co., 1959. 456 pp.

Musil, Alois. *The Manners and Customs of the Rwala Bedouins*. American Geographical Society, Oriental Explorations and Studies, No. 6. New York: The American Geographical Society, 1928. 712 pp.

Nadel, S. F. *The Nuba*. London: Oxford University Press, 1947. 527 pp.

Nastrucci, Mario. "Preparazione delle bevande alcooliche abissine nell'Harar," *L'agricoltura coloniale*, XXXIV (1940), 408–25.

Nicholson, G. Edward. "A Note on Ethiopian Cottons," *The Empire Cotton Growing Review*, XXXV (1958), 160–67.

Nicholson, G. Edward. *Cotton in Ethiopia*. Addis Ababa: Ministry of Agriculture, Imperial Ethiopian Government, 1956. 70 pp.

Nistri, Pier Francesco. *Dalla valle dell'Obel agli altipiani dell'Uogherà*. Relazioni e monografie agrario-coloniali, No. 42. Florence: Istituto Agricolo Coloniale Italiano, 1937. 77 pp.

Nowack, Ernst. *Land und Volk der Konso*. Bonner Geographische Abhandlungen, Heft 14. Bonn: Geographischen Instituts der Universität Bonn, 1954. 60 pp.

Ortiz, Fernando. *Cuban Counterpoint*. New York: Alfred A. Knopf, 1947. 312 pp.

Parkyns, Mansfield. *Life in Abyssinia*. London: John Murray, 1868. 446 pp.

Paulitschke, Philipp. *Ethnographie Nordost-Afrikas. Die Materielle Cultur der Danâkil, Galla und Somâl*. Berlin: Geographische Verlagshandlung Dietrich Reimer, 1893. 338 pp.

Pavari, Graziella. "L'abitazione umana nell'A. O.," *L'universo*, 17 (1936), 317–45.

Pearce, Nathaniel. *The Life and Adventures of Nathaniel Pearce*. Edited by J. J. Halls. London: Henry Colburn and Richard Bentley, 1831. 2 vols.

Peck, E. F. "Agriculture in the Somaliland Protectorate," *The East African Agricultural Journal,* IX (1943–44), 42–46.

Pelzer, Karl J. *Pioneer Settlement in the Asiatic Tropics.* American Geographical Society, Special Publication No. 29. New York: American Geographical Society, 1945. 290 pp.

Perham, Margery. *The Government of Ethiopia.* London: Faber and Faber, Ltd., 1948. 481 pp.

Piccoli, Gualfardo. "Sull'utilità della coltivazione del Fico d'India, quale risorsa foraggera, nelle nostre colonie," *L'agricoltura coloniale,* 37 (1943), 267–75.

Plowden, Walter C. *Travels in Abyssinia and the Galla Country.* London: Longmans, Green, and Co., 1868. 485 pp.

Prassolov, L. I. "Soils of Abyssinia and Erythrea," *Pochvovedenie* (Moscow), 28 (1933), 367–73.

Rassam, Hormuzd. *Narrative of the British Mission to Theodore, King of Abyssinia.* London: Murray, 1869. 2 vols.

Ratzel, Friedrich. *The History of Mankind.* Translated by A. J. Butler. Vol. II. London: Macmillan and Co., 1897. 562 pp.

Rava, Maurizio. *Al lago Tsana.* Rome: Reale Società Geografica, 1913. 270 pp.

Rawlinson, George. *The History of Herodotus.* London: J. M. Dent and Sons, Ltd., 1910. 2 vols.

Reale Società Geografica Italiana, Rome. *L'Africa Orientale.* Bologna: Zanichelli, 1936. 407 pp.

Rey, C. F. *In the Country of the Blue Nile.* London: Duckworth, 1927. 296 pp.

Rey, C. F. *The Real Abyssinia.* London: Seeley Service and Co., 1935. 291 pp.

Rochet d'Héricourt, C. E. X. *Voyage sur la côte orientale de la mer Rouge, dans le pays d'Adel et le Royaume de Choa.* Paris: Arthus Bertrand, 1841. 439 pp.

Rock, Joseph F. *The Ancient Na-Khi Kingdom of Southwest China.* Harvard-Yenching Institute, Monograph Series, Vols. VIII–IX. Cambridge, Mass.: Harvard University Press, 1947. 2 vols.

Salt, Henry. *A Voyage to Abyssinia and Travels into the Interior of that Country.* London: F. C. and J. Rivington, 1814. 506 pp.

Sauer, Carl O. *Agricultural Origins and Dispersals.* Bowman Memorial Lectures, Series Two. New York: The American Geographical Society, 1952. 110 pp.

Schoff, Wilfred H., trans. *The Periplus of the Erythraean Sea.* New York: Longmans, Green, and Co., 1912. 323 pp.

Scott, Hugh. "Journey to the Gughé Highlands (Southern Ethiopia), 1948–9; Biogeographical Research at High Altitudes," The Linnean Society of London, *Proceedings,* Vol. 163, Part 2 (1952), pp. 85–189.

Seyffert, Carl. *Biene und Honig im Volksleben der Afrikaner.* Veröffentlichungen des Staatlichsächsischen Forschungsinstitutes für Völkerkunde in Leipzig, Reihe 1, Band 3. Leipzig: R. Voigtländer, 1930. 209 pp.

Showalter, Ada Elizabeth. "Customs, Food Habits, and Diet Evaluation of Ethiopian People." Unpublished M.S. thesis, The Ohio State University, 1950. 118 pp.

Simmons, James Stevens, Tom F. Whayne, Gaylord W. Anderson, Harold Maclachlan Horack, and Ruth Alida Thomas. *Global Epidemiology. A Geography of Disease and Sanitation.* Volume Two. Philadelphia: J. B. Lippincott Co., 1951. 652 pp.

Simmons, James Stevens, Tom F. Whayne, Gaylord W. Anderson, Harold Maclachlan Horack, and Ruth Alida Thomas. *Global Epidemiology. A Geography of Disease and Sanitation.* Volume Three. Philadelphia: J. B. Lippincott Co., 1954. 357 pp.

Simoons, Frederick. "The Agricultural Implements and Cutting Tools of Begemder and Semyen, Ethiopia," *Southwestern Journal of Anthropology,* 14 (1958), 386–406.

Simoons, Frederick. "Notes on the Bush-Pig (*Potamochoerus*)," *The Uganda Journal,* 17 (1953), 80–81.

Simoons, Frederick. "The Non-Milking Area of Africa," *Anthropos,* 49 (1954), 58–66.

Smeds, Helmer. "The Ensete Planting Culture of Eastern Sidamo, Ethiopia," *Acta Geographica,* 13, No. 4 (1955), pp. 1–39.

Snowden, J. D. *The Cultivated Races of Sorghum.* London: Adlard and Son, Ltd., 1936. 272 pp.

Sollas, W. J. *Ancient Hunters and Their Modern Representatives.* New York: The Macmillan Co., 1924. 689 pp.

Statistical Office of the United Nations. *Yearbook of International Trade Statistics, 1956.* Vol. 1. New York: Statistical Office of the United Nations, 1957. 629 pp.

Steer, G. L. *Sealed and Delivered: A Book on the Abyssinian Campaign.* London: Hodder and Stoughton, 1942. 254 pp.

Steudner, Hermann. "Herrn Dr. Steudner's Bericht-Reise von Adoa nach Gondar. Dec. 26, 1861–Januar, 1862," *Zeitschrift für Allgemeine Erdkunde,* Berlin: Neue Folge, Band 151 (1863), pp. 43–141.

Stiehler, W. "Studien zur Landwirtschafts- und Siedlungs-geographie Äthiopiens," *Erdkunde,* II (1948), 257–82.

Sylvain, Pierre G. "Ethiopian Coffee—Its Significance to World Coffee Problems," *Economic Botany,* 12 (1958), 111–39.

Taīye, Balambaras Mengistu. "A Short History of Gondar." Manuscript in the hands of the author, Gondar, Ethiopia. 1944 (Eth.).

Tax, Sol, Loren C. Eiseley, Irving Rouse, and Carl F. Voegelin. *An Appraisal of Anthropology Today.* Chicago: The University of Chicago Press, 1953. 395 pp.

Tothill, J. D., ed. *Agriculture in the Sudan.* London: Oxford University Press, 1948. 974 pp.

Tothill, J. D., ed. *Agriculture in Uganda*. London: Oxford University Press, 1940. 551 pp.

Trimingham, J. Spencer. *Islam in Ethiopia*. London: Oxford University Press, 1952. 299 pp.

Ullendorff, Edward. *The Semitic Languages of Ethiopia*. London: Taylor's (Foreign) Press, 1955. 273 pp.

Van de Wall, G., and E. D. Alvord. *A Survey of the Food and Feed Resources of the Union of South Africa*. Pretoria: J. L. Van Shaik, 1954. 312 pp.

Vavilov, Nicolaï Ivanovich. "Studies on the Origin of Cultivated Plants," *Bulletin of Applied Botany and Plant-Breeding*, XVI (1926), No. 2, 139–248.

Vavilov, Nicolaï Ivanovich. *The Origin, Variation, Immunity and Breeding of Cultivated Plants*. Translated by K. Starr Chester. *Chronica Botanica*, Vol. 13, 1949–50. 364 pp.

Vitali, Giovanni, and Enrico Bartolozzi. *Strumenti agricoli indigeni dell'Africa Orientale Italiana*. Relazioni e monografie agrario-coloniale, No. 52. Florence: Regio Istituto Agronomico per L'Africa Italiana, 1939. 76 pp.

Wainwright, G. A. "Iron in the Napatan and Meroitic Ages," *Sudan Notes and Records*, XXVI (1945), 5–36.

Walker, Craven Howell. *English-Amharic Dictionary*. London: The Sheldon Press, 1928. 236 pp.

Watt, George. *Dictionary of the Economic Products of India*. Vol. IV. London: W. H. Allen and Co., 1890. 643 pp.

Werth, Emil. *Grabstock, Hacke, und Pflug*. Ludwigsburg: Verlag Eugen Ulmer, 1954. 435 pp.

Wolda Mariam, Yohanis. *World History*. Addis Ababa: Ministry of Education and Fine Arts, 1940 (Eth.). 482 pp.

Wylde, Augustus B. *Modern Abyssinia*. London: Methuen and Co., 1901. 497 pp.

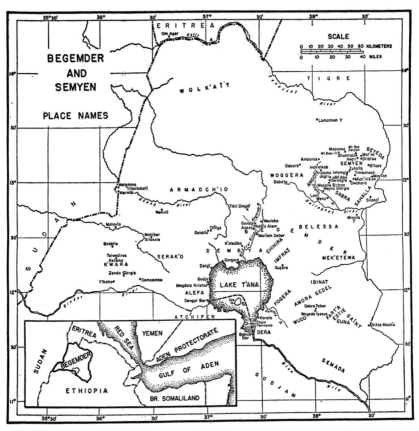

MAP 9

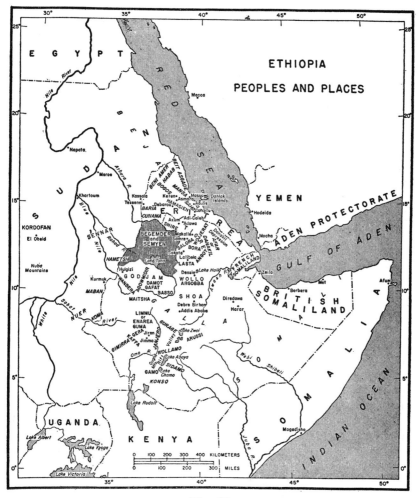

MAP 10

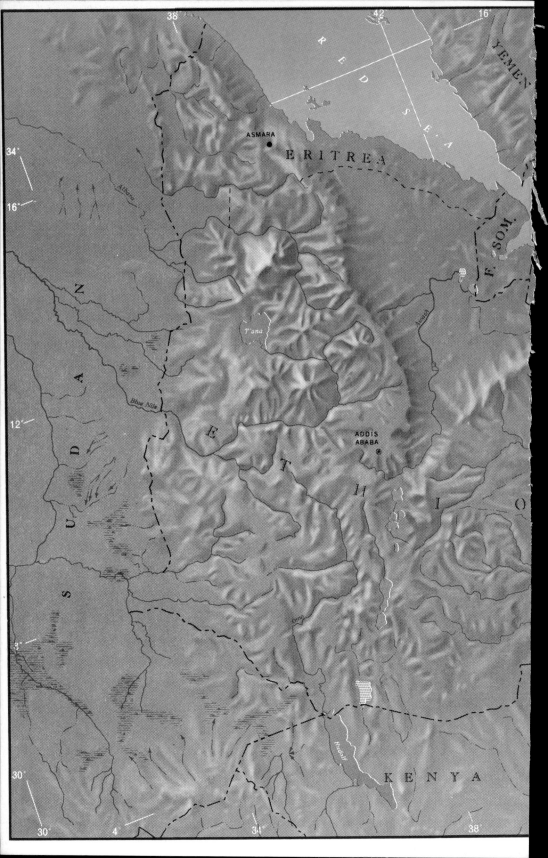